TM

References for the Rest of Us!™

BESTSELLING BOOK SERIES

Do you find that traditional reference books are overloaded with technical details and advice you'll never use? Do you postpone important life decisions because you just don't want to deal with them? Then our *For Dummies*® business and general reference book series is for you.

For Dummies business and general reference books are written for those frustrated and hard-working souls who know they aren't dumb, but find that the myriad of personal and business issues and the accompanying horror stories make them feel helpless. *For Dummies* books use a lighthearted approach, a down-to-earth style, and even cartoons and humorous icons to dispel fears and build confidence. Lighthearted but not lightweight, these books are perfect survival guides to solve your everyday personal and business problems.

> **"...Dummies books consistently live up to their brand-name promise to transform 'can't into can.' "**
> — *Ottawa Citizen*

> **"...clear, straightforward information laced with a touch of humour."**
> — *The Toronto Star*

> **"...set up in bits and bites that are easy to digest, full of no-nonsense advice."**
> — *The Calgary Herald*

Already, millions of satisfied readers agree. They have made For Dummies the #1 introductory level computer book series and a bestselling business book series. They have written asking for more. So, if you're looking for the best and easiest way to learn about business and other general reference topics, look to For Dummies to give you a helping hand.

CDG BOOKS
C A N A D A
TM

Investing Online For Canadians

FOR DUMMIES®

2ND EDITION

by Andrew Dagys
and Kathleen Sindell, PhD

CDG BOOKS CANADA

CDG Books Canada, Inc.

◆ Toronto, ON ◆

Investing Online For Canadians For Dummies® 2nd Edition

Published by
CDG Books Canada, Inc.
99 Yorkville Avenue
Suite 400
Toronto, ON M5R 3K5
www.cdgbooks.com (CDG Books Canada Web Site)
www.idgbooks.com (IDG Books Worldwide Web Site)
www.dummies.com (Dummies Press Web Site)

National Library of Canada Cataloguing in Publication Data

Dagys, Andrew

Investing online for Canadians for dummies

2nd ed.
Includes index.
ISBN: 1-894413-35-0

1. Investments — Computer network resources. 2. Electronic trading of securities. I. Sindell, Kathleen. II. Title.

HG4515.95.D33 2001   332.6'0285'4678   C2001-901774-X
KF750.K47 2000

Printed in Canada

1 2 3 4 5 TRI 05 04 03 02 01

Distributed in Canada by CDG Books Canada, Inc.

For general information on CDG Books, including all IDG Books Worldwide publications, please call our distribution centre, HarperCollins Canada; Tel: 1-800-387-0117. For reseller information, including discounts and premium sales, please call our sales department; Tel: 1-877-963-8830.

This book is available at special discounts for bulk purchases by your group or organization for resale, premiums, fundraising and seminars. For details, contact CDG Books Canada, Special Sales Department, 99 Yorkville Avenue, Suite 400, Toronto, ON M5R 3K5; Tel: 416-963-8830; Fax: 416-923-4821; e-mail: spmarkets@cdgbooks.com.

For press review copies, author interviews, or other publicity information, please contact our marketing department: Tel: 416-963-8830; Fax: 416-923-4821; e-mail: publicity@cdgbooks.com.

For authorization to photocopy items for corporate, personal, or educational use, please contact Cancopy, The Canadian Copyright Licensing Agency, One Yonge Street, Suite 1900, Toronto, ON M5E 1E5; Tel: 416-868-1620; Fax: 416-868-1621; www.cancopy.com

is a trademark under exclusive license to CDG Books Canada, Inc., from Hungry Minds, Inc.

CDG BOOKS CANADA

About the Authors

Andrew Dagys, CMA, is a professional accountant and principal of Treetop Investment Advisors, providing specialized investment management services for high-technology and health-care sector investors.

Andrew is a bestselling author who has written and co-authored several books, including *The Internet For Canadians For Dummies* Starter Kit (first and second editions), *The Internet for 50+, The Financial Planner for 50+,* and *The Ontario Retirement Handbook.* Andrew is an investment columnist for *Forever Young* and a contributor of technology-related articles to *Canadian Living.*

An avid online investor, Andrew uses the Internet as a powerful investment tool. He also enjoys speaking to business and general audiences about the latest developments in computer technology, and about how the Internet can empower Canadians. He lives in Toronto with his wife, Dawn-Ava, and their three children, Brendan, Megan, and Jordan.

Kathleen Sindell, PhD, an expert on electronic commerce, is a popular speaker and an adjunct faculty member at the Johns Hopkins University MBA Program. She is the author of numerous popular, academic and professional books, articles, and Web sites. She is the founder of a firm that provides consulting and authoritative publications about management, finance, and real estate in the e-commerce environment.

Dr. Sindell is the author of *Loyalty Marketing in the Internet Age* (Dearborn, October 2000), the *Unofficial Guide to Buying a Home Online* (IDG/MacMillan 2000), and *A Hands-On Guide to Mortgage Banking Internet Sites,* a separate directory published by *Mortgage Banking Magazine* (2000, 1999, 1998, 1997).

Dr. Sindell has taught more than 25 graduate-level courses, she lectures for the New York Institute of Finance, and she is a well-known speaker at regional and national conferences where she addresses the development of online customer loyalty, online-investing and mortgage-lending topics, and electronic customer-relationship-management issues.

Dedication

Andrew dedicates his part of this book to the memory of those who lost their lives in the World Trade Center tragedy.

Kathleen dedicates this book to her husband, Ivan Sindell, whose enthusiasm added a lot to this work.

Acknowledgements

Andrew thanks Robert Harris, who once again gave him the opportunity to write a book about one of his favourite topics — online investing. He also thanks Melanie Rutledge, his editor, who provided tremendous value to this title with her great care, insights, and suggestions. Andrew appreciates the ongoing writing advice provided by Joan Whitman, whom he has had the pleasure of working with for years. He is grateful to Kelli Howey and others at CDG Books Canada who worked behind the scenes and who helped shape the final product.

Andrew gives special thanks to Ron Hew, a friend and fellow investing enthusiast. With years of professional investment experience behind him, Ron volunteered to review this book and provided valuable feedback.

As always, Andrew is grateful to his wife, Dawn-Ava, who makes his life wonderful to live.

Kathleen thanks Joyce Pepple, acquisitions editor, for her thoughtful guidance and support. She also thanks her literary agent, Carole McClendon, and all the folks at Watershide Productions for their encouragement. She also appreciates Andrea Boucher's dedication to high quality. She thanks Rowena Rappaport, too, for her fine editing. And thanks to everyone behind the scenes, especially all the people listed on the credits page. Thank you for making this book happen.

Kathleen gives special thanks to her brother-in-law, Gerald Sindell, for his profound counsel on everything relating to the business of publishing.

And finally, Kathleen thanks the folks who put investing information online for the public. They have changed the financial community forever.

Publisher's Acknowledgements

We're proud of this book; please send us your comments through our Online Registration Form located at www.hungryminds.com.

Some of the people who helped bring this book to market include the following:

Acquisitions and Editorial

Editorial Director: Joan Whitman

Associate Editor: Melanie Rutledge

Copy Editor: Kelli Howey

Production

Director of Production: Donna Brown

Production Editor: Rebecca Conolly

Layout and Graphics: Kim Monteforte, Heidy Lawrance Associates

Proofreader: Allyson Latta

Indexer: Belle Wong

General and Administrative

CDG Books Canada, Inc.: Ron Besse, Chairman; Tom Best, President; Robert Harris, Vice-President and Publisher

Hungry Minds Consumer Reference Group

Business: Kathleen Nebenhaus, Vice President and Publisher; Kevin Thornton, Acquisitions Manager

Cooking/Gardening: Jennifer Feldman, Associate Vice President and Publisher; Anne Ficklen, Executive Editor; Kristi Hart, Managing Editor

Education/Reference: Diane Graves Steele, Vice President and Publisher

Lifestyles: Kathleen Nebenhaus, Vice President and Publisher; Tracy Boggier, Managing Editor

Pets: Kathleen Nebenhaus, Vice President and Publisher; Tracy Boggier, Managing Editor

Travel: Michael Spring, Vice President and Publisher; Brice Gosnell, Publishing Director; Suzanne Jannetta, Editorial Director

Hungry Minds Consumer Editorial Services: Kathleen Nebenhaus, Vice President and Publisher; Kristin A. Cocks, Editorial Director; Cindy Kitchel, Editorial Director

Hungry Minds Consumer Production: Debbie Stailey, Production Director

Contents at a Glance

Cartoons at a Glance

By Rich Tennant

"No, that's not a pie chart. It's just a corn chip that got scanned into our portfolio summary."

page 267

COACH SPAULDING AND HIS WIFE CHECK THE STOCK MARKET

"Get ready, Mona — I think I found a winner."

page 101

Wanda had the feeling that her husband's new portfolio management program was about to become interactive.

page 215

"I'm not saying I believe in anything. All I know is since it's been there, our online investment picks have been posting 50% higher returns."

page D-1

"I couldn't get this stock-screening software to work on my PC, so I replaced the motherboard, upgraded the BIOS, and wrote a program that links it to my personal database. It told me I wasn't technically inclined and should set up a meeting with a financial adviser."

page 179

"Oh yeah, he knows what he's doing online. When he tries to check his investments, he gets a computer message saying there's 'Insufficient Memory' to complete the task."

page 9

Fax: 978-546-7747

E-mail: richtennant@the5thwave.com

World Wide Web: www.the5thwave.com

Table of Contents

Introduction

Welcome to the second edition of *Investing Online For Canadians For Dummies.* The Internet offers an astounding amount of financial information, and this edition of *Investing Online For Canadians For Dummies* provides clear advice and ample illustrations to help you navigate the Internet. With the assistance of this book, you can learn about your investment options, develop personalized and effective investment strategies, and start investing online.

Plenty of books are available about online investing, but most assume that you are a practised investor who enjoys talking in "Bay Street–speak." This book is different; it doesn't include statements like "Our goal is to maximize after-tax returns at a controlled risk level" or "Even though the stock has done well, it remains cheap at mid-year, trading at 40 cents on the dollar of net worth and a third of the market's P/E." In other words, this book is a "big picture" guide to online investing that explains the basics and shows how to build wealth for beginning online investors of all ages and income levels.

In this book, you find out how to get started, what you really need to know, and where to go on the Internet for more information. You don't need to memorize complex commands or formulas. We describe everything in plain English, and we leave the Bay Street–speak out in the street, where it belongs.

Who Are You?

In writing this book, we assume the following:

- ✔ You would like to take advantage of all the timely investment information and useful tools available on the Internet.
- ✔ You want to get some investment work done using the Internet. (Online research, analysis, and monitoring of investments can be time-consuming — online investing really is work.)
- ✔ You intend to invest mainly in Canadian and U.S. securities markets.
- ✔ You are not interested in becoming the next Warren Buffett — at least not this week.

About This Book

Many online investing books are written by individuals who maintain Web sites, and these books often promote their authors' investment systems, products, and services. Other investment books are written by professional money managers to promote their newsletters or their mutual funds. This book, however, has no hidden agenda. It focuses on common-sense ways to create and build wealth with the Internet. It has no bias.

We've designed *Investing Online For Canadians For Dummies,* 2nd Edition, for novice online investors, but it can also benefit industry experts such as financial professionals and planners. Each chapter stands alone and provides the instructions and information you need for solving an investment problem or making an investment decision.

Most online investors will read this book in chunks, diving in long enough to solve a particular investment problem ("Hmm, I thought I knew how to contact an electronic brokerage, but I don't seem to remember . . .") before putting it aside. However, the book is structured so that if you want to read it through from beginning to end (even though it's primarily a reference tool), you can. That's because we've crafted it in a way that mimics the process people often follow to make an investment decision — starting with research and ending with monitoring and selling an investment. Discussing online investment topics in a logical way makes it a lot easier to learn the essentials of online investing.

Here's a quick rundown of some of the topics we cover:

- ✔ Using the Internet to help you make and keep money
- ✔ Getting up-to-the-minute equity quotes and company data 24 hours a day
- ✔ Finding the best savings rates and bond data on the Internet
- ✔ Locating Internet resources for selecting mutual funds
- ✔ Working with Internet tools for researching, analyzing, and selecting stocks and bonds
- ✔ Trading through an online broker and paying the lowest commissions possible
- ✔ Monitoring and tracking your equity or mutual fund portfolio
- ✔ Discovering down-to-earth strategies that can build wealth with small investments

As well, we give warnings to help you avoid dangerous or costly traps, and we point out excellent online investment resources. Most resources presented are Canadian in origin, but many of these deal with both Canadian and foreign investment options. *Investing Online For Canadians For Dummies,* 2nd Edition, is your road map to using the Internet as a potential wealth-building tool. It provides the Internet knowledge that you need to get the edge on investors who rely only on old news found in newspapers and magazines.

How to Use This Book

If you have a question about an online investing topic, just look up that topic in the table of contents at the beginning of the book or in the index at the end of the book. You can get the help you're seeking immediately or find out where to look for expert advice. Don't hesitate to use the table of contents and the index often.

Investing has become a specialized field that isn't particularly easy for the average person. Luckily, the Internet offers plenty of sites where you can research the basics of investing before you buy or trade.

If you want to get your feet wet before jumping into online electronic trading, visit the Investor Learning Centre of Canada (www.investorlearning.ca). You can read their educational "Money School" Web pages that show you how the world of investments works.

If you're new to investing on the Internet, check out the first three chapters in Part I. They give you an overview of the Internet and some important investor tips. To become more familiar with the Internet, try some of the activities that we suggest in these chapters.

If you are new to the Internet, we recommend that you get a copy of *The Internet For Canadians For Dummies,* 2nd Edition Starter Kit, written by Andrew along with John R. Levine, Carol Baroudi, and Margaret Levine Young (CDG Books Canada, Inc.). It can help you hook up with Canadian Internet providers, surf the Net, download free software, and join mailing lists or discussion groups.

If you're a new investor, check out Chapter 17, which offers warnings about online fraud and shows you where to turn for more help. When you start participating in investor discussion forums or subscribing to online publications, you're likely to receive e-mail stock tips and investment offers. Treat these messages as you would any telephone cold call. Thoroughly examine the investment and get a second opinion from an independent investment expert you respect before you trade.

How This Book Is Organized

This book has five parts. Each part stands alone — that is, you can begin reading anywhere to get the information you need for investment decision-making. Or you can read the entire book from cover to cover.

Here are the parts of the book and what they contain.

Part I: Online Investing Fundamentals

In Part I, you find out how and why you should use the Internet as a tool to help you invest. Some handy technical tips are presented right away. For example, you learn the essentials of downloading and decompressing certain types of files. (Other tools that are more specific to online investing are presented in other parts of this book.) You also get a brief overview of the foundation, or building blocks, of all investments — fixed-income investments, stocks, and mutual funds. A good understanding of these elements is essential if you are to be an effective online investor. In addition, some of the more sophisticated variations of these investments are introduced. Part I also presents Web sites that specialize in bonds, stocks, or mutual funds, and discusses online banking.

Part II: Finding the Right Investments

The chapters in Part II show you how to research and find the right investments. This part of the book shows you how to research fixed-income, stock, and mutual fund choices online. You find out how to wield the Internet as an information-gathering tool. You are also introduced to the world of online discussion forums — where you can "talk" to other investors who share, or even compete with, your interests! You see why online investment discussion forums are some of the most popular places to be on the Net! You can start anywhere in the book, but we suggest you begin with the type of investment that intrigues you the most.

Part III: Tools of the Online Investing Trade

The chapters in Part III cover how to screen, select, and analyze individual stocks and mutual funds online. This part details how to calculate a bond's value and create a yield curve. It introduces and describes key criteria used to screen securities. It also points you to further online sources for annual reports, economic data, industry standards, and more.

Part IV: Trading and Tracking Online

Part IV covers online trading of stocks, mutual funds, and bonds, and includes instructions on how to open a cash account with an electronic broker. An important part of your success is keeping an active eye on your investment portfolio, so Chapter 16 features online tools you can use to make sure you're on top of your progress. In the last chapter in this part, check out important information about avoiding online fraud, with key tips to keep your investments safe and sound.

Part V: The Part of Tens

Part V provides handy top-ten lists packed full of ready online references. The chapters in this part discuss comparing online investing misconceptions and reality, knowing when to buy and sell, planning for a comfortable retirement, and finding tax help online.

Special features

Check out this book's Internet Directory, which includes the latest and greatest investor sites on the Internet. The focus of this directory is on the Canadian (and U.S.) sites you're most likely to use when you allocate your capital among domestic and foreign mutual funds, stocks, and bonds.

The Internet is in constant flux. Thousands of new Web pages are added each day. Some sites listed in this directory (and elsewhere in the book) may change or disappear because of mergers with larger sites. Some Web sites just vanish for no reason. If a site has moved, you may find a link to the new location. If not, try a search tool (such as Google or Yahoo!) to locate the resource you need.

What's in Store

In this second edition of *Investing Online For Canadians For Dummies,* we describe dozens of the latest and greatest Internet resources that are available to assist you in your wealth-building efforts. These Web sites include the newest online investing information, research sources, calculators, spreadsheets, shareware, freeware, and product demonstrations.

The content of *Investing Online For Canadians For Dummies,* 2nd Edition, is both updated and comprehensive, with chapters and information on current topics such as:

- ✔ Moving from saver to investor
- ✔ Bulletproofing your online investing
- ✔ Picking a rising star: New online tools for analyzing stocks
- ✔ Checking out technical analysis, market timing, and other online methods of analyzing stocks
- ✔ Researching online information about fixed-income securities and bonds
- ✔ Practising (cost-free) trading strategies for futures and commodities with online simulations
- ✔ Day trading online for beginning investors
- ✔ Reading the big buy and sell signals

And so much more!

Technical Requirements

The following list details the minimum computer requirements for connecting to the Internet. This list describes all the hardware and software you need:

- ✔ An IBM PC-compatible computer with a minimum of 16MB of RAM, 12MB available hard disk space, any Pentium processor, and a Windows 95/98/ 2000 or Windows Me, NT, or XP operating system. Or . . . a Macintosh or Mac clone with a minimum of 16MB of RAM, 10MB available hard disk space, a Power PC processor, and System 7 or higher.
- ✔ Any Internet browser (such as Netscape Navigator 4.7 or Microsoft Internet Explorer 5.0).
- ✔ A SLIP or PPP Internet connection, with a modem that runs 56 Kbps or faster, or a direct connection.

Icons Used in This Book

In *Investing Online For Canadians For Dummies,* 2nd Edition, we use icons to guide you through all the suggestions, solutions, cautions, and World Wide Web sites. We hope you find that these icons make your journey through the world of online investment strategies smoother.

This icon indicates an explanation for a nifty little shortcut or time-saver.

This icon points out riskier investment strategies plus other things to watch out for.

This icon directs you to a resource on the World Wide Web that you can access with Netscape Navigator, Internet Explorer, or other Web software.

Think of this icon as a mental string around your finger. It reminds you of things you won't want to forget when you're finding your way around the world of online investing.

Feedback, Please

If you have any comments, suggestions, or questions, Andrew, who wrote this Canadian edition, would love to hear from you. Please feel free to contact him in care of CDG Books Canada, Inc., 99 Yorkville Ave, Suite 400, Toronto, Ontario, M5R 3K5. Better yet, send him an e-mail message at `aj-dagys@home.com`.

Part I
Online Investing Fundamentals

The 5th Wave   By Rich Tennant

"Oh yeah, he knows what he's doing online. When he tries to check his investments, he gets a computer message saying there's 'Insufficient Memory' to complete the task."

In this part . . .

You find out why you should use the Internet as a tool to help you invest. Some useful resources are presented. The chapters give a brief overview of the foundation, or building blocks, of all investments — fixed-income investments, stocks, and mutual funds. Part I also introduces you to Web sites specializing in bonds, stocks, or mutual funds, and discusses online banking.

Chapter 1

Why Look to the Internet for Investment Information?

• •

In This Chapter

▶ Taking full advantage of Internet investment opportunities

▶ Picking winning investments online

▶ Visiting an Internet investor supersite

▶ Getting started with Internet resources

• •

*T*imely, high-quality information has always made the difference between making money and not making money. In the past, big-time investors had tickertape machines in their offices churning out the latest Bay Street stock prices. Now you can have a personalized stock ticker automatically run on your desktop computer, or have your cellphone beep a stock price to you while you vacation at Mont-Tremblant.

In this chapter, we kick-start your journey into the world of investing online by providing short examples of how the Internet can help you navigate each fundamental step of the investing process. Specifically, the Internet can help you

1. **Learn about new investments.**

2. **Research investment options.**

3. **Analyze investment candidates using online tools.**

4. **Trade online: Buy and sell investments.**

5. **Track and monitor your investments.**

To help you get started, we point you toward some helpful online investment resources, and we offer examples of the types of investment information you can find on the Internet. (We assume that you're already connected to the Internet at work, at school, or at home. However, we briefly discuss some important computer hardware, Internet connection, and software issues in Chapter 2, to reflect recent changes in technology since the last edition of this book.)

If you need help getting started on the Internet, pick up a copy of the second edition of *The Internet For Canadians For Dummies* Starter Kit, by Andrew Dagys, John R. Levine, Carol Baroudi, and Margaret Levine Young (CDG Books Canada, Inc.). *The Internet For Canadians For Dummies* Starter Kit, describes what the Internet is (and what it is not), introduces you to Internet terminology and concepts, explains different Internet services, shows you how to navigate the Web, and provides details about how to download some nifty software and other types of files from sites on the Internet.

Can You Earn Big Bucks by Investing on the Internet?

Imagine that it's Monday around 7:00 a.m. You have more than enough time to read the newspaper and check your e-mail before you head out to work. With your cup of coffee in hand, you go to your computer and read your morning e-mail newspapers: *TheGlobeandMail.com* or *National Post Online* (www.globeandmail.com) and (www.nationalpost.com), or *Barron's Online* (www.barrons.com).

You're interested in the Canadian banking industry and have watched the large chartered banks try to merge during the past few years. You notice that XYZ Bank's stock has taken a slight tumble. You find news and a few rumours about possible banking and trading irregularities, but no additional information. The share price has declined from $40 per share to $31, and now it's in your price range. Is XYZ Bank's declining stock price an investment opportunity for you? If you're an online investor, here's what you do:

1. **Go to the Canada NewsWire service and National Post Online (www.newswire.ca and www.nationalpost.com, respectively) and get more information about XYZ Bank.**

   You find more news about the irregularities but no company press releases or additional information.

2. **Go to Adviceforinvestors.com (adviceforinvestors.com) or SEDAR (www.sedar.com) and get an in-depth company report.**

   The report indicates that the bank hasn't experienced any recent management, staff, or financial problems.

3. **Go to XYZ Bank's home page and get a copy of the bank's most recent annual report.**

   You review the multi-year summary of financial figures, stock prices, and dividends, on the lookout for unusual trends.

4. **Compare XYZ Bank's performance to the industry average at Yahoo!** (`finance.yahoo.com`).

   The bank's return on equity (ROE) is 19 percent. Bad-loan write-offs and investment income levels are also fine, and are in fact better than most Canadian banks.

   Note: ROE is one gauge of overall shareholder return. It measures an investor's gain or loss for a particular stock. ROE is determined by taking a company's annual after-tax profit and dividing it by the equity in the company. (Equity is what's left over — hopefully a lot — when you subtract all of a company's liabilities from its assets). A high ROE rate is good and means that the company is giving back lots of income to the shareholders who invested in the company.

5. **Check what Standard & Poor's has to say about XYZ Bank at** `www.standardpoor.com`.

   Standard & Poor's, a North American equity analysis and rating service, indicates that XYZ Bank's growth in profits and operating income has consistently improved. Its analysts have not discovered and commented on any unusual events.

6. **Check what the experts have to say at Zacks** (`my.zacks.com`).

   They still recommend buying the stock and expect earnings to jump ahead early next year.

7. **Crunch a few numbers, perform your fundamental analysis with the help of the Internet (as we discuss in Chapter 8), and decide that future returns will pay for the risk you're taking now.**

8. **Contact your online brokerage and place your order.**

   When the market opens, you want to purchase 100 shares of XYZ Bank stock because you believe that the rumours about banking and trading irregularities were just that — rumours. Your online broker will e-mail you notification later in the day that your trade was executed. You can check on it at lunch.

So does online investing sound complicated? It's not, and thousands of people invest online every day — men and women in all walks of life. If you have a computer and Internet access, you can do it, too. This book shows you how.

Picking a Winning Investment Online

You may be a beginning investor who is unsure about how to leap into the finance world, or you may be an experienced investor looking for an extra edge or something new. Whatever category you fall into, the Internet can provide you with the tools and resources you need.

You don't have to be a technical genius to access all the available Internet tools, research sources, and financial data. You don't even have to be an experienced investor. The Internet can help you pick winning investments that match your financial objectives. Here are just a few of the many ways the Internet can assist you in picking winning investments:

- ✔ You can find investment opportunities in the news, discussion forums, and mailing lists to subscribe to.

- ✔ You can receive daily tailored and personalized news reports by using services such as My Yahoo! (`my.yahoo.com`). (We discuss tailored news providers in chapters 9 and 11.)

- ✔ You can subscribe to investor supersites to study specific industries and general conditions of the market and to watch what professionals say and do. (We offer examples of these supersites later in this chapter. More examples are scattered throughout this book.)

- ✔ You can study the past-performance data and review earnings estimates of investment candidates online (see chapters 7 to 10).

- ✔ You can create your own analyses and make decisions based on your own online research (see Chapter 9).

What Can Investors Find on the Net?

The Internet is the most comprehensive and useful tool ever placed in the hands of the individual investor. With it, you don't need to be a Bay Street insider to build your small savings into a solid investment portfolio. All you need to be is online. Here are a few examples of what you can find:

- ✔ Company annual reports, 24-hour access to U.S. Securities Commission filings (reports required by securities regulators for publicly traded companies south of the border), 24-hour access to filings with the securities commissions overseen by many Canadian provinces, other in-depth industry and company data, earnings estimates, and broker recommendations for companies you're considering as candidates for investment.

- ✔ Alerts for when the prices of your chosen stocks reach predetermined buy or sell targets. The alerts may come through your instant messaging service (such as AOL Instant Messenger — also called AIM), or through an Internet-ready cellphone.

- ✔ All the information you need for buying and selling treasury securities and government, agency, and corporate bonds.

- ✔ Internet programs to sort through thousands of Canadian and U.S. mutual funds to find those few special mutual funds that meet your investment criteria.

A word of caution

Some Internet investments may sound too good to be true. Well, they are. Just like any place, the Internet has its share of frauds, schemes, and deceptions. Investments in stocks, mutual funds, and bonds are not guaranteed to $60,000 the way Canada Deposit Insurance Corporation (CDIC) savings deposits are. If your legitimate investment loses money or if someone deceives you in some type of "get rich quick" scheme, no CDIC insurance payments exist to cover your losses.

✔ Internet screening tools to sift through thousands of North American stocks to find the ones that meet your predefined needs and financial goals.

✔ Online portfolio management programs that automatically update your portfolio each evening.

✔ Real-time and delayed stock quotes displayed on your desktop.

✔ Very low commission fees for your online trades.

Don't invest until you determine your personal financial goals and decide how much risk you can take. You should also give some consideration to spreading your investments around to diversify your risk. After you set these goals, online investing allows you to take control of your finances and start building wealth.

Where Should You Start?

According to several surveys, the average online investor uses the Internet about 12 hours each week. The average time non–online investors spend on the Internet is about 9 hours per week. As this comparison indicates, if you use the Internet to do your own investing, you won't spend a significantly longer time in front of your computer than other people do.

Connecting to the Internet gives you access to millions of documents, a vast variety of software programs, and high-calibre information that in the not-too-distant past only large financial institutions could access. The World Wide Web provides an easy-to-use interface that allows you to access the Internet's many financial resources. This interface lets individual investors (1) acquire an education in investing, (2) avoid costly financial services, and (3) conduct high-grade online research. Picking your first investor resources is an important task. You can get a good feel for what's available on the Internet at compilation sites called investment *supersites*. Here are a few examples:

✔ **Canada Stockwatch** (`www.canada-stockwatch.com`) offers delayed quotes (quotes are communicated about 15 to 20 minutes after the trade really occurs), detailed charts, news, industry research, earnings estimates, and more.

✔ **The Canadian Online Investor** (`www.stockreviews.com`) is a daily online newsletter that provides investors with Canadian and U.S. market commentaries and overviews, as well as information about currencies, interest rates, and commodities. Each issue details market movers, stocks to watch, breaking news, and a company highlight.

✔ **CANOE Money** (`www.canoe.ca/money`), shown in Figure 1-1, is a collection of links and guides to online resources that deal with investor education, stocks, mutual funds, financial planners, reference material, risk reduction, and investment clubs.

✔ **IE:Money** (`www.iemoney.com`) is the online version of Canada's national personal finance magazine. It's a big-picture resource to help get financial advice on investing and more. From here, you can access investment tools, news, and links to other investment information (see Figure 1-2).

✔ **Investment Basics** (`www.fidelity.com`) is a site where Peter Lynch, a successful investor, former fund manager, and author, freely offers his expert advice on topics such as the key things that every investor should know; how to design your investment strategy; and ways to implement your investment plan.

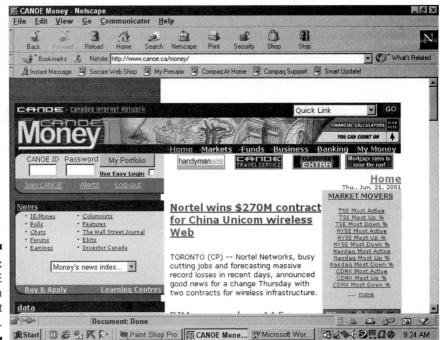

Figure 1-1: CANOE Money can help you get started.

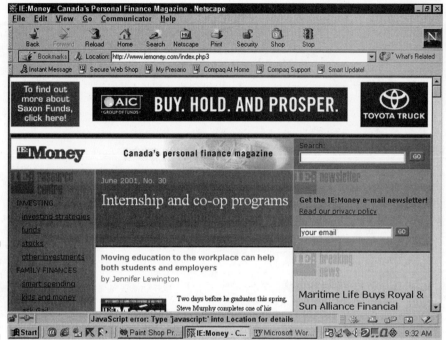

Figure 1-2:
IE:Money
can give you
valuable
advice.

✔ **INVESTools.com** (`www.investools.com`) provides newsletters, portfolio workshops, quotes and news, research reports, and data on Canadian and U.S. securities.

✔ **Investorguide** (`www.investorguide.com`) features newsletters, research, a thousand answers to frequently asked questions, and a well-organized investor and educational directory with links to thousands of investor Internet sites.

✔ **Microsoft Investor** (`www.investor.msn.com`) offers investment research, news and feature articles, portfolio tracking and management, and stock and mutual fund screens. Microsoft Investor provides a free stock ticker that you can personalize and add to your Microsoft Active Desktop component or your Web page.

✔ **Money & Investing** (`www.eldernet.com/money.htm`) is geared to investors over age 50. This site provides tutorials on the basics of investing, mutual funds, stocks, and bonds. Also included is sound advice on how to select a financial adviser.

✔ **Quicken.ca** (`www.quicken.ca`) is an investor supersite with portfolio management, delayed quotes with graphs, newsletters, prospecting tools, breaking news and alerts, research data, and investor education.

Avoiding information overload

When you're just starting out on the Internet, it's easy to be overwhelmed by the huge amount of business and financial data available. The best way to avoid information overload is to divide these resources into specific categories. Add these categories to your browser's book-mark file. For example, this chapter provides information for these bookmark categories:

✔ Investment news and market commentary

✔ Investment publications

✔ Investment tutorials, training, and simulations

Bookmarks offer a convenient way to retrieve Web pages. To bookmark a Web page, all you have to do is click the bookmark (or favourites) icon in your Internet browser, which leads you to a drop-down menu. To make a new category, just click New Folder and enter the title in the folder text box. For example, to bookmark a page,

click File→Bookmark. If you make a mistake, just click Edit→Bookmark and make your correc-tion. Bookmarks are stored in a list that's saved on your computer's hard disk. Once you add a bookmark, it stays on your list until you remove it or change lists. For more information about bookmarks, refer to *The Internet For Canadians For Dummies,* 2nd Edition Starter Kit by Andrew Dagys, John R. Levine, Carol Baroudi, and Margaret Levine Young (CDG Books Canada, Inc.).You can find more investor news, finance, and investment organizations on the Internet. Competition is high, so many groups are willing to give away a large amount of high-quality infor-mation, downloadable software, and online tools for free. These organizations hope you become a fan of their great services. Those that charge fees, or those that support themselves, want to acquire you as a steady paying customer for their products or services.

✔ **U.S. Securities and Exchange Commission** (www.sec.gov) articles are available for beginning investors. The Securities and Exchange Commission (SEC) is an American government regulatory agency. Its feature articles aim to inform and protect first-time investors.

FAQs sources

The Internet is continually flooded with newbies. To keep up with the demand for beginner information, experienced online investors have devel-oped frequently asked questions (FAQs) Web sites to answer questions that are asked again and again. These sites are convenient and can often save you much time and effort (even if you are an experienced investor).

If you're seeking the answer to just one question, use your Internet browser's Find Word in Page function. For example, go to the FAQ Web site you select from the list of sites below. Click Edit at the top of your Internet browser.

A drop-down menu appears. Choose Find Word in Page. Enter your keywords and press Enter. Your Internet browser searches the page for the words you entered. This makes your page search more efficient and shortens your research time.

The accumulated answers in these FAQs present a solid personal finance seminar, highlighting the stock market and investing. Here is a listing of some of the best sites available at this time:

✔ **The Investment FAQ (**`www.invest-faq.com`**)** site answers your questions about investment and personal finance matters (see Figure 1-3). Alternatively, you can browse categories for the answers you're seeking. Don't miss the regularly updated tours for beginning, intermediate, and experienced investors.

✔ **The Syndicate (**`www.moneypages.com/syndicate/faq`**)** lists FAQs from investment newsgroups (see Figure 1-4, on the next page). The Web site is designed to help beginning or experienced investors better understand investing.

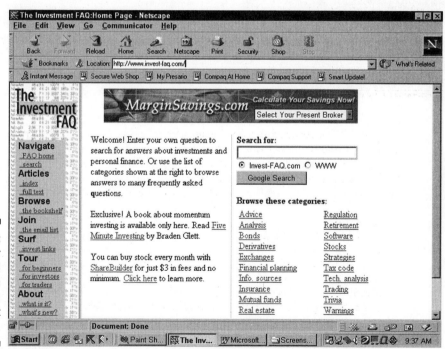

Figure 1-3:
Enter your question and get answers at The Investment FAQ.

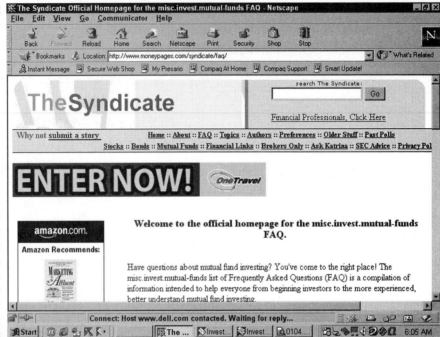

Figure 1-4:
The
Syndicate
has the
answers
you're
looking for.

Glossaries

As you cruise the Internet, you may encounter Web sites that discuss stocks, online trading, technical analysis, and *derivatives* (financial instruments such as options and futures whose price is derived from the price of an underlying financial asset). The language may seem arcane and undecipherable; however, the Internet can help. You can find many online glossaries to assist you in stretching your vocabulary. The following are a few examples:

✔ **Equity Analytics, Ltd. (**`www.e-analytics.com/glossary/glossar1.htm`**)** provides a technical analysis glossary. (Technical analysis is a statistical approach for valuing stocks and forecasting stock prices.) Go to `www.e-analytics.com/glossdir.htm` to find other financial glossaries.

✔ **Web Investors (**`www.webinvestors.com`**)** provides a fast and easy way to research investment concepts on the Web. It includes definitions, definitions with links, and new features each month. Type in the words "investment glossary" in this Web page's search tool to get a list of more glossaries.

✔ **Yahoo! Financial Glossary (**`biz.yahoo.com/f/g/g.html`**),** shown in Figure 1-5, offers a convenient glossary with hyperlinks that define words used in the text. For example, if a definition uses the word *option*, you can click the hyperlink and get the definition.

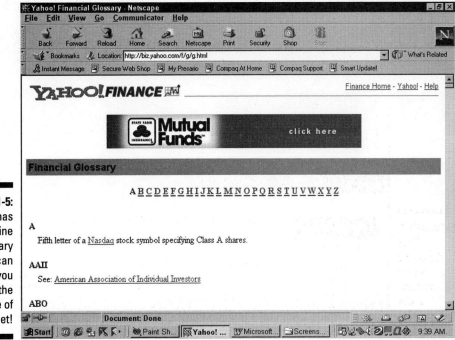

Figure 1-5:
Yahoo has an online glossary that can help you speak the language of Bay Street!

Chapter 2

Internet, Here I Come

• •

In This Chapter

▶ Evaluating your computer system

▶ Considering your Internet connection

▶ Downloading files

▶ Opening your downloaded files

• •

*T*he Internet can assist you in getting the information you need to be a savvy investor. For the most part, this is very easy. To start, you need the right equipment, software to run it (and run on it), and a good Internet connection. Also, files are sometimes sent to your computer in a funny format, and they have to be deciphered. At other times, you may need to download special trading software (for example, Nasdaq Level II) or data from your broker that you want to transfer online to a spreadsheet program on your computer. This chapter explains how to do these types of things. It's more straightforward than it sounds.

The Right Stuff: Hardware and Software

If you want to invest online, you'll need to get on the Web. To do that, you'll need certain computer hardware and software. If you're already a computer whiz, and an Internet veteran, then simply compare your current computer system with the following technologies just to make sure that you're up to speed. If you are just starting out, then we recommend that you consider computer systems with the specifications outlined next.

Certain online-investing-related software packages (discussed throughout this book) require a minimum level of computer processing power. Virtually all of today's new computers (PCs or Macintoshes) pack enough firepower to get the job done quickly. If you are looking for a Pentium-based PC system, opt for a Pentium II or higher. You can expect to pay around $2,000 for a

Pentium III system, including software and a monitor. Equally fast processors (300 MHz CPU speed or higher) offered by Apple (Power PC), AMD, and Cyrix are also fine. Super-fast systems, boasting 1,500 MHz and rivalling those used by Bay Street traders, are also available. Undoubtedly, you will see many systems available for much less money, but you usually get what you pay for. If the price is cheap, most likely the components — held together by multicoloured rubber bands — are as well!

Purchase as much PC or Mac as you can afford. Memory of 64 MB or more and hard disk space exceeding 20 GB should serve you well. Buying computer power and memory is especially important if you intend on doing some day trading (which we discuss in Chapter 15). Don't skimp on the basic package, which consists of a monitor, processor, and memory. Instead, feel free to skimp on the glow-in-the-dark printer, or that insurance company software application that predicts your date of death!

One other note: Most current online-investing software mentioned in this book will run on any of the following operating systems: Windows 95, 98, NT, 2000, Me; XP; OS/2; or Linux. Most will also run on Macs with a Mac OS 8 operating system or better.

The Connection

Different Internet service providers (ISPs) offer different types of connections. The key word here is *broadband* — or, in plain English, fast speed!

There are several methods available to connect your computer to the Internet. Each method has a different speed. The speed of an Internet connection, or the *data receipt transfer rate*, is measured in bits per second (bps). Modems list their connection speed in kilo (thousand) bits per second (Kbps). The faster ISPs list their connection speed either in mega (million) bits per second (Mbps) or giga (billion) bits per second (Gbps).

Plain-vanilla connections

Most Canadians still use dial-up modems, which use a copper telephone line to access the Internet. But asking Granny to hang up when you want to pick up a quick 200 shares of E*Trade today may cost you your inheritance tomorrow! Many online investors prefer more flexible and much faster Web-access options.

DSL

DSL is short for *digital subscriber line*. This technology, or Internet conduit, also uses your existing telephone line. However, it's able to significantly increase the bandwidth over the lines between your home and the telephone company. DSL gives you 24-hour access to the Internet and does not interfere with incoming and outgoing telephone calls from, and to, Granny. Your computer is connected to the Internet 24 hours a day, and you can use your telephone anytime you wish.

One important point about DSL: To get maximum benefit by way of speed, you need to live less than four kilometres from your phone company's switching stations. (A switching station is a phone company facility where tiny robots figuratively "pull" a phone line cable from one switchboard socket and insert it into another socket. Unlike back in the days of Bell Canada switchboard operators, these little robots pull about 10 million switches per second!) Anyway, the closer you are to these switching stations, the faster the data transfer rate. Data transfer rates range from 128 Kbps to 8.5 Mbps.

Sympatico High Speed Edition (www.hse.sympatico.ca) is an example of a DSL Internet service. A friendly technician named Gus will arrive on your doorstep to deliver, install, and configure the DSL high-speed modem, the Ethernet card, the phone filters, and the special software. The tip is extra! Okay, they aren't all named Gus, but they are all pretty friendly.

Cable modems

A cable modem may be an alternative for you, if you have cable TV and your cable company supports the service. A special cable modem allows you to connect your computer to the "box" that connects your TV to the cable. (Don't feel guilty if you had to re-read that last sentence. We had to re-read it three times!) The data receipt transfer rate for a cable modem is about 27 Mbps, but it depends on the cable company's connection to the Internet and how many people in your neighbourhood are using it — just like it says in the TV commercials!

ISDN

Integrated services digital network (ISDN) is another Internet option some people consider. Where a regular vanilla-flavour phone modem uses your current analog telephone line, for ISDN service the telephone company installs a new "digital" line. ISDN service is typically allocated in 64 Kbps channels; so, one channel gives you a 64 Kbps connection, two channels gives you a 128 Kbps connection, and so on. ISDN is used mostly by businesses since it's quite expensive and annoyingly complicated to install.

Using FTP to Get Investment Information Online

Some online investors develop complex spreadsheets containing company data. They use the spreadsheets to analyze companies from many angles. Sometimes a company is analyzed for financial strength. At other times, the spreadsheet is used for technical analysis, where the investor tries to predict which way a stock will move. Many investors are now sharing their spreadsheet creations online with other interested investors.

Lots of investment-related software programs, called *freeware* or *shareware*, now reside on the Internet. These programs help online investors make investment decisions. Many investment supersites point you to these resources.

Not all data files are available from a Web site. In many cases, a spreadsheet or software program can be accessed only through a file format called *FTP — file-transfer protocol.* You need to know how to deal with an FTP download.

Silly FTP tricks

To use an FTP server, you have to log in with a username and password. What happens if you don't have an account on the FTP server machine? No problem, if it's a publicly accessible FTP server. You log in as anonymous and type your e-mail address as your password. *Voilà!* You have access to lots of files! This method of using public FTP servers is called *anonymous FTP.* There's nothing sleazy about it; public FTP sites expect you to use anonymous FTP to download files.

Where do I go?

Anonymous FTP sites are a type of Internet bulletin board. They are a rich resource of information and software on thousands of topics. The Internet has several repositories of anonymous FTP files. One repository that you'll want to visit is TILE.NET (www.tile.net/ftp).

Once there, you can find anonymous FTP sites in one of several ways. FTP resources are listed by subject, country, and site name. You can also use the built-in search engine to fine-tune your quest for a specific anonymous site.

The URL of FTP

To get your Web browser to transfer files by using FTP, you use a special kind of URL. You have probably typed URLs that begin with www, which allow browsers to talk with Web servers. To tell your Web browser to log in to an FTP server, you type a different kind of URL — an FTP URL. An FTP server's URL looks like this:

```
ftp://servername/directoryname/filename
```

You can leave out the directory name and filename, if you like, to get to the top-level directory of that FTP server. For example, the URL of the Microsoft FTP server (at ftp.microsoft.com) is

```
ftp://ftp.microsoft.com/
```

This URL has no filename part: If you omit the filename, the server displays the top-level directory to which you have access.

No matter which Web browser you use, you follow the same general steps to retrieve files via FTP.

1. **Run your Web browser as usual.**

2. **To tell your browser to load the URL of the FTP server, type the FTP URL (in much the same way you would type in a Web site URL) in the Address, URL, or Netsite box, just below the toolbar, and then press Enter.**

   The browser logs in to the FTP server and displays its home directory. Each file and directory in the current directory appears as a link. If you're asked for a login name, type anonymous in lowercase letters.

3. **Move to the directory that contains the file you want, by clicking the directory name.**

   When you click a directory name, you move to that directory, and your browser displays its contents.

4. **Download the file you want by clicking its filename.**

   If you download text, a spreadsheet, a computer program, or another file that your browser knows how to display, the browser displays it after downloading. If you click the filename readme.txt, for example, the browser displays the text file. If you want to save the file after you look at it, choose File→Save As from the menu and tell your browser the filename to use.

5. **If your browser asks what to do with the file, tell it to save the file, and choose the directory and filename in which to save it.**

   Your browser downloads the file.

As mentioned earlier, with FTP you can download investment freeware and shareware programs to install and use them. Many financial companies promote their investment products by offering free or time-limited demo versions. You may need a few well-chosen software tools, including a program to decompress compressed files. (Useful little programs like this one are called *utilities* in the jargon.)

Installing FTPed software usually requires three steps.

1. **Using FTP, download the file that contains the software.**

2. **If the software isn't in a self-installing file, it's usually in a compressed format, so decompress it.**

3. **Run the installation program that comes with it, or at least create an icon for the program.**

You already know Step 1, the FTP part. The rest of this discussion describes Steps 2 and 3: decompressing and installing. Here goes!

Decompressing and unzipping

Most financial and other software on FTP servers is in a compressed format, to save both storage space on the server and transmission time when you download the file. An increasing amount of software is *self-installing* — the file is a program that does the necessary uncompressing and installing. Self-installing Windows files end with .exe; non–self-installing compressed files end with .zip.

If a file is compressed, you need a program to deal with it. Files with the file extension .zip identify compressed files (these files are called, amazingly, *ZIP files*). Luckily, someone (a guy named Nico Mak) wrote a nice little Windows program called WinZip that can both unzip and zip things for you, directly from Windows. Mac users can get a program named unzip.

If you already have WinZip (which is also available through the mail or from various shareware outlets), you can skip this entire section.

To get WinZip on the Web, go to www.winzip.com. Click on the link called Download Evaluation to get to the download page. On that page, download either the Windows 3.1 or the Windows 95/98/NT/2000/Me version, as appropriate.

To install WinZip:

1. **Run winzip31.exe or winzip80.exe.**

   That's the program you just downloaded.

2. **Follow the installation instructions that WinZip gives you.**

   Although you have a bunch of options, you can accept the suggested defaults for all of them.

Running WinZip

Give it a try! Double-click that icon! To open a ZIP file (which the WinZip folks call an *archive*), click the Open button and choose the directory and filename for the ZIP file. Poof! WinZip displays a list of the files in the archive, with their dates and sizes.

Unzip it!

If you want to use a file from a ZIP file, after you have opened the ZIP file you extract it — that is, you ask WinZip to decompress it and store it in a new file.

To extract a file:

1. **Choose it from the list of files.**

   You can choose a group of files that are listed together by clicking the first one and then Shift+clicking the last one. To select an additional file Ctrl+click it.

2. **Select the directory in which to store the unzipped files, and click the Unzip Now button.**

3. **Click OK.**

   WinZip unzips the file. The ZIP file is unchanged, and now you have the uncompressed file (or files) also.

Mac users say StuffIt

Mac users can download an unzip program from `ftp.uu.net` in the `/pub/archiving/zip/MAC` directory. More popular than zip and unzip for the Mac crowd, however, is a shareware program called StuffIt. StuffIt comes in many flavours, including a commercially available version called StuffIt Deluxe. StuffIt files of all varieties generally end with the extension .sit.

For decompression, you can use the freeware programs UnStuffIt and StuffIt Expander.

With all this technical information under your belt you're ready to try your hand at the exciting world of investing online. Now, on to the really fun stuff!

Chapter 3

Investing Basics

••

In This Chapter

▶ Moving from saver to investor

▶ Understanding risk

▶ Setting your goals and objectives

▶ Diversifying your portfolio

▶ Using Internet resources to get you started

▶ Bulletproofing your investing

••

*I*f you've been an investor for a while, Part I of this book may seem like old hat to you. You may even want to skip it altogether. But if you're somewhat new to the investment game and are thinking about taking a dip in the world of GICs, fixed-income investments, mutual funds, high-octane stocks, or other sophisticated investment alternatives, then read on. You have to have a firm understanding of investment basics as a springboard to investing online!

In this chapter, we explain what you need to do before you begin investing, as well as how the Internet can help you get started. We spell out how you can move from saver to investor. We show you how to determine your investment objectives and decide how much you need to earn to meet those goals. We also help you figure out your risk-tolerance level so you can make a plan to maximize your personal wealth now.

Equity Investing and Risk

The concept of *investing* means different things to different people. If part of your wealth is already locked into securities such as stocks, mutual funds, or any similar type of liquid financial instrument, you are considered to be an "equity" investor. However, if your money is kept almost entirely in bank accounts, GICs, or Canada Savings Bonds, you are considered to be a "fixed-income" investor, or saver. Investing may or may not take place in Canada. It may also involve things like real estate and art. The line between investing and saving is often a blurred one.

Understanding risk

If you step into the world of equity investing, in whole or in part, you step into various types of equity risk. It is important to cultivate an ongoing awareness of these risks, just as the captain of a ship needs to know where the reefs are at all times.

One of the fundamental concepts associated with equity investing is that the higher the investment risk you take on, the higher the potential return on your investment. So the trick is obviously to balance your personal tolerance for risk (how much money you are willing or able to lose) with the amount of the risk you actually assume when you invest. The more risk you take on, the more aware of it you should be.

Types of risk

The first risk you have to deal with is *stock market risk*. During the recent *bear market* (where stocks trend downward in price over a period of several months), we have seen the values of equities trading on the Nasdaq, the TSE, and to some extent the Dow, plummet. That's market risk! To mitigate it, consider the current position of the stock market. If you think that markets are *oversold* — when people panic and drive down prices well below their value — it may signal a good environment to buy equities. However, if stock "price-to-earnings" ratios and other market-value drivers, like the economy, are unfavourable, you may think twice about investing. Remember that the position of the markets today is often linked to where the economy will likely be six months down the road.

Another type of risk is *business risk*. For example, if you're investing in a high-technology company, the business risk associated with the company is very high. This is because the company is exposed to stiff competition, or demand weakness (nobody wants to buy the company's product or service). Business risk differs by industry and company. The competition within the high-tech industry is fierce, and barriers to entry are often low. This results in more volatility, which in turn drives up overall investment risk. But if you invest in a utility such as Hydro Quebec or Bell Canada Enterprises, the associated business risk is lower due mostly to fixed demand.

Liquidity risk is another investment risk factor to consider. Favour highly liquid securities, where the volume of trading of the stock or mutual fund is sufficient to enable you to buy or sell quickly — with minimum price volatility. In some cases, the volumes associated with some securities are so low that any attempt to buy or sell the security may result in your paying too much — or receiving too little.

If you're investing in foreign stocks or mutual funds, you are exposed to *currency-rate risk*. If the Canadian loonie goes up or down relative to the foreign currency, you may win or lose, depending on the direction of the rate change.

Consider *interest-rate risk* as well. Bank of Canada and U.S. Federal Reserve lending rates are a very important consideration — for both bond and equity investors. Financial stocks, like banks, tend to rise when interest rates go down. When rates go up, these issues tend to stagnate.

Take your attitudes about risk into consideration when you invest. Your risk tolerance often depends on your investment knowledge, your investment experience, and your personality. Each Canadian investor has his or her own investing style and objectives. Knowing exactly what your risk-tolerance level is can help you select investments that offer the highest return for the investment's level of risk.

Planning Your Investment Portfolio

Before you can build an investment portfolio, you need to look at your own circumstances. This plan should work for you and for your family members. Simply put, where do you want your money to take you? It isn't difficult or scary to put yourself to this test; it should be exciting and fun. With a comprehensive plan, some good advice, and a pinch of luck, you can make your dreams come true.

The first step in designing your investment portfolio is to establish your long-term goals. Do you want to retire and travel the world? If so, then your investment strategy may have to be more aggressive. The lifestyle of the rich and famous doesn't come cheap! If you have kids heading to university in a decade, you'll want to stock up on investments you can get at when the time comes. For every plan you can cook up, there are investments that make perfect ingredients. But if you already saved a lot, and want to preserve it, you may be focusing on safer and longer-term investments. Take out a piece of paper and start writing. Make a wish list of what you'd like to happen. We'll work you through how your goals need to match up with the financial choices you make.

Defining Your Investment Objectives

Once you have a clear picture of your personal goals, you need to set investment goals that can make your dreams a reality. Matching your investment style to your personality takes a bit of thinking. After all, we're all different, and there are as many possible investing permutations as there are people!

Some investors seek growth in their portfolios. They want to make a good buck from the funds they invest. And for the sake of that buck, they're willing to roll the dice by investing in riskier investments. Other investors may want to generate payouts from their cash, as interest or dividends, because they need the money to meet day-to-day obligations. Many investors' needs fall somewhere between the two.

The lower the risk you take, the lower your return will be. Investing aggressively — taking a chance with your hard-earned cash — is risky in another way. You run the risk of not getting *investment returns* — the profit you make on your money — that work for you. In fact, you could lose all or part of your initial investment. The level of risk assumed is what distinguishes investing from saving. No single investment will fulfill all your objectives. It is critical that you align your investment goals with your personal goals.

Diversifying Your Investments

Diversification is something you do to diffuse some of your investment risk. Different investments behave differently in various economic and market scenarios. By diversifying your investments, you create some stability in the way your investments behave when changes in the economy or stock market occur.

The best way to describe diversified investing is to think of the cliché "Don't put all of your eggs into one basket." Keep in mind that diversification among assets is not meant to *eliminate* the risk of negative returns. For example, you may diversify asset classes to include a mix of cash, fixed-income investments, stocks, real estate, and other investments. But if your cash and fixed-income returns are reasonable and your stocks plummet drastically, your overall return can still be negative. This occurs in spite of the fact that you diversified your portfolio. This is exactly why a lot of mutual funds provide negative returns even though they are diversified investments.

So we see that there is no one perfect mix of investments to balance risk and reward when you're building your portfolio. Your portfolio asset mix will depend on your risk tolerance, current market conditions, and outlooks for the future economies of Canada and foreign countries.

Another example of a diversified investment portfolio is one where your investment funds are placed in a mix of cash, Canadian fixed-income securities, Canadian stocks, foreign stocks, international mutual funds, and income trusts. The actual proportion can vary — the mix is up to you or your financial adviser after you determine your risk tolerance and investment objectives.

For example, if you want to accept more risk — to try to get really high returns — more of your diversified portfolio pie will be allocated to stocks as opposed to cash. If you're risk-averse, more of your funds will go toward cash and GICs and other more conservative investments. To diversify, you also need to know what your investment alternatives are. People often consider investing to be risky in general, simply because they don't understand how the investment world works and what their options are. Perhaps that's why so many Canadians shy away from investing altogether. Spreading your money around is a powerful way to protect your investments.

Determining How Much You Can Invest

Deciding how much you can invest isn't based on guesswork. It requires some analysis and setting up a budget. A budget is a blueprint that guides you through the process of paying bills, purchasing needed items, putting money into savings, and knowing how much you can invest. Where you can often run into problems is not budgeting for predictable but occasional expenses. Occasional expenses can include car repairs, annual life insurance premiums, tuition, and so on.

 Gaining a good understanding of how much money you can expect to earn and where your cash goes is the first step to determining how much you can invest. Prepare a budget using pen and paper, Internet tools, or personal financial software like Microsoft Money 2001 Deluxe (www.microsoft.com/money) or Quicken Deluxe 2001 (www.quicken2001.com) to track your finances. Because the pen-and-paper method is too time-consuming, and personal software programs can be costly and difficult to learn, we recommend using Internet tools. The Internet offers many online budgeting resources that are free, easy to use, and quick.

Using the Internet to control your finances

Whatever your personal situation, you can find investments that are tailor-made for your requirements. Determining how much money to invest (or whether you have any money to invest) is a big step in the right direction.

The hundreds of existing online calculators can make setting up a budget almost painless. Using the online calculators at the following sites, you can determine your retirement income needs and more:

  ✔ **AGF (**www.agf.ca**)** has several calculators, one of which determines the income you will need when you retire, based on lifestyle assumptions you make.

- **Altamira** (www.altamira.com) can, among other things, show you the savings you need to retire with "X" amount of dollars.

- **Clarica** (www.clarica.com) helps determine your expected income at retirement.

- **Ernst & Young** (www.ey.com/can) provides an online calculator that shows you taxes saved by contributing to an RRSP.

- **FinanCenter** (www.financenter.com) offers a "How Much Am I Spending?" calculator that you can access by clicking on the Budget icon. This calculator shows your income, how much you're spending, and the amount available for investment. The online calculator even derives the future value of your investments if invested for ten years.

- **Retireweb** (www.retireweb.com) is outstanding on the "number crunching" side of things and has several calculators to help manage finances as you move toward retirement. For example, it calculates RRSP contributions versus mortgage paydowns. It also has an assortment of cash-flow calculators to tell you how much you have to save now in order to get "X" amount of dollars in the future. One of the more nerve-racking features of this Web site is the life-expectancy predictor. You enter your vital statistics anonymously and out comes your age of death!

- **Understanding and Controlling Your Finances** (www.bygpub.com/finance/CashFlowCalc.htm) provides an online cash-flow calculator that shows your income and expenses and determines whether you're living within your means.

Most calculators ask you to provide some financial information that is used as a basis for their calculations. Be wary of the fact that calculators sometimes make mistakes. Don't use them as a substitute for professional advice. Rather, use them as a learning tool and a reality check!

Using the Internet to get investment advice and to access government program information

If you want to access a directory of retirement or financial planning advisers, look no further than the Financial Advisor Pages (www.fapages.com), one of Canada's largest directories of financial advisers.

If you want to be your own adviser, you can always take a course. Such courses are available through the Canadian Institute of Financial Planning (www.mutfunds.com/cifp) and the Canadian Securities Institute (CSI) (www.csi.ca). One of the CSI's mandates is to promote investment knowledge.

You can enroll online for one or more of these courses offered by the CSI: Canadian Securities Course (CSC), Financial Management Advisor Program, Canadian Investment Manager Program, Derivatives Program, Management Training, and Specialty Learning. The CSC is geared to individuals who wish to become investment advisers, financial planners, and mutual fund representatives. However, a large proportion of Canadians with the CSC designation are people who just wanted to learn about investing and how to manage their portfolio.

TV and radio are also not to be forgotten! Consider checking out the CBC's Web site (cbc.ca/onair). It has links to business news and more.

If you seek advice from a retirement planner or financial adviser, consider several things. Is the planner trained? How is the planner compensated? Does the planner have experience in areas of concern to many Canadians, such as annuities and Registered Retirement Income Funds (RRIFs)? Canadians who close their Registered Retirement Savings Plans (RRSPs) can further defer the resulting taxes by transferring the RRSP funds into annuities or RRIFs. However, with annuities and RRIFs you have to take a minimum amount of cash out of the plan each year. Those withdrawals are taxed. The preceding Web resources will provide useful advice and help you understand these issues.

The Internet is an efficient and effective way to link to information about government programs and services. The major programs for retiring Canadians, otherwise known as entitlements, are delivered at the federal level. The Web pages devoted to these on the Human Resources Development Canada (HRDC) Web site can be found through the home page at www.hrdc-drhc.gc.ca. This site contains a large selection of information about federal income security and other programs such as,

- ✔ Old Age Security (OAS)
- ✔ Guaranteed Income Supplement (GIS)
- ✔ Spouse's Allowance and Widowed Spouse's Allowance (SPA/WSPA)
- ✔ Canada/Quebec Pension Plan (C/QPP)

Go to www.canada.gc.ca/depts/major/depind_e.html to access a handy master list of all federal programs, agencies, and departments. To find information about the Quebec Pension Plan and other province of Quebec income security plans, go to www.rrq.gouv.qc.ca.

Investing in Securities that Meet Your Goals

Investors often receive hot tips from neighbours, e-mail messages, and message boards or chat rooms. However, studies indicate that chasing these investments — even if they are top performers — rarely produces the returns investors expect. Keep in mind that each security purchase is part of your investment plan, which is tied to your long-term goals. Specifically, how you choose to invest your capital (in mutual funds, stocks, bonds, treasury securities, money market funds, and other types of investments) depends on the following:

- ✔ Your required rate of return
- ✔ How much risk you can tolerate
- ✔ How long you can invest your capital
- ✔ Your personal tax liability
- ✔ Your need for quick access to your cash

The Internet provides many sources of information that can assist you in developing your investment approach. For example, Mutual Funds Online magazine (`www.mfmag.com`) provides information and advice about mutual funds and investing in general. This Web site has scores of archives of online columns dating back to 1999. They are sorted by month and focus mostly on mutual funds. This site also has several handy online analytical tools to help you with your investment decisions.

Checking Out What the Experts Are Doing

After factoring all the elements of this chapter into your investment plan, you may want to find out which stocks are creating the biggest buzz on the Internet and how the experts are responding. Keep in mind that you can follow investment candidates cost-free for years. Following, we list some of the best Internet investment starting points:

- ✔ **The Gordon Pape Web Page** (`www.gordonpape.com`) includes assessments of several companies' retirement planning online resources.
- ✔ **Investorguide** (`www.investorguide.com`) offers links to thousands of investor-related sites. This well-organized guide includes site reviews, summaries, and investment research.

- ✔ **StockHouse (**www.stockhouse.ca**)** is a Canadian investment Web site that includes daily market wrap-ups, newsletters, information about stocks and mutual funds, easy-to-use screening tools, and research sources.

- ✔ **Zacks Investment Research (**www.zacks.com**)** specializes in free and fee-based investment research. Get American (and many Canadian) company reports, broker recommendations, analysts' forecasts, earnings announcements, and more.

Tracking and Measuring Your Success

After selecting, analyzing, and purchasing securities, your work still isn't done. Managing your investment portfolio can help you squeeze every bit of profit from your investments and realize your financial goals. You need to find information on changing market conditions, study analytical techniques, and update your financial plan regularly. The Internet provides many portfolio-management tools that include all these features. (See Chapter 16 for more details about online portfolio tracking and monitoring.)

If you want to calculate your returns or expected returns with pencil and paper, it's relatively easy, assuming that no additional purchases or redemptions were made during the period you're calculating (other than the reinvestment of dividends, interest payments, or capital gains distributions). To calculate your return, start with the ending balance and subtract the beginning balance. Divide this number by the beginning balance and then multiply by 100 to determine a percentage. This percentage is your return. The formula is as follows:

$$\text{Total Return} = \frac{(\text{Ending Balance} - \text{Beginning Balance})}{\text{Beginning Balance}} \times 100$$

Suppose that you invest $10,000 in stocks on January 1, 2002, and on December 31, 2002, your account has a value of $12,174:

1. **Start with the ending balance and deduct the beginning balance.**

   $12,174 − $10,000 = $2,174

2. **Divide the result by the beginning balance:**

   $2,174 / $10,000 = 0.21740

3. **Multiply the result by 100:**

   0.2174 × 100 = 21.74%

   Your return is **21.74%**.

Setting realistic expectations

When you start your investment program, don't expect to become a millionaire overnight. History has shown that the market has many ups and downs. However, when looking at the long term (five years or more), investors have been rewarded for their patience. Additionally, riskier investments held over the long term provide higher rewards than low-risk investments. As you can see from the following statistics, less risk equals less return. For example, from 1970 to 1997, $1 invested in treasury bills grew to $6.22. For bonds, $1 invested from 1970 to 1997 increased to $11.07, and $1 invested in stocks for the same period grew to $22.62.

A return of 21.74 percent in one year (by anyone's standard) is pretty good. This rate means that for each dollar invested, you earned $0.22. To determine whether this rate of return "beat the market," you need to compare it to the appropriate benchmark.

Bulletproof Investing

This chapter details the beginnings of the investment process, and if you glanced through, you can see that selecting securities isn't the first thing investors do. Choosing investments is just one of many elements in the process. To bulletproof your investing, you need to complete the many tasks detailed in this chapter. The following is a checklist that outlines how you can bulletproof your investment plan:

- ✔ **Determine where you stand.** Gain a good understanding of what your financial commitments are for now and the future. Make certain you have an emergency fund and a savings plan.

- ✔ **State your financial goals clearly.** How much do you need? When do you need it? How much risk can you tolerate? If you lost the principal of an investment, could you mentally recover and invest again?

- ✔ **Determine the appropriate allocation of your personal assets for your age (young adult, middle-aged, retiree, and so on).** Develop a regular investing program and stick to it regardless of market volatility.

- ✔ **Select the investments that meet your financial goals and risk tolerance level.** How much time do you have (in years) to invest? Should you be an active trader and invest often during the day, or a passive investor with a buy-and-hold policy?

Bear market basics

While you are probably familiar with the term *bear market,* you may be confused about what it actually means — lots of investors are. Some financial experts and market watchers apply the term to an *index,* like the Dow Jones or Nasdaq; others apply it to a *sector,* like technology. Still others apply it to North American or world stock markets as a whole.

One sure-fire indicator of a bear market is a continual stock index price decline of 20 percent or more, over at least a two-month period. By this measure, since the mid-1950s there have been ten bear markets in stocks trading on American exchanges. That translates into about one bear market every five years in U.S. equity markets, as measured by the Standard & Poor's 500 Index. Bear markets can even strike bonds, although infrequently. An example of a recent bear market is the one that hit the Nasdaq — or the technology sector — early in 2000.

During the darkest days of the Great Depression, the markets in the U.S. fell 89 percent. Between January 1973 and October 1974, the U.S. market lost an incredible 48 percent of its value. The most recent bear market in the technology sector wiped out up to 95 percent of the value of some shares, compared to their peak-level value. That's worse than the Depression from a percentage point of view!

Investment tips during a bear market include these:

✔ **Continue to invest in companies.** During a bear market, babies are often thrown out with the bath water. Identify companies with good *fundamentals* (good revenue growth, expectations of real cash profits, solid management, and positive analyst coverage). You may be pleased to find yourself snatching up stocks trading at lower-than-reasonable prices — real bargains!

✔ **Don't make sudden trades.** Shift investments within your portfolio(s) gradually. Remember that a market recovery can happen anytime. Selling securities too low is as tragic as buying them too high.

✔ **Be realistic.** The days of massive run-ups in high-tech stocks will not recur in the short term. Investors won't easily forget how much it stings to lose personal savings.

✔ **Be patient.** Bears don't turn to bulls overnight. Some rebounds have been known to come about quickly, but others take longer. Having said that, we believe that while bear markets are temporary, market greed is permanent! That's why you can expect an eventual turnaround after most bear markets.

✔ **Analyze your investment candidates.** Before you call your online broker, make certain that you can explain to a child in two minutes or less why you want to own a particular investment. Determine how long you plan to hold the security and decide at what price you will sell (and take your profits or cut your losses).

✔ **Select an online broker that suits your needs.** Avoid mutual fund loads and high fees. Use automatic investment plans, dividend reinvestment programs, investment clubs, and other programs to reduce brokerage commissions (see Chapter 15 for more information).

✔ **Monitor your portfolio and re-evaluate your goals on a regular basis.**
Rank the performance of your investments and make the appropriate
changes. You can expect that the introduction of new products and new
technology, as well as changes in general market conditions, will affect
how established businesses operate. Use this information to know when
to hold and when to fold.

Check out Investor Home at `www.investorhome.com` for more information
about the investment process and bulletproofing your portfolio.

Some investments are simple. Others are a bit more complex. So to lay the
groundwork for your ability to invest online, we introduce three of the basic
types of investment classes. These are the roots and common denominators
associated with virtually all other, more complex investment options.

The first investment class is the fixed-income instrument. The second class of
investment involves stocks. The third type of investment pertains to mutual
funds. Stay tuned; the next three chapters deal with these investment options.

Chapter 4

Fixed-Income Investments

● ●

● ●

*F*ixed-income investments are an important part of the global financial plan. In this current era of volatile markets, there is a very strong demand for safe, income-yielding, fixed-income investments. *Fixed-income investments* are just that — investments that legally entitle you to a fixed amount of interest income. Depending on what you want your money to do for you, fixed-income investing could be just the right thing for all or part of your portfolio.

This chapter presents the basics of fixed-income investing and points you to Internet resources that can tell you even more. Since the gateway to many fixed-income investments is often through your bank, we introduce you first to the basics of online banking.

Saving for that Rainy Day

Let's start by being blunt — a savings account earns very little in the way of rate of return on the money you park there. To make matters worse for many Canadian bank account holders, interest rates are slowly creeping down. In addition, you have the "privilege" of paying service charges for using the account. Putting too much money in a bank account is a very poor investment choice. In fact, it's not much of an investment decision at all.

Even with all of the warts associated with savings accounts, you still have to deal with the issue of banking in general. Many Canadians complain — rightly so — about the myriad of service and other charges that banks levy. What can you do? The best plan is to shop around for the best deal. Good banking deals do exist. The Internet can help you find those deals and may even compel you to bank on the Web!

Managing your bank accounts

To start, examine your banking needs and then match the range of service packages available from various banks to meet those needs. Make sure you get value for the service fees you pay. If you don't, look for a bank that provides this value.

Never in Canadian history has the banking landscape been so competitive. Every week, banks offer you more services. It's hard to keep up. But why does it still seem that your overall banking fees haven't gone down as much as you would like? In our opinion, the answer is simple: banks, like any business, will try to get away with whatever they can charge you. As long as a competitor does not charge less for a product or service, expect to pay more.

Despite the competitive environment, there is still a notable lack of consistency among the banks. Some banks charge less for servicing your finances, whereas others offer better rates on your cash balance. This presents an opportunity for you to find the bank — or banks — that offers the highest return on your deposits and the lowest service charges. Easy enough — if you're willing to dedicate hours to phone calls or bank visits! The Internet saves the day! How? It's a seriously powerful information-gathering tool.

Why Canadians bank on the Web

The Internet gives you access to two things. The first is information about all financial institutions. The second is your bank account and other personal financial information — all from the comfort of your home.

With the Internet, you can locate, assess, and comparison-shop a wide variety of services, financial products, and fees. Services vary tremendously from bank to bank — more than you may have thought.

Another key reason to bank online is the fact that most financial institutions allow their customers to access the details of their bank accounts electronically, anytime and anywhere. This means that you can access your account with your PC to pay bills, transfer funds, get a statement, and verify balances.

The Web's Brink's truck

Secure Internet transactions are already available, making online banking a reality. Security software is getting better all the time. In fact, most Internet analysts agree that there is now a lower risk of your being a victim of Internet fraud than, say, of having someone look at your credit card number (or take your duplicate credit card slip) in a store and use it for fraudulent purposes. This extra security should help us all sleep a little easier.

Online banking may also provide a seamless link to your broker, especially if that broker is affiliated with the bank. For example, TD Waterhouse provides an online brokerage service that is affiliated with the Toronto-Dominion Bank.

As well as advertising a multitude of services, most bank Web sites post current interest rates and service fees. Most allow you to apply for a bank account online. It's convenient and quick, and banking through the Internet allows you to access information that you might not find in your branch. Check it out!

- ✔ **The Bank of Montreal** (www.bmo.com) provides budget calculators that are useful to anyone who wants to control their expenses.

- ✔ **The Canadian Imperial Bank of Commerce** (www.cibc.com) offers its customers access to an online financial planning magazine called *Net Worth*. A retirement calculator is available to help you determine the future value of your investment savings.

- ✔ **Scotiabank's** (www.scotiabank.ca) Web site, shown in Figure 4-1 on the next page, has links to several RRSP calculators that you can access to perform "RRSP reality checks." Other calculators on this site allow you to determine your net worth and cash flow — essential information to know before you invest.

- ✔ **TD Canada Trust** (www.tdcanadatrust.com) provides access to comprehensive and timely reviews of the Canadian economy. This Web site also features a market update, and a comprehensive online library of economic reports. This big-picture information is helpful for investment decision-making.

When choosing to bank through the Internet, remember to compare online access fees, transaction fees, online service packages, and the overall sophistication of the online service.

The big banks aren't the only players in town. If you are looking for the URL for a bank, trust company, or credit union, Yahoo's financial services directory at www.yahoo.com/Business_and_Economy/Companies/Financial_Services/Banking can give it to you.

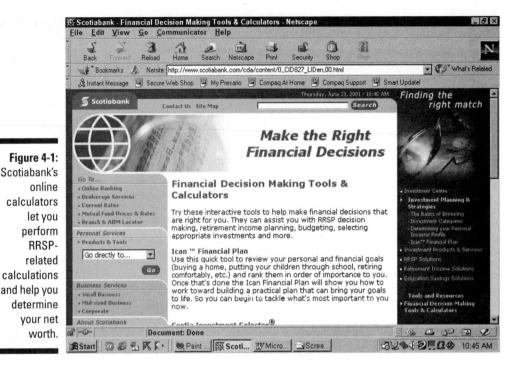

Figure 4-1:
Scotiabank's online calculators let you perform RRSP-related calculations and help you determine your net worth.

The Canadian Financial Network (CFN) (www.canadianfinance.com) is a repository of more than 6,300 international online financial resources. According to CFN's home page, the resources are outlined in enough detail to ease your search and target the information you want. CFN is geared to Canadian investors. Once you find the CFN Web site, you notice that most financial institutions provide locators (directories) of their branches and services.

Comparing accounts

If you wish to compare accounts at various Canadian financial institutions (including trust companies and credit unions), Industry Canada's Financial Service Charges Calculator (www.strategis.ic.gc.ca), shown in Figure 4-2, can help. This Web tool analyzes your banking habits based on a series of questions and evaluates the cost of your banking transactions with a selection of accounts. This shows how flexible the Web can be in taking individual differences into account.

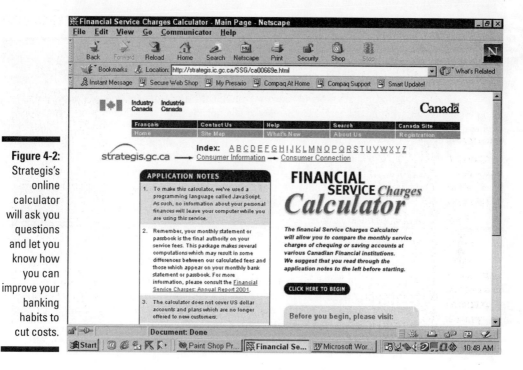

Figure 4-2:
Strategis's online calculator will ask you questions and let you know how you can improve your banking habits to cut costs.

PC versus Internet banking

Not all interactive banking services are created equal. As well as banking through the Internet, a public domain, you can use a system of online banking called "PC (direct-dial/private network) banking." In this private system, you use your modem and computer, but you dial the bank directly rather than using the Internet. PC banking is a good alternative for Canadians who feel a little uneasy about the Internet — especially when their lifetime savings are involved! The end results for both options are the same: efficient and informed banking.

Should you switch banks?

Don't hesitate to re-evaluate your current banking habits. Stay with your bank only if it offers discounts and the best returns on savings available to Canadian customers. The Internet can change how you handle your finances. Instead of passively being a long-standing bank customer, you can be empowered, actively managing your funds from the comfort and convenience of your home.

The Canada Deposit and Insurance Corporation

You may have built up a substantial nest egg or you could be just getting started in the investing game. Either way, you want to be sure that your life savings are protected. You may have heard a little about the Canada Deposit and Insurance Corporation (CDIC), which offers $60,000 worth of protection to your hard-earned cash. But did you know that there are ways to double the amount they'll insure? Did you know that not all financial instruments are protected? A visit to CDIC at www.cdic.ca is a lot easier than slogging through the maze of voice mail that is typical of many "information lines." At the CDIC site, you can access information on how your savings are protected from loss, and put it to work for you.

Get a "feel" for an institution by studying its financial products and services. Decide which institution best suits your needs. A newly discovered bank or trust company that is sensitive to your needs should be at least as acceptable to you as your current one. Be a vigilant consumer of banking services!

Finally, don't just consider the size or origin of a financial institution. The Internet is universal, allowing for large and small participants. As long as you have CDIC or equivalent protection, consider smaller Canadian banks, foreign institutions operating in Canada, and local credit unions. Canadians like a personal touch and want to feel that the people behind the Web sites are accessible. Some Canadians may prefer service in another language. For example, HSBC (www.hsbc.ca) excels at addressing the international finance and language needs of its Asian clientele.

Term Deposits

Term deposits are a popular form of fixed-income investment. Part of their popularity stems from their simplicity. They pay interest on the face value of the certificate. Interest is guaranteed, and is slightly higher than what you'd get with a bank savings account. Term deposits are offered by banks and credit unions. They range in term from 30 days to 5 years. Usually, a minimum deposit is made, the amount depending on the term. You can redeem term deposits prior to maturity, but the level of interest you earn is much lower if you do.

Like savings accounts, term deposits earn very little interest. When interest rates were high, they may have been a good option. With today's lower interest rates, however, it's not a good idea to make them your only type of investment. Their low returns pretty well force most Canadians to look at other investment options.

Guaranteed Investment Certificates (GICs)

Guaranteed investment certificates (GICs) are another type of fixed-income investment. GICs pay rates of interest that are slightly higher than the rates paid by term deposits. With most GICs, you won't actually get the cash *principal* — the amount you originally invested — until the GIC matures. The maturity date occurs when the legal obligation to pay interest to you expires, and the principal and remaining interest is returned at that time. However, some GICs might be sold or transferred at market value. It's also possible to purchase monthly GICs, and this eliminates the problem of not getting cash until maturity. Monthly GICs have a simple term of one calendar month, so you're never without cash for long. However, the *yield* (interest divided by principal) on these is much lower than traditional, longer-term GICs. Generally, you can obtain a GIC with a term ranging anywhere from 30 days to 5 years.

Lately, there has been a flurry of new GICs. For example, it's now possible to get multiple terms within one single GIC — at different rates of interest. You can also get GICs that allow you to take some money out at regular intervals.

Index-linked GICs

Index-linked GICs link your GIC to the growth of stock markets. There is potential for growth through capital gains. Capital gains are what you get when you subtract all costs of an investment from the proceeds of disposition (sale or legal transfer). Linked GICs came about to allow investors the opportunity to have the security of a risk-free fixed-income investment and still play the market. There are many types of index-linked GICs available today. More variations and indexes are coming out all the time. Make certain you read the fine print before investing in any one of these. There can be some surprises in the form of restrictive rules and punishing limitations.

Typical terms for index-linked GICs are three to five years. In most cases, there is no limit on the maximum return. Many are eligible for inclusion in your Registered Retirement Savings Plan and will help you gain some valuable tax breaks (more on RRSPs, a popular tax deferral tool and savings vehicle, in Chapter 21). Keep in mind that with this type of GIC your cash will be tied up for an extended period of time. So find out what it will cost you to exit from this type of GIC. Be aware that the return a GIC of this nature gives you is considered interest, not capital gains. Interest is taxed at a higher rate.

More like saving than investing

Index-linked GICs are more like savings than investments. They are better than regular GICs when Canadians experience low inflation, almost at the doorstep of deflation. E-mail a bank and have it send you its literature on its index-linked GICs (bank home page URLs are listed earlier in this chapter).

CIBC is one of several banks with Web pages on index-linked GICs (see Figure 4-3). CIBC has an online worksheet to help you calculate the value of your index-linked GIC. Go to `www.cibc.com/products/investment/rrsp/sell/marketMixGIC.html` for a detailed description of GIC products.

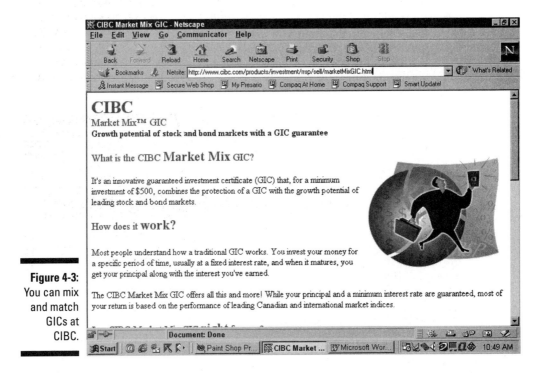

Figure 4-3:
You can mix
and match
GICs at
CIBC.

Treasury Bills

Treasury bills, also known as *T-bills,* are fixed-income, money market bonds. Both the federal and provincial governments issue T-bills. *Federal government* T-bills carry the highest credit rating and are very liquid. Issued in large denominations, the Bank of Canada auctions treasury bills every other week. They can mature in anywhere from 91 days to 1 year. Treasury bills are sold at a discount to their face value. Say you buy a $10,000 treasury bill for $9,150. When it matures, you are entitled to the face value of $10,000. The difference of $850 ($10,000 less $9,150) is the interest you earn over the term of the treasury bill.

Treasury bills are very good investments if you're looking for safety — the government guarantees them 100 percent and there is no limit on the amount they'll cover. T-bills do not increase your wealth at a rapid pace — they only protect it.

Treasury bills can be in Canadian or American dollars. A minimum investment is usually $10,000 U.S. for an American T-bill. For Canadian T-bills, the minimum purchase or investment amount is $5,000. Most financial institutions sell them. You can get more information about Canadian treasury bills by going to the Bank of Canada's Web site (`www.bankofcanada.ca`), shown in Figure 4-4. You can also access information about exchange rates, convert currency online, access an online inflation calculator (useful for calculating future savings requirements), and even see if there is an unclaimed bank account in your name!

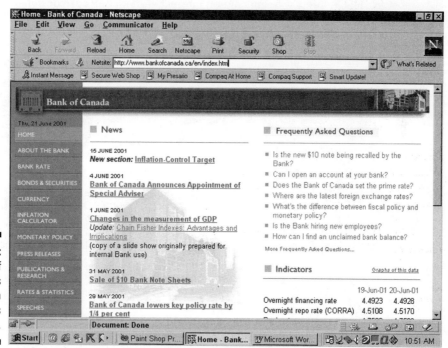

Figure 4-4:
The Bank of Canada has information about T-bills and more.

Provincial T-bills are guaranteed by the issuing province and range in credit-worthiness from mid- to high-quality. The minimum investment amount varies from $5,000 to $100,000 par value, depending on the issue. The yield is usually 10 to 20 basis points higher than government of Canada T-bills.

Savings Bonds

You've heard about savings bonds. You've probably got some already. If you haven't heard about them, check out the Bank of Canada's Web site (`www.bankofcanada.ca/en/securities.htm`) to find out about the many different types of Canada Savings Bonds (CSBs) available (see Figure 4-5). After inflation and taxes are factored in, however, we think that savings bonds are more of a savings vehicle than anything else. Here's why. . . .

CSBs are yet another form of fixed-income investment. They pay holders a stated rate and amount of interest. Some CSBs pay *compound interest,* where the interest is reinvested instead of being paid out. Compounding effectively results in interest being paid on interest earned. CSBs are designed to provide security of capital invested. Although they can be cashed in at any time,

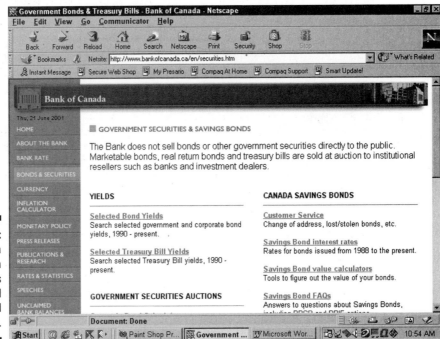

Figure 4-5: There's a Canada Savings Bond designed just for you.

there is no secondary market. This means that you can't sell CSBs to someone else on the open market. They are registered in your name. (So you don't have to worry about losing one, because it's not tradable.) Also, the savings bond is not designed to change in value. It's worth the same amount — its face value plus interest. Regular CSBs pay interest annually, but if you cash them within three months of purchase, no interest is payable to you.

You can get all the information you need about Canada Savings Bonds through the Bank of Canada's home page (www.bankofcanada.ca). The Canada Savings Bond Web pages feature calculators to help you invest wisely.

Government Bonds

Government bonds are issued by governments and are traded by brokerage houses on Canadian and U.S. stock exchanges. The purchase date and maturity date and the interest rate are indicated on the certificate you receive when you purchase one of these bonds.

Government bonds can change in value, just like stocks. So you can earn a capital gain if the change in value goes in your favour. You also receive income in the form of interest payments. Since you can count on a rate of return, these are a safe, relatively sure investment.

You can buy bonds valued in U.S. dollars, or any other foreign currency, or bonds whose rate of interest changes as prime rates do. Such bonds are called *floating rate debentures* — they will increase the rate of your return every six months when the rate moves up, or drop it regularly during periods of decline.

Bond prices are very sensitive to news. For example, when the U.S. Federal Reserve chairman, Alan Greenspan, or Canada's central banker, David Dodge, decides to tighten or loosen credit, the respective government bond prices move as well. This means that bonds with a longer maturity are more volatile than bonds closer to maturity. The behaviour of Canadian government bonds often tracks the behaviour of U.S. bonds.

Bonds are quoted at par, which means 100. When a bond's interest rate is more than the prevailing interest rates, the bond will sell for more than par. In other words, it's worth more! That's because you do better holding on to the bond than you would if you had to settle for a lower "market" (going value) interest rate elsewhere. However, a bond may sell at less than par because you do worse holding a bond that has an interest rate that is lower than the market rate of interest for bonds. The market discounts or places a premium on government bonds based on three key drivers:

✔ **Length of time remaining to maturity:** The longer the time to maturity, the more volatile a bond will be. That makes its value less predictable.

✔ **Interest rate:** Interest rates on bonds are compared to the prevailing interest rates on similar bonds, and are discounted or sold at a premium accordingly.

✔ **Issuer of the bond:** The better the financial strength of the issuer, the more creditworthy the bonds are likely to be. This reduces the risk that the issuer of the bond will default on the obligation. Lower risk will translate into a higher bond value, and vice versa.

There are other marginal factors that affect price as well:

✔ **Bond prices move in a direction opposite to interest rates.**

✔ **Bonds with lower yields are more volatile than bonds with higher yields.** For example, if rates go up, a bond with a 6-percent coupon rate will decline more in value than one with a 7-percent rate.

✔ **Bonds are more volatile when rates are low.** For example, if a bond yield dips from 7 percent to 5 percent, this affects price less than a drop from 4 percent to 2 percent, which is more pronounced.

There is another kind of government bond, called a *municipal bond*. Municipal bonds are debt securities issued by municipalities, counties, cities, or townships to raise money for projects that benefit the Canadian public. They are popular in the U.S., too. Municipal bonds are explained in more detail in Chapter 7.

Strip Bonds

Banks, brokerage houses, and other dealers create strip bonds by purchasing large blocks of good-quality bonds and then "stripping" them apart into their two components — the interest coupons and the principal. Once stripped, the principal amount (residue) and interest payments (coupons) are considered to be separate investments.

If you buy a strip bond, you don't receive interest. Rather, you can make a capital gain by keeping it until maturity; or you can sell it prior to maturity and, if interest rates have fallen since you bought, make a capital gain. In other words, when interest rates go up above the yield of a strip bond, its market price will generally fall. But when current interest rates fall below the yield of a strip bond, its market price tends to rise — because the strip is worth more. Because of this seesaw behaviour, strip bonds can be somewhat volatile.

Strip bonds sell at a discount to face value. The extent of the discount depends on the issuer's creditworthiness. The difference between the discounted purchase price and the value at maturity represents your return. To demonstrate the concept of discounting once again, a Government of Canada strip bond maturing in ten years to provide $15,000 can be purchased today for about $8,400. The difference between these two amounts is your investment return — about 6 percent compounded annually. This example demonstrates the power of compound interest.

Strip bonds can be cashed in anytime. They are risk-free because governments back them. It's possible that the federal government can default on the obligation, but at the moment it's unlikely. Their return to maturity is superior to GICs by a few basis points, depending on general market conditions. Terms range from 6 months to 30 years. They are flexible investments.

Money market strips are essentially like strip bonds, in that the two components of money market strips — principal and interest coupons — can be stripped from each other and sold separately. They too are sold at a discount to face value, and are highly liquid. They're a really safe bet because the federal or provincial governments back them. Terms to maturity for money market strips are shorter, varying from one month to two years.

Any form of bond — stripped or not — is a better investment than a GIC. Bonds can play an important part in the investment strategy of Canadians. They won't give you the type of returns you might get in the stock market; but they don't have the same downside either. You can own a bond directly or through a bond mutual fund.

You can buy bonds of most types from these sources:

- ✔ Banks
- ✔ Brokerage houses or discount brokers
- ✔ Full-service advisers
- ✔ Qualified financial advisers

Corporate Bonds

Corporate bonds are like government bonds. They are available with slightly better yields than government bonds, but that's because of their relatively higher risk. Currently, corporate bonds are selling well. Many Canadians expect corporate bonds to sell well because interest rates continue to fall or stay low and the supply of government bonds is going down. Bell Canada and TD Canada Trust bonds are examples of issuers of corporate bonds.

You need to be able to assess whether a company will have enough money to pay you interest and the full principal back at maturity. Rating agencies, such as the Canadian Bond Rating Service (www.cbrs.com/cbrs) and the Dominion Bond Rating Service (www.dbrs.com), are there to help you along. Give it a try (see Figure 4-6). Type in Nortel and view the results! Remember that you can buy corporate bonds that are rated AAA (the best quality), AA (very good), A (good), down to a basement-level C or D (speculative or default).

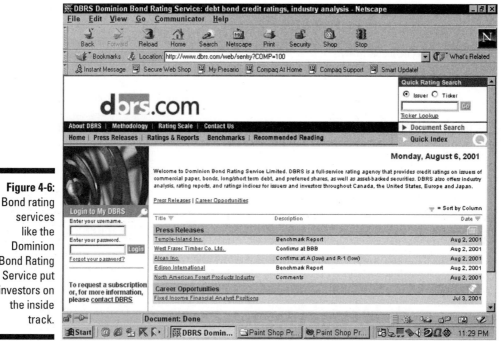

Figure 4-6: Bond rating services like the Dominion Bond Rating Service put investors on the inside track.

Where to Go for Canadian Bond and T-bill Information

There are several Web sites that provide information about various forms of Canadian fixed-income investments. These sites provide primers, show you current interest rates, and even let you trade.

E-Bond Ltd. (www.ebond.ca) is a Canadian, independent brokerage/investment firm and online discount bond broker. E-Bond provides most fixed-income security buyers/sellers with rates for required terms. At E-Bond's site, you can access live rates, investor news, and your account — 24 hours a day.

You can trade online or by phone. E-Bond deals with all areas of the bond markets and reviews a variety of other investment vehicles as well, including federal government bonds, provincial and federal zero coupons, and a selection of high-grade corporate debt.

Bondcan.com (`www.bondcan.com`) is an investment Web site that specializes in fixed-income instruments. Its daily commentary feature provides a summary of the day in the marketplace. It gives daily quotes and end-of-session valuations. Believe it or not, there is even a discussion forum on bonds! As well, you can read the Bonds 101 primer that introduces you to the fixed-income investment marketplace. A glossary teaches you bond-market jargon. Bondcan.com has links to the Bank of Canada and Statistics Canada Web sites, both of which publish bond-market–related articles and historical yields — critical information for any bond investor.

Commercial Paper and Bankers' Acceptance

Commercial paper is issued by very large corporations, and is essentially a short-term unsecured promissory note. The maturity of commercial paper is typically less than 270 days. The most common maturity ranges from 30 to 50 days. Credit ratings vary from high to low quality. The minimum investment is $50,000 par value, and the yield advantage is 20 to 25 basis points higher than Canadian treasury bills. This yield spread varies, depending on the issuer, market conditions, and term to maturity.

Asset-backed commercial paper usually involves a financial company setting up a trust with an aim to acquire financial assets such as leases, loans, and accounts receivable, from Canadian corporate sellers. Trusts, such as Summit Trust, then fund these purchases by issuing asset-backed commercial paper to the public market. This type of commercial paper usually carries a high credit rating and has a minimum investment amount of $50,000. Its yield advantage over Canadian treasury bills is about 30 to 35 basis points.

A *bankers' acceptance* is much like it sounds — a debt instrument that is guaranteed, or accepted, by the borrowing corporation's bank. The credit-worthiness of such issues ranges from high to medium quality. With a minimum investment of $50,000, the yield advantage over Canadian treasury bills is 10 to 20 basis points.

Fixed-income investments at a glance

Fixed-income investments are a lot more complex than many Canadian investors think. There are many types to choose from, each with different features and levels of risk. Following is a list of some of the choices available in the world of fixed-income investing, and a brief description of each.

Bird's-Eye View of Fixed-Income Investments

Investment Type	Quality	Liquidity	Income Timing	Suitability
Guaranteed investment certificates (GICs)	Highest if less than $60,000	Low to none	Annual, semi-annual, monthly, or compounded	Buy and hold
Treasury bills (T-bills)	Highest	Highest	Discounted; no interim payments	Short term/ liquidity
Savings bonds	Highest	Moderate	Varies	Quality/liquidity
Government bonds (including provincial and municipal bonds)	High	High	Semi-annual	Quality/liquidity
Strip bonds (government)	Highest/high	High to moderate	Discounted; no interim payments	Wide range of terms; compound interest
Strip bonds (corporate)	Varies	High to low	Discounted; no interim payments	Wide range of terms; compound interest
Corporate bonds	Varies	High to low	Semi-annual	Higher yield than government bonds
NHA mortgage-backed securities	Highest	High	Monthly: principal and interest	Monthly income; higher yield than Canada Savings Bonds

Chapter 5

The Basics of Stocks

*N*ow let's get acquainted with stocks and some Internet resources that will help you get even more insights into this classic investment vehicle. The savvy online investor reviews all possible stock candidates, looking for companies that are exceptional in some way and positioned to perform well in the future.

In this chapter, we present a primer on stocks and discuss using the Internet to decide which types of securities are right for you. We also show you how to read a stock table and find the ticker symbols of securities online, and we introduce you to stock valuation so that you can make wise investment decisions.

In Part II of this book, we show you how to dig a little deeper when researching stocks. But for now, we begin with the essentials.

Taking Stock of Yourself . . .

Most people spend the bulk of their income on no-frills necessities such as housing, food, transportation, and education. People who don't invest often believe that they can't afford to do so. Investing today usually means giving up some immediate pleasure, such as going on a European vacation, taking the family to see a play, or dining at that great new restaurant. However, even a small amount of money invested each month can make a big impact on your long-term financial security.

Investing can help you stay ahead of inflation and assist you in accumulating real personal wealth with the power of compounding. Successful investing has several key factors, some of which were introduced previously in this book. But before you begin racking your brain trying to remember where exactly these factors were introduced, take heart; we recount them here:

- ✔ **Know yourself.** How much risk to your savings can you tolerate and still sleep at night? How much experience, technical knowledge, and time do you have to make investment decisions?

- ✔ **Know your goals and the time you have to accomplish them.** Understand exactly what's needed to achieve your financial objectives.

- ✔ **Decide how you want to allocate your assets into the three fundamental classes: stocks, bonds, and cash.** You decide how much you want to invest in each class based on how much risk you can tolerate, your required rate of return, and your investment time horizon.

- ✔ **Select specific investment candidates in the three asset classes.** Bear in mind the importance of compounding and the impact of taxes and fees on your returns.

- ✔ **Determine how much risk you can take and other investment criteria for selecting the right investments.** For example, how long can you invest your cash? What is your required rate of return?

- ✔ **Keep current with changes in the economy and other factors that affect your investments.** Strive to make proactive rather than reactive investment decisions. You can keep current by using the online news services listed in this chapter and in this book's Internet Directory. We offer additional how-to information in chapters 9 and 11.

- ✔ **Decide how you plan to define success for your investment selections.** Monitor your investments and keep good financial records.

You can find many asset-allocation worksheets on the Internet. These worksheets help you determine the percentage of your total investment that you will place in various types of investment vehicles. The Financial Pipeline (www.finpipe.com/strategy) has a free, easy-to-use worksheet, shown in Figure 5-1, which can immediately match your risk tolerance to your financial goals. This is a commercial site, however, so be forewarned that Financial Pipeline will try to point you to advertiser services or try to sell you something. Try a financial Web site, such as the one at Canada Life (www.canadalife.ca), shown in Figure 5-2. This site's version of an asset allocation worksheet is an online questionnaire that helps you determine how and where to invest, by looking at your personal investment style.

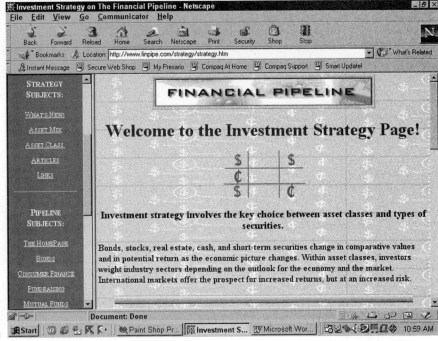

Figure 5-1:
Financial
Pipeline has
worksheets
to help
determine
your
investment
style.

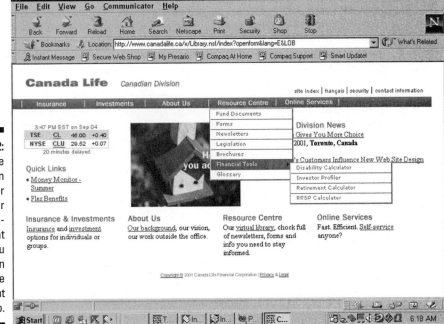

Figure 5-2:
Canada Life
has an
Investor
Profiler
question-
naire that
can help you
develop an
appropriate
investment
portfolio.

Understanding Stocks

When you buy shares of a company, you purchase part ownership in that company. As a shareholder, you also expect to receive *capital appreciation* on your investment — that is, the difference between your purchase price and the market price of your shares. If the company prospers, your shares of stock increase in value. If company performance declines, the market value of your shares decreases.

As a shareholder, you're entitled to periodic cash dividends. (The board of directors decides whether dividends are paid.) The amount of cash dividends paid per year can vary, but they're generally predictable.

Some successful firms, like Dell Computer and Microsoft, do not pay dividends. These companies usually plow all of their earnings back into the company to finance its expansion and innovation. In theory, this increases the value of the company and the price of shares shareholders own. In other words, if all goes as planned the shareholders get capital appreciation instead of a dividend cheque. Some investors in high tax brackets prefer this approach. They don't have to pay taxes on capital appreciation until they sell the stock. With dividends, investors have to pay the Canada Customs and Revenue Agency (CCRA) right away.

The *annual return* is the percentage difference of the stock price at the beginning of the year from the stock price at the end of the year and any dividends paid. The price at which you can buy or sell a share of common stock can change radically. As a matter of fact, stock prices are so volatile that accurately predicting annual returns is impossible. (If we had this gift, we would all be rich!)

For answers to questions like "What is a stock?" "Why does a company issue stock?" "Why do investors pay good money for little pieces of paper called stock certificates?" "What do investors look for?" and "What about ratings and what about dividends?" go to `invest-faq.com/articles/stock-a-basics.html` and read Investor FAQ (Frequently Asked Questions). For answers to questions like "What is a derivative?" "How do you reduce risk?" and "How do we join an investment club?" go to `www.canoe.ca/MoneyStocks/index_knowledge.html`, the site for CANOE Money, shown in Figure 5-3.

Types of Stocks

Just like other investments, several types of stocks are available to try. Each stock type has characteristics, benefits, and drawbacks that you should be aware of before you invest. The following is a quick summary to help you gain an understanding of these financial instruments.

Common stocks

When we think about investing, we tend to think primarily of common stocks. After all, it's difficult not to be bombarded daily with stock market news and commentary. As well, Canadian history is filled with stories about how the Bronfmans, Blacks, and other entrepreneurial industrialists made their fortunes on Bay and Wall streets with common stocks.

Both new and old companies sell common stock to raise capital to fund operations and expand their businesses. *Common stocks* represent shares of ownership in a corporation. Shareholders have a right to dividends and can vote on mergers, acquisitions, and other major issues affecting the corporation. Shareholders also have a voice in the election of the board of directors. Dividends are paid at the discretion of the board of directors. The liabilities of being a shareholder are limited. Shareholders can't lose any more than the amount of their investments.

Preferred stocks

Preferred stocks are also equity stocks in a corporation. However, preferred shareholders cannot cast their votes on issues regarding company management. For this trade-off, the shareholder gets another benefit: a fixed dividend. Preferred stock is sold at *par value* (face value). The par value of preferred stocks is usually $25, $50, or $100. The company assigns a fixed dividend. Preferred stocks (sometimes called hybrids because they include the features of both stocks and bonds) compete with bonds and other interest-bearing financial instruments, which means that the amount of the dividend is affected by the current interest rate at the time that the preferred stock is issued. Higher dividends tend to be issued when interest rates are high. Lower dividends are issued when interest rates are low. Preferred shareholders are paid their dividends regularly and the stock has no maturity date. Canadian banks such as TD Canada Trust and Scotiabank are examples of companies issuing preferred shares to the investing public.

Stock rights and warrants

Stock rights are derivative financial instruments that are similar to stock options. Stock rights allow current shareholders to purchase stock ahead of the public and directly from the company with no commissions or fees, and usually at a discount of 5 to 10 percent. The life of a stock right is generally only 30 days. During this time, the investors can exercise their rights, purchase shares at a discount, and sell them for a quick profit. If investors don't want to purchase the shares outright, they can sell the stock rights for a profit. After the expiration date, stock rights have no value, so stock-right investors need to be quick.

Warrants are a way to gain control of a large amount of stock without having to purchase it outright. Warrants are options to purchase a pre-set amount of stock at a pre-set price, during a specified time period (5 years, 10 years, 20 years, or perpetually). At the time the warrant is issued, the price is fixed above the market price. Warrants have no voting rights or claims on corporate assets. When the warrant expires, it has no trading value. Warrants have value only if the stock is trading at a price that is above the amount stated on the warrant. Warrants are often sold with bonds, as part of an initial public offering, or as part of a merger or acquisition.

For more information about the topics covered in this section, go to www.canoe.ca/MoneyStocks and check out the Markets and other sections. Click an icon or a hyperlink (Learn About Markets, a headline, and so on) to jump directly to the subject matter.

Picking the Right Stock for the Right Goal

Selecting your own stocks can be hard work. The exciting thing is that the Internet has much of the information you need, and most of this information is free. With the power of your computer, you can use Internet data to gain real insight. As you start to determine which stocks you're interested in, you should be aware of the different types of stocks. Stocks have distinct characteristics, and as general economic conditions change they behave in special ways.

Write a short list of your financial goals and then investigate how different types of stock relate to those objectives. Different stocks have different rates of return — some are better for young, aggressive investors; others are better for retirees or for people in high tax brackets. Here are a few examples of the different types of stocks:

- **Blue-chip stocks:** Usually the most prestigious stocks on Bay Street. These are high-quality stocks that have a long history of earnings and dividend payments. These stocks are considered by many to be stable long-term investments — as long as no stock scandal breaks out to undermine that stability!

- **Cyclical stocks:** Stocks of companies whose fortunes rise when business conditions are good. When business conditions deteriorate, their earnings and stock prices decline. These companies are likely to be manufacturers of automobiles, oil and gas companies, and industrial goods plants.

- **Seasonal stocks:** Similar to cyclical stocks; their fortunes change with the seasons. Good examples of seasonal companies are retail corporations whose sales and profits increase during the holiday season.

- **Defensive stocks:** Tend to be stable and relatively safe in declining markets. Defensive stocks are from companies that provide necessary services. For example, utilities prosper during both cold Canadian winters and hot summers. They provide essentials that everyone needs regardless of the economic climate. Companies in this category also provide products such as drugs and food, so their sales remain stable when the economy is depressed.

- **Growth stocks:** Growth companies are positioned for future growth and capital appreciation. However, their market price can change rapidly, as we witnessed throughout much of 2000 in the technology sector. Rather than pay dividends, growth companies typically spend their profits on research and development to fuel future growth. These stocks are good for aggressive, long-term investors who are willing to bet on the future. If you're in a high tax bracket, these stocks may be for you; low dividends mean less taxes. However, if expected earnings don't match analyst predictions, expect a big decline in stock price.

✔ **Income stocks:** Purchased for their regular, high dividends, income stocks usually pay bigger dividends than their peers do. Income stocks are attractive to retirees who may depend on their dividends for monthly expenses. Income stocks are often utility companies, banks, and similar firms that pay higher dividends than comparable companies. These companies are often slow to expand because they spend most of their cash on dividend payouts. During times of declining interest rates, bonds are better investments.

✔ **International stocks:** Investors who put their money in these stocks often believe that Canadian domestic stock markets are underperforming relative to certain foreign markets. These investors are seeking better returns overseas. However, international stocks include some risks that Canadian stocks don't have, such as trading in another currency and using accounting standards that do not follow generally accepted Canadian principles. Additionally, public information may have to be translated, which causes delays and sometimes miscommunication. All these elements add cost and risk to foreign stocks.

✔ **Speculative stocks and initial public offerings:** Speculative stocks are easy to identify because they have price-to-earnings (P/E) ratios that are between 50 and 70 when other stocks have multiples of 15 to 20. A second type of speculative stock is an *initial public offering (IPO)*. An IPO is a company's first sale of stock to the investing public. The company is seeking equity capital and a public market for their stock. Investors purchasing stock through IPOs generally have to be prepared to accept higher levels of risk in exchange for the possibility of large gains. A stock issued under an IPO often has no track record. A good example of a speculative stock is Loudcloud; the stock price of this new public company is volatile, and profits are small.

✔ **Value stocks:** Some Wall Street analysts consider these stocks to be bargains. These stocks have sound financial statements and increases in earnings but are priced less than stocks of similar companies in the same industry.

You can find additional information about Canadian and U.S. stock sectors at Briefing.com (www.briefing.com). Each stock sector has a descriptive narrative, rating, and review date. You can also access free quotes and charts, and set up a portfolio.

How to Read a Stock Chart or Table

Most newspapers and many Internet sites, such as the *Globe and Mail* (www.globeandmail.com) and Canada Stockwatch (www.canada-stockwatch.com), have a listing of the day's stock activities. Table 5-1 shows the type of information you find in a listing for Compaq stock from Canada Stockwatch. (The values in the table are hypothetical.)

Table 5-1	Reading the Stock Pages at Canada Stockwatch
Entry	**Value**
Date	December 17, 2001
Last	67.75 (close)
Change	+3
Volume	14,122,200
Time	4:21 p.m. EST
Exchange	TSE
Day open	64.75
Day high	68.25
Day low	64.125
52-week high	79.50
52-week low	28.75

Here's how to interpret all this information about Compaq's stock:

- **Date: December 17, 2001.** The date that the stock activity is recorded.

- **Last: 67.75 (close).** The dollar amount of the last price for the stock at close of trading. (U.S. stock prices are customarily shown in fractions instead of decimals.)

- **Change: +3.** This change compares the current price to the previous day's closing price. It is the amount of today's gain or loss.

- **Volume: 14,122,220.** The volume or number of shares traded that day or time of day.

- **Time: 4:21 p.m. EST.** The time of the price quote. Some Internet quote services provide real-time quotes; others may be delayed as much as 20 minutes.

- **Exchange: TSE.** The stock exchange that the security is traded on; in this case, the Toronto Stock Exchange (TSE).

- **Day open: 64.75.** The price of the stock at the beginning of the day. The stock may open higher or lower than the previous day's close.

- **Day high: 68.25.** The highest stock price of the day.

- **Day low: 64.125.** The lowest stock price of the day.

- **52-week high: 79.50.** The highest stock price in the past year.

- **52-week low: 28.75.** The lowest stock price in the past year.

Canada Stockwatch is continually updated. See `www.canada-stockwatch.com` for more about how this financial Web site is structured. (This home page lets you see the services they offer.)

Finding Ticker Symbols and Stock Prices Online

A ticker symbol is the letter code representing the company's name in the listing for a publicly traded security. For example, if you want to find the current price for a share of Nortel's stock, look for the company's ticker symbol — NT. On second thought, looking at Nortel's volatile price may be a bit nerve-racking! Ticker symbols for companies traded on the Toronto Stock Exchange (TSE) and the New York Stock Exchange (NYSE) have between one and three letters; stocks traded on the Nasdaq have four or five letters.

Many commercial organizations provide ticker symbols and quotes on the Internet. Canada Stockwatch (`www.canada-stockwatch.com`) is a quote service that has other features that make it a good place to start researching stock prices. For example, you can look up a stock symbol by typing in the name of a company, and Stockwatch automatically finds the ticker symbol. Canada Stockwatch offers various levels of service. For example, free services include daily North American market statistics, gold/silver prices, company information, recent news bulletins for every Canadian public company, multiple company quotes and recent bulletins, price/volume charts for every Canadian public company, a searchable database of certain insider trading reports, and a daily summary of your companies' closing prices and bulletin list.

Canada Stockwatch's fee-based services are charged based on usage. For example, historical Canadian stock prices can be downloaded from as far back as 1986 for 40 cents per year. You can get a list of all bulletins for any company or by bulletin type for 20 cents per company. A list of all bulletins for any date (including today) can be purchased for $1. You can access a list of all the roles a particular individual is involved with in all companies for $1.

In addition to Canada Stockwatch, other online quote services include

✔ **AlphaTrade.com** (`www.alphatrade.com`), a mostly fee-based Web site that provides, for $30 per month, a financial toolkit that gives you flash quotes, a scrolling ticker, news links, and a portfolio tracker. You can customize these tools to track only the markets and securities that interest you. For example, you can track Canadian markets and specific Canadian stocks by customizing the toolkit to do so. A free demo is offered on the Web site.

✔ **Briefing.com** (`www.briefing.com`) provides a free introductory service that includes market comments, quotes, charts, portfolio tracking, sector ratings, and an economic calendar. Briefing.com has two levels of premium service. The first level, called Stock Analysis, is $6.95 U.S. per month (with a free trial) and includes stocks on the move, technical stock analysis, earnings calendar, splits calendar, stock ratings, upgrade/ downgrade reports, and company reports. The highest level of service, called Professional, is $25 U.S. per month (with a free trial) and includes many advanced investor services.

✔ **Canstock** (`www.canstock.com`), shown in Figure 5-4. Canstock requires you to register, provides unlimited free quotes, allows you to set up a personalized portfolio of up to ten stocks, and lets you personalize market information. Canstock also provides fee-based financial content and analytical tools for individual and professional investors.

Enhanced services include real-time and delayed stock quotes, analytical tools, business news, detailed company information, comprehensive mutual fund data and profiles, and currency exchange rates. You can get a 30-day free trial subscription to check out the services.

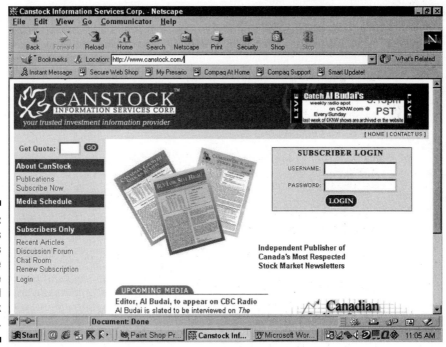

Figure 5-4:
Canstock's services include real-time and delayed stock quotes.

✔ **QuotesCanada (**www.quotescanada.com**)** is another free and for-fee Web site that offers free historical and real-time (up to 50 a day) quotes, index information, newsletter, and portfolio tracking. Enhanced services, at about $30 per month, include real-time scrolling news headlines, real-time customizable streaming quotes, commodity information, detailed charts and graphs, and an oil and gas index.

✔ **Yahoo! (**finance.yahoo.com**)** provides a stock locator feature that covers both Canadian and U.S. stocks. You can search by typing in a company name or by accessing its alphabetical index of companies.

What Does the TSE 300 Have to Do with Anything?

You can measure how good or bad an investment is by comparing it to a market index. For example, the TSE 300 tracks a broad group of large-capitalization stocks that are traded on the Toronto Stock Exchange. Go to www.tse.com to see the TSE Web site.

Each stock in the TSE 300 index is weighted by the relative market value of its outstanding shares. Overall, the index represents the performance obtained in the stock market for large-capitalization stocks. (We define the term *large-capitalization stocks,* or *large-cap stocks,* in Chapter 8.) This index provides performance information so that you can compare the stocks in your portfolio to "the market." If your returns are better than the market, you're doing well. If your returns are lower than the market, you need to re-evaluate your stock selections.

When you compare the performance of your stock to a market index, you can determine whether the stock outperformed the market, maintained the market rate, or underperformed. As Table 5-2 shows, not all market indexes are alike. For example, the U.S. Dow Jones Industrial Average is the most well-known index, but it includes only 30 large, mature, consumer-oriented companies. The Wilshire 5000 is the most comprehensive index of common stock prices regularly published in the U.S. and may be the best indicator of overall market performance. As you can see in Table 5-2, the Standard & Poor's (or S&P) 500 index tracks the performance of large-capitalization American stocks traded on the New York Stock Exchange and the Nasdaq. In other words, the S&P 500 isn't the ideal index for evaluating the performance of your Canadian small-capitalization stock.

Table 5-2	Comparing Apples to Apples with the Right Index
Index	**Type of Security**
Australian All Ordinaries	Large- and medium-capitalization Australian stocks
Dow Jones Industrial Average	Large-capitalization stocks
Financial Times (FTSE)	Large- and medium-capitalization United Kingdom stocks
Lehman Bros. Bond Index	Variety of bonds
Russell 2000	Small-capitalization stocks
S&P 500	Large-capitalization stocks
TSE 35	Large-capitalization stocks on the Toronto Stock Exchange
Wilshire 5000	Entire market

Valuing Stocks

Stocks are more difficult to value than bonds. Bonds have a limited life and a stated payment rate. Common stocks don't have a limited life or an upper dollar-limit on cash payments. This uncertainty makes stocks harder to value than bonds. Despite this, many ways exist to value common stock. Overall, the value of a stock is the current value of all its future dividends. However, common shareholders aren't promised a certain dividend each year. The dividend is based on the profitability of the company and the board of directors' decision to pay dividends to shareholders.

The second source of return for a stock is the increased market price of the stock. If the company decides not to pay dividends and reinvests profits in the firm, the company's future profits and dividends should grow. This additional value should be reflected in a stock price increase in the future.

Fundamental analysis seeks to determine the intrinsic value of securities based on underlying economic factors. It is the most widely accepted method for determining a stock's true value, which you can then compare to current prices to estimate current levels of mispricing. Fundamental analysts usually forecast future sales growth, expenses, and earnings.

To determine the intrinsic value (and what some people feel is the real value) of a stock, many investors turn to the *Value Point Analysis Model,* which uses 12 key factors to value a stock. Overall, the Value Point Analysis Model, which was designed 20 years ago, is used to evaluate a stock's worth in terms of its fundamental economic underpinnings and the general money market. The key factors used are as follows:

1. **Corporate name, ticker symbol, and exchange that the stock is traded on.** This information is used to identify the specific stock you are analyzing.

2. **Number of the corporation's shares outstanding (in millions).** This number represents how many other common shareholders will be paid dividends.

3. **Long-term debt (in millions).** Long-term debt is the amount of any loans or bonds outstanding that mature in one year or more. Debts with terms of one to four years are considered short- or mid-term liabilities.

4. **Current dividend payout ($ per share).** This number is the annualized amount of this year's dividend. For example, imagine that we are in the middle of the second quarter. The first quarter dividend is $0.25. The company pays dividends each quarter. The annualized current dividend is $1.00. (In other words, 4 × $0.25 = $1.00).

5. **Book value or net worth ($ per share).** Many company reports have calculated this number for you. This value is often listed at the bottom of the balance sheet. The formula to calculate net worth is total assets less total liabilities. For example, total assets ($100 million) less total liabilities ($75 million) equals a net worth of $25 million. Net worth divided by the number of outstanding shares equals the book value per share.

6. **Projected earnings ($ per share).** Many company reports include expert forecasts of expected earnings. For example, if earnings for one year are $1.00 and next year the earnings are $1.10, the growth rate is 10 percent.

   You can use experts' earnings forecasts or the amount you believe is correct for your analyses. Remember that each quarter you may see "earnings surprises," and individual investors have often outsmarted the so-called experts.

7. **Projected average growth in sales and earnings (percentage).** Without revenue (sales), you have no profits (earnings) — and corporate earnings are what make stocks valuable. At the beginning of each company's annual report is a letter from the CEO. In this letter, the CEO usually states what he or she expects sales to be for the next year. You may or may not agree with this statement. Enter the percentage amounts that, in your judgment and based on your research, are correct.

8. **Current earnings ($ per share).** Current earnings are often called earnings per share and are calculated for you at the bottom of the income statement. In case you have to do your own math, take net after-tax income and divide it by the number of outstanding shares of common stock. For example, $1.5 million net after-tax income divided by 1 million shares is $1.50 per share.

9. **Current sales price ($ per share).** Check with an online quote server for the current sales price of a share of stock.

10. **Number of years the earning growth rate is expected to be sustained (1.0, 1.5, 2.0 years, and so on).** Some companies have variable growth rates and others have a steady increase that can go on for ten years or more. You need to decide whether the company will sustain its growth rate and for how long. This decision is a judgment call that investors have to make.

11. **Current yield of AAA bonds (percentage).** Luckily, the Value Point Analysis Model fills this number in for you.

12. **Projected change of AAA bonds (percent, 100 basis points = 1 percent).** The Value Point Analysis Model enters a default amount here. If you agree with the amount, don't change it.

If you are averse to math, then the Value Point Analysis Financial Forum at www.eduvest.com can help. The Value Point Analysis Financial Forum includes a community of Canadian and American investors who share information about their stock picks and analyses using the Web site's valuation model. To use the model, click Value Point Analysis Model at the home page. Just enter the 12 factors into the fundamental analysis model. For additional insight, you can post your results and get feedback from others. All this at a price you can't beat — it's free.

Valuation model input and results

No investor wants to pay more for a stock than it is worth. The following mini-table illustrates the input data and results for an online stock valuation using the Value Point Analysis Model, which can help you determine a stock's fair value. An example of user input and results looks like this:

Description	*Model Input*
1. Stock name, ticker symbol, and exchange	Example corporation, EXCC, NYSE
2. The number of shares in millions, greater than 0	1010.00
3. The long-term debt in millions of dollars	28200.00
4. Current dividend in $/sh (xx.xx), annual	8.00
5. Book value or net worth in $/sh	20.12
6. Projected earnings in $/sh, annual	8.80
7. Projected average growth in earnings (%)	5
8. Projected average growth in sales (%)	5

9. Current earnings in $/sh, annual amount   8.17

10. Current price in $/sh, greater than 0   138.00

11. Number of years the earnings growth rate is expected to be sustained (for example, 1.0, 1.5, 2.0, and so on)   1.0

12. Current yield of AAA bonds, greater than 0   6.55

13. Projected change of AAA bonds (%)   0

Description	*Stock Evaluation Results*
NAME SYM EXCH	Example name, Example symbol, NYSE
VALUE POINT ($/sh)	133.55
PROJECTED EARNINGS ($/sh)	8.80
PROJECTED P/E	15.18
VALUE POINT/CURRENT PRICE	0.97
CURRENT P/E	16.89
CURRENT YIELD (%)	5.8
CURRENT PRICE. ($/sh)	138.00
RELATIVE RISK FACTOR	0.90

This table indicates that the Value Point–determined fair value for the stock is $133.55. As well, the model forecasts earnings of $8.80 and a projected P/E ratio of 15.18. The Value Point price is 0.97 of the stock's current price. The stock's current P/E ratio is 16.89. The current yield is 5.8 percent and the current price is $138. The model assigns a relative risk factor of 0.90 to its estimate of the stock's fair value.

In summary, this table indicates that the stock's intrinsic value is $133.55. The stock is currently selling for $138.00. This amount is greater than $133.55, which indicates that the stock is overpriced. If we were you, we wouldn't even think about buying this expensive stock. However, if you already own the stock, it might be a good time to sell.

You can visit the following Web sites for more about fundamental analysis and valuing stocks:

- ✔ **J & E Research, Inc. (**www.jeresearch.com**)**, a group of PhDs and MBAs who specialize in financial modelling, research, and analysis. Try their stock analysis program. It uses an Excel spreadsheet that can assist you in completing the fundamental analysis of any stock.

- ✔ **Simtel (**www.simtel.net**)** offers many downloadable investment programs that can help value stocks and other securities.

Double-checking your Internet-derived valuations

Working with a pen and pencil is okay, but using a spreadsheet program (Excel, Lotus 1-2-3, and so on) is quicker and better. We suggest that you create the table and enter the formulas that follow into your spreadsheet program. Let your computer do the math for you.

To use this fair-value model, create a table with seven rows and five columns. The first column is a description; the next columns are for different stock factors in the next four years.

1. In the first row, first column, type `Current Sales Price`. In the next column, enter the current sales price. The next three cells leave blank.

2. In the second row, first column, type `Dividends (A)`. In the next cell, enter the current dividend. In the following three cells, enter the projected dividends for the next year, the second year, and the third year.

3. In the third row, first column, type `Earnings (B)`. In the next cell, enter the current earnings. In each of the next three cells, enter earnings forecasts for each of the next three years.

4. In the fourth row, first column, type `Payout % (C) (A/B = C)`. In the next cell, type `N/A` (not applicable). In the following cell (using the example), divide the next year's projected dividends (A) by the projected earnings (B) to create the payout percentage (C). The example uses $6.50 / $11.50 = 0.56 = 56%.

5. In the fifth row, first column, type `Earnings Growth`. In the next cell, type `N/A` (not applicable). In the following cell, enter the percentage of earnings growth from one year to the next. The example uses $11.50 (projected earnings) divided by $10.00 (current earning) equals 1.15, which is a growth rate of 15% over last year.

6. In the sixth row, first column, type `Investors Required Rate of Return`. You determine this amount. It is your personal level of return. The example uses 15% for all four years, but your requirements may be different.

7. In the seventh row, first column, type `Projected Growth Rate of Dividends and Earnings`. This is the estimate of how fast the company is growing. The example uses 10% for all four years. Using the example, just "plug and chug." That is, just plug the numbers used in the example into your spreadsheet program and let it chug away, doing the work for you. Multiply the formula's Price-to-Earnings Ratio by the Current Dividend. The result is the stock's Fair Value. In our example the Fair Value is $110.00.

Summing it up, the formula's results are used to compare the fair market value to the current price of a stock. The example has a Fair Value of $110 and the stock's Current Sales Price is $109. If the current stock price is less than the fair market value, then the stock is undervalued and possibly a bargain. The stock in the example is selling for $1 less than the Fair Value and might be a good purchase. (If the current stock price is greater than the fair market value, then the stock is overvalued, which means it's too expensive and not a good buy.)

The type of valuation shown in the formula (and all financial valuation models used in this chapter) should be used with caution. Your good judgment is required for any successful investment. Paying the right price is only one aspect of good investing. For more information on how to pick winners, see Chapter 13.

Options, Options

In North America, an equity option represents the right to buy (a call option) or sell (a put option) an underlying financial asset at a pre-determined price (referred to as a "strike price") at or before a set time (the expiry date). Options can be traded on a stock exchange, just like stocks.

Buying 'em

When purchasing options, you pay a premium for the right to exercise that option at the agreed-upon price and time. For example, one call option contract to buy shares of Micron Technology (a semiconductor manufacturer) at $50 per share, in January 2002, would cost you a "premium" of about $5 per share today. You are not obliged to exercise that right. But if it works out in your favour (the price of Micron rises above $55 by the expiry date), you may exercise it. If not, you would not exercise it.

Option prices relate mostly to risk (price volatility), time frame, and the markets in general. If the options contract (one contract may buy 100 shares) does not work to your favour, you may let the option expire worthless. Your losses are fixed. You can't lose more than the amount you paid for the option. The potential loss is something that you can calculate before you enter into a contract.

Selling 'em

Whenever you write or sell an option, you're undertaking an obligation. This commitment to honour the option, if it is exercised, exposes you to large or even unlimited loss. When you write or sell an option, you'll *receive* the premium paid for that option, but you'll have to leave this premium on deposit with your broker until the option has expired. Brokerages often demand a margin requirement as well. This margin is not like the one used to buy stocks with a broker, since it's not a loan. *Margin* in this sense is a down payment on the commitment you have made. It's a form of security, because if you maintain the contract, you will have to deliver on the obligation, in full.

Eventually, you'll either have to take delivery of the underlying asset at the agreed price (if you are a buyer) or deliver the underlying asset at the agreed price (if you are a seller) at the agreed delivery time. You are not forced to keep that commitment until expiry time. You can terminate your position by selling your commitment to someone who is prepared to buy it from you. In liquid markets this is fairly easy to do.

The big picture

If you believe that a certain stock is likely to make a significant price move and could be a good candidate for an option trade, you are only getting started. You also have to deal with a wide array of choices to execute an options trade. What strike price? What expiry month? Do you trade puts or calls? The list of decisions goes on!

When trading options, first consider several interrelated factors. In addition to stock market risk, other factors include the current share price, option strike price, option premium, the economy and industry, and time to option expiration. In the volatile arena of options trading, it's a must to get a handle on these factors.

How the Web Can Give You More Options

Check out the following Web sites for more information about options:

- ✔ **Chicago Board Options Exchange** (www.cboe.com) is such a comprehensive Web site that the volume of content can be overwhelming at times. But it has great primers on options, and offers free delayed quotes with multiple option quotes and bid/ask spreads.

✔ **NumaWeb** (www.numa.com) is a clearinghouse, or portal, for option (and other financial derivative) Web sites. It has option strategies, calculators, and links.

✔ **Options Industry Council** (www.optionscentral.com) has a mandate to educate the investing public about the benefits and risks of options. This free Web site also has primers about options strategies and answers to frequently asked questions.

✔ **Quote.com** (www.quote.com) offers basic delayed option quotes and new listings free of charge. Some of the enhanced services, like detailed and real-time quotes, are reserved for subscribers.

✔ **Thomson Investor Network** (rtq.thomsoninvest.net) offers free real-time options quotes.

✔ **Yahoo!Finance** (finance.yahoo.com) provides free delayed stock option prices and option chains (different premiums and dates) on individual stocks.

Chapter 6

What's So Great about Mutual Funds?

- -

In This Chapter

▶ Understanding mutual fund types, fees, and risks

▶ Discovering why mutual funds are popular

▶ Finding mutual fund primers on the Internet

▶ Opening a mutual fund account with as little as $25

▶ Checking out segregated funds, index funds, and wrap accounts

- -

*W*ant to participate in potential stock market gains but afraid of the risks? Don't want to pay high brokerage commissions and initial fees? Want to get your portfolio diversified? Well, a *mutual fund* (a pool of investors' money and investments that is managed professionally to meet a particular set of investment objectives) may be for you. When you buy shares in a mutual fund, you are really buying shares of an investment company. A fund manager does all the research. She makes all the decisions to buy or sell stocks, bonds, GICs, or other securities in the fund on your behalf.

Mutual funds are one of the most popular investment vehicles among Canadians — which is pretty amazing, considering that before the 1920s mutual funds didn't even exist in North America. Today, more than 11,000 mutual funds exist in Canada and the United States combined. Total mutual fund assets invested in Canada are valued at $375 billion. In the U.S., that figure is close to $3 trillion. About 25 percent of all Canadian and U.S. households invest in mutual funds. In Canada, individuals are collectively investing about $1.5 billion per month in mutual funds.

In this chapter, we present some general information about mutual fund investment, including types of funds, fees, and potential risks. We explain how you can use the Internet to learn even more about mutual funds, and how to find mutual fund facts and figures online. We also introduce you to special kinds of financial instruments called segregated funds (distinct types of mutual funds offered by insurance companies); index funds, such as exchange-traded funds (ETFs); and wrap accounts. These are all kissing cousins to basic mutual funds.

Mutual Fund Mania

Mutual funds are a good solution for individuals who don't have the time or technical knowledge to track individual stocks. Mutual funds offer a convenient way of investing in stocks, bonds, cash, money market instruments, commodities, and so on. The goal of a mutual fund company is to make more money for individual investors. In return for handling the investments, a fee is paid to the manager of a mutual fund for supervising the investment portfolio and administering the fund. Management fees are normally calculated as a percentage of the total assets of the fund. The fees are referred to as *management expenses*.

Often, the fund manager and technical analysts invest in a collection of about 40 securities. However, any one fund can include anywhere from 20 to 250 securities. The fund manager expects these investments to earn interest from bonds, dividends from stocks, capital gains from buying and selling stocks at opportune times, and any other spin-off profits that can increase the value of the mutual fund. The mutual fund doesn't pay any taxes directly because it is considered by the Canada Customs and Revenue Agency to be a "mutual fund trust." All of the fund's profits are distributed as dividends and capital gains to the investors (the *unitholders*). Income and gains — yes Virginia, gains are indeed possible in bear markets — are taxed at the unitholder level, in the unitholder's hands.

The unitholder pays the annoying management fee, registration fees, expenses for annual meetings, custodial bank and transfer agent fees, interest and taxes, brokerage commissions, marketing costs, and sometimes expenses related to the distribution of fund materials — prospectus, annual statement, and so on. (On the bright side, the fund manager's baby-sitting expenses will not likely be passed on to you. That's due more to the fact that many fund managers are in their early twenties than that they are nice!) Anyhow, these fees and expenses are usually deducted from the dividends paid to unitholders.

Visit the *Globe and Mail*'s GLOBEfund Web site at www.globefund.com for more information about mutual funds. This Web site offers primers for beginners interested in mutual fund investing. Figure 6-1 shows the Online Investing section. There is also a learning page, a Getting Started section, a glossary, and a variety of mutual fund articles by well-known Canadian mutual fund authors.

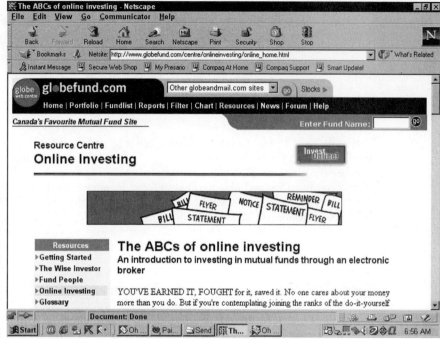

Figure 6-1:
GLOBEfund's
Web site is
a good first
stop to learn
more about
mutual
funds.

Mutual funds can be a good choice of investment because they offer individual investors several benefits:

- ✔ **Diversification:** Mutual funds add securities to a portfolio so that the portfolio's unique risk is lowered. In other words, mutual funds allow you to spread out your risk by purchasing several types of investments in one fund.

  Before you purchase a fund, read the prospectus to see how the assets are allocated. Well-diversified funds provide lots of investor protection. If one stock loses half its value in one day, the effect on the entire fund is small. On the other hand, if one stock skyrockets, the effect is equally small — you won't be able to run out and buy that yacht you've been dreaming about. It is important for all mutual fund investors to understand this.

- ✔ **No broker required:** If you're confident about your investment choices, you'll likely purchase no-load mutual funds directly from the mutual fund sponsor, instead of paying a load (a broker's commission).

- ✔ **No investor homework:** The mutual fund does the tracking and record keeping for you.

✔ **Professional management:** The fund managers, employed by the fund, search for promising investments on your behalf. Having these professionals working for you full-time is supposed to give you a competitive advantage over other investors.

Mutual Fund Basics

With more than 11,000 North American funds to choose from, selecting a mutual fund has become a complex process — meaning that online screening tools are more important than ever before. Many of the Web sites mentioned in this chapter provide basic screening tools based on the type of fund and historical performance. However, mutual fund screening tools are from the Dark Ages compared to the *stock* screening tools introduced in Chapter 12.

When you select your investment criteria for mutual funds, you need to consider several factors:

✔ How long do you plan to own the mutual fund?

✔ How much risk to your principal can you tolerate?

✔ Which mutual fund category best meets your personal financial objectives?

The funds you select will be based on the answers to these questions. If you need your money in a year and can't afford much risk — for example because you plan to use the money to purchase a house — you want to consider a safe, short-term bond fund. However, if this money is your retirement fund that you don't plan to tap for ten years, and you can stomach some ups and downs, you should consider a growth stock fund.

Before you start considering mutual fund candidates, you need to understand some general information: mutual fund fee structures, ways to minimize fees, the types of risk associated with mutual funds, the types of funds you can choose, and how to read a prospectus.

Open-end and closed-end mutual funds

An *open-end mutual fund* has an unlimited number of shares. You can buy these shares either through the mutual fund company itself or your broker. The Canadian Office of the Superintendent of Financial Institutions and provincial regulators require that each mutual fund company calculate the *net asset value* or *NAV* (the market value of all the assets less the liabilities of the fund) of each fund every day at the close of business. Regulations for U.S. mutual fund companies are similar.

A *closed-end mutual fund* is a hybrid — part mutual fund and part stock. A closed-end mutual fund is a publicly traded investment company with a limited number of shares. It doesn't stand ready to redeem its own shares from shareholders, and rarely issues new shares beyond its initial offering. That's why it's a "closed" fund. You can buy or sell these shares only through a broker on the major stock exchanges. The value of these shares isn't calculated by using the NAV methodology. Instead, shares are valued by using a method similar to bonds and are traded at either a discount or a premium. Market prices of publicly traded closed-end mutual fund shares are published daily.

Types of closed funds include closed-end stock funds; investments in common and preferred stocks; closed-end bond funds; investments in a range of bonds; and closed-end convertible bond funds, which have portfolios of bonds that can be converted to common stocks. Closed-end single country funds that specialize in stocks from one country or geographical region are yet another type of closed fund.

Minimizing fees

Loads are the fees with which mutual fund companies compensate the broker who sold the fund to you. About half of all Canadian and U.S. stock and bond funds have loads; money market funds normally don't have loads. Loads and other fees are very important considerations because they reduce your investment returns.

Loading it on

The dreaded *front-end load* is the most common type of fee that mutual fund companies charge. Investors pay this fee when they purchase shares in the mutual fund. No additional fees are charged for redeeming or selling the mutual fund shares. Canadian securities law sets limits on the extent of loads. Loads average about 5 percent for stock funds and 4 percent for bond funds in Canada and the U.S.

The less common *back-end load* fee is charged when you sell or redeem the shares. Back-end fees are usually based on time, starting at 5 percent during the first year and declining a percentage point a year — by year five, no fees are charged. Industry fees range from 0.20 percent to 0.35 percent but can be as high as 1.25 percent.

Generally, funds with back-end loads are more expensive than funds with front-end loads. However, if you are willing to hold your investment for five years or more (which you really ought to, if you're investing in stocks), you pay no load, since back-end loads usually disappear after five years.

What does all this fee information mean? If you purchase 300 shares at $10 per share with an 8-percent front-end fee, you're purchasing only $2,760 worth of shares instead of $3,000. The other $240 goes to compensate the broker who sold you the fund. In other words, your investment needs to increase by $240 just to break even.

Taking it off

Some funds have no loads, which means that they have no front-end or back-end fees. These no-load funds generally don't have a sales force, so you have to contact the investment company directly to make a purchase. Nevertheless, no-load funds do charge service fees, proving that there's no such thing as a free lunch. Mutual fund companies charge annual fees for their management services, deducting these amounts before calculating the NAV.

Annual fees for the fund managers are about 0.50 percent of the fund's net assets. Other service fees include legal and auditing fees, the cost of preparing and distributing annual reports and proxy statements, director's fees, and transaction expenses . . . yada, yada, yada. When added to the management fee, a fund's total yearly expenses can range from 0.75 to 1.25 percent of its assets. This number is also known as the *management expense ratio (MER)*.

Experienced mutual fund investors typically avoid funds with MERs greater than 1.25 percent. Excessive MERs often represent rip-offs.

Some mutual fund companies may have low up-front fees but charge high rates for managing fund operations. The prospectus tells you whether the mutual fund charges these fees. Always be on guard for the tricky accounting games that mutual funds tend to play.

For a great primer on mutual funds, pick up a copy of *Mutual Funds For Canadians For Dummies*, by Andrew Bell, published by CDG Books Canada, Inc. We're pretty sure there's a copy or two stocked in your local bookstore.

Rating Mutual Funds

Mutual funds provide statements about their objectives and risk posture (which is briefly explained in qualitative terms in the prospectus). Rather than provide precise information to help you evaluate the riskiness of a mutual fund, however, these statements often offer vague, general explanations of a fund's approach to risk. For more precise, statistical evaluations of the risks involved with a particular fund, you can turn to independent mutual fund rating services such as Morningstar Canada (www.morningstar.ca) for Canadian mutual funds, and Morningstar (www.morningstar.com) for U.S. mutual funds. Morningstar Canada's BellCharts service, available with a subscription fee, is a powerful tool that can help you compare and assess Canadian mutual funds and more. Go to www.morningstar.ca/Products/ProdBCPlus.asp.

Morningstar Canada and other independent rating services calculate statistics such as the standard deviation of a fund's return and the beta. The standard deviation and beta help you judge how volatile, or risky, a mutual fund is. Specifically, the *beta* is the measure of a mutual fund's (or stock's) risk relative to a market index or other benchmark. A beta of 1.5 means that if the annual equity market return is 10 percent, then we expect the equity fund return to be 15 percent.

Consider standard deviation as an example. Standard deviation offers a clear indicator of a fund's consistency over time. A fund's *standard deviation* is a simple measure of its highest and lowest returns over a specific time period. Just remember this point: The higher the standard deviation, the more volatile the fund, and the higher the risk.

For example, if the three-year return on a fund is 33 percent, that statistic may mean that the fund earned 11 percent in the first year, 11 percent in the second year, and 11 percent in the third year. Or, the fund may have earned 28 percent in the first year, 5 percent in the second year, and 0 percent in the third year. If your financial plan requires an 11-percent annual return, this fund is not for you!

A fund for you, a fund for me

You can choose from a wide variety of mutual fund categories. As a matter of fact, so many types of funds are available that you're almost guaranteed to find a fund that is an excellent fit for your personal financial objectives. You can divide mutual funds into nine groupings:

- ✔ **Aggressive growth funds:** Aggressive growth funds tend to invest in small, young companies and may involve the use of options and futures to reap greater profits. Aggressive growth funds primarily seek increases in capital gains. If the stock market is hot, these funds often provide the biggest return of all mutual funds, mostly because of the capital gains of the stocks in the fund. They also drop the most when the market is cold. Their volatility makes them a poor choice for the short-term investor.

- ✔ **Balanced funds:** Balanced funds are a mix of stocks, bonds, and treasury bills, and possibly some foreign assets. Each fund has a different strategy for determining its *asset allocation mix* (the decision regarding how an institution's funds should be distributed among the major classes of assets in which it may invest).

- ✔ **Bond funds:** Investment-grade bond funds usually have less risk than funds with stocks, but they are not risk-free. These types of bond funds are usually good investment choices for short-, medium-, and long-term investors who desire low risk. Investment-grade bond funds focus on current income. For more information on bonds, see Chapter 4.

✔ **Dividend funds:** Dividend funds are investments in common and preferred stocks offered by corporations that generate a high, steady stream of dividend income. Dividends from Canadian mutual funds usually qualify for a dividend tax credit, thereby increasing the after-tax yield to the unitholder. Dividends from U.S. mutual funds do not have the same benefit. This makes Canadian dividend funds more attractive to Canadian investors. Also, if you earn dividend income, you pay lower tax rates than you do on interest income. This is yet another advantage of investing in dividend funds.

✔ **Equity funds:** Equity funds are funds that invest in the stock market. They are higher risk than money market or bond funds, but they can also offer the highest returns. An equity fund's NAV can rise and fall quickly over the short term, but historically stocks have performed better over the long term than other types of investments. Not all equity funds are the same. For example, some equity funds specialize in growth or technology stocks.

✔ **Growth funds:** Growth funds are similar to aggressive growth funds but have less risk. They may invest in larger, well-established firms with a long track record of earnings that may continue to grow faster than average. These funds also seek stocks with capital gain potential. In addition to stocks, these funds generally include bonds and cash equivalents. Growth funds are best for investors with medium- to long-term objectives.

✔ **Growth and income funds:** Funds in the growth and income category target a steady return with capital growth potential. They often invest in companies that are growing, as well as in companies that are paying high or increasing dividends. Growth and income funds are more diverse than growth funds — they may include bonds — and are less risky, which means that these funds reap fewer rewards if the stock market soars, and lose less if the stock market drops.

✔ **International funds:** International funds include a mix of stocks and bonds from other nations or governments. These funds are subject to several types of risks that domestic mutual funds don't experience, such as political risk and exchange-rate risk (losing money because of changes in the currency exchange rate).

✔ **Money market funds:** Money market funds provide less return and less risk than other types of mutual funds and are good investments for short-term investors. The principal advantage of these funds is their safety. Also, if you ever need to get to your money fast, money market funds allow you to do so.

Table 6-1 provides a brief overview of the time period and risk-tolerance level of the major mutual fund categories.

Table 6-1	Choosing the Right Type of Mutual Fund	
Investment Time Period	*Risk-Tolerance Level*	*Category of Mutual Fund*
Less than 2 years	Minimum risk to principal	Money market fund
	Some risk to principal	Bond fund (short to intermediate bond fund)
Between 2 and 4 years	Minimum risk to principal	Money market fund
	Some risk to principal	Bond fund (short to intermediate term)
	Moderate risk to principal	Bond fund (intermediate to long term)
Between 4 and 6 years	Minimum risk to principal	Money market fund
	Some risk to principal	Bond fund (short to intermediate)
	Moderate risk to principal	Growth and income funds
	Excessive risk to principal	Growth funds and international funds

Setting realistic expectations for your investment choices is important. The Internet provides many information sources about the average rates of return for different categories of mutual funds. You can find out how the fund category you select stacks up against other categories of funds at GLOBEfund (www.globefund.com), shown in Figure 6-2, or Fundata Canada (www.fundata.com), shown in Figure 6-3, both on the next page.

Locating and reading the prospectus

At SEDAR (www.sedar.com) you can access information — including prospectuses — for almost all Canadian mutual funds. If you know the name of the fund you're interested in, you can investigate its activities on this "system for electronic document analysis and retrieval." Target your search by determining the range of dates you want, which filing forms (quarterly, annually, and so on) you want to read, and the name of the specific fund.

After you find the prospectus or other document that you want, you can read it immediately. You can also download it as a special file to your computer or print it out so that you can read the information later. The printed product will look much the same as it did in its original form, before it was transmitted

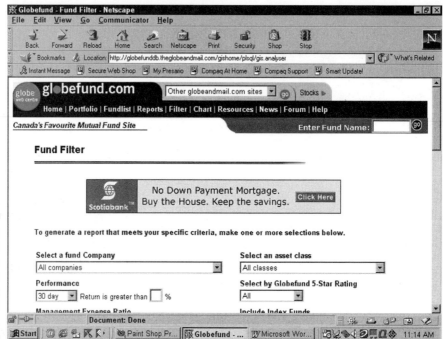

Figure 6-2:
GLOBEfund
lets you
compare
different
mutual
funds.

Figure 6-3:
Fundata
Canada
has lots of
helpful
performance
statistics
that you can
browse.

through the Internet. SEDAR only accepts documents in PDF format, and recommends the Adobe Acrobat Reader program to read the PDF documents. (A *PDF file* is a method for distributing formatted documents over the Internet.) The Adobe Acrobat Reader is available for free at www.adobe.com.

You can easily download the Adobe Acrobat Reader software by following the download instructions from the Adobe home page (www.adobe.com). Once you've found and printed the document you're interested in from SEDAR, you can go to your favourite coffee shop to read it at your leisure!

When you read the prospectus you have downloaded, look for the following information:

- **Investment objectives:** The first paragraph of the prospectus describes the fund's investment objectives and lists the types of securities the fund invests in. If the fund doesn't meet your investment objectives, you can stop reading and start evaluating another fund.

- **Fees:** Canadian securities law requires mutual funds to list all fees, costs, and expenses in a table at the front of the prospectus.

- **Additional hidden expenses:** Extra expenses may be for services such as printed shareholder materials, toll-free telephone numbers with 24-hour service, accumulation plans that reinvest your distributions (shareholder profits), and related support and guidance.

- **Performance:** Brief financial statements give year-to-year data for the past ten years (or less if the fund isn't that old) to show the fund's performance. Statistics track the fund's NAV, shareholder distributions, and expenses. For funds that include stocks, dividends and price information may also be included. Many funds provide graphs that show how a $1,000 investment increased or decreased over a ten-year period.

  Don't rely exclusively on past performance as an indicator of future performance.

- **Statement of additional information:** This section of the prospectus covers fund details and other items such as the biographies of the fund's directors, the fund's objectives, and fund sponsors.

Finding Mutual Fund Information on the Internet

The Internet provides many mutual fund supersites that are timely, interesting, and best of all useful. Here are a few examples of these all-purpose sites:

- **CANOE Money** (www.canoe.ca/money) provides information on Canadian mutual funds. It has archives of mutual fund articles (click on Funds) that have appeared in its affiliated chain of news dailies. This site has online tools to assist you in making your mutual fund selections.

- **Schwab Canada** (www.schwabcanada.com) provides mutual fund investors with a comprehensive list of mutual funds to choose from.

- **The Fund Library** (www.fundlibrary.com) has background information on most Canadian mutual funds. It lists strategies for using funds to meet your investment goals, among many other things. You can participate in discussion forums about mutual fund investing. You can download brochures (in Adobe Acrobat format) on an array of Canadian mutual funds. Just about anything you want to know about Canadian mutual funds is available at this site.

- **Fundata Canada** (www.fundata.com) provides daily information about Canadian mutual funds. It ranks funds over several time periods, some as long as five years. It also has online articles, news, market data, fund research, and links to fund sites.

- **GLOBEfund** (www.globefund.com) provides concise overviews of most Canadian mutual funds. You can link to the fund's Web site to get more details. GLOBEfund lets you access published articles about a particular fund. You can even generate a chart that examines the performance of a fund based on a variety of criteria. The site has a news centre, information about the new tax rules (such as capital gain/loss inclusion rates), links to mutual funds, and a research centre that allows you to track performance from a list of more than 1,000 funds.

Canadian Mutual Fund Companies

There are several mutual fund players in Canada. They include the following:

- **Mutual fund companies:** Some companies are exclusively involved in the selling of mutual funds. Altamira, AGF, Mackenzie Financial, Trimark, AIC, and Templeton are some of the names you've probably been bombarded with in the media.

- **Bank and trust company subsidiaries:** All of Canada's chartered banks and trust companies offer mutual funds to their clients. You can buy a fund from them directly through one of their branches. However, you are not really dealing with your bank or trust company. You're actually dealing with a separate affiliated company. This structure gives you some protection in the event that the unthinkable happens, and a Canadian bank fails. (Never in Canada, you say?) An example of this structure is the "Royal Mutual Fund" family of funds, sponsored by Royal Mutual Funds Inc., a member of the Royal Bank. (No, insider tips are not included in the management expense.) TD Canada Trust is another fund sponsor with its own family of funds.

✓ **Insurance companies:** Some insurance companies sell their funds in much the same way as banks and trust companies do. In addition, they offer a special type of "segregated fund," discussed later in this chapter.

More Mutual Fund Information

Let's face it: mutual funds are risky. The Canada Deposit Insurance Corporation (CDIC) doesn't insure mutual funds — not even the mutual funds sold by your bank. Even mutual fund portfolios consisting only of guaranteed Canadian treasuries contain some element of risk. On the other hand, mutual funds can give you a much better return than savings accounts, money market deposit accounts, or guaranteed investment certificates. Returns for North American stock mutual funds average about 11 percent per year, whereas savings accounts may earn only about 4 percent. Although your savings account pays 4 percent year after year, your mutual fund may be up 35 percent this year and down 10 percent the next.

Over the years, the stock market has outperformed any other investment. However, individual investors frequently can't purchase a large number of different securities to diversify their investment risk as easily as they can with mutual funds. Buying shares in a mutual fund solves this problem. When you invest in a mutual fund, the diversity of the portfolio reduces the risk of losing your total investment. Selecting the right fund may be difficult, but you can find plenty of online help.

Assume that you have $1,000 to invest in a mutual fund. With your investment, you're purchasing a share of the total assets in the fund. If the share price of the fund is $10 per share, you can purchase 100 shares. The price of each share is the *net asset value (NAV)*. The fund manager calculates the NAV of the mutual fund by adding up the value of the securities in the fund and dividing it by the number of outstanding shares.

The NAV increases and decreases as the market fluctuates. Canadian and American securities regulators require that the NAV of each mutual fund be calculated and published for investors at the end of each business day. Here are a few examples of online quote servers that provide mutual fund NAV information and more:

✓ **The Fund Library.com** (www.fundlibrary.com), shown in Figure 6-4, on the next page, is a repository of all kinds of mutual fund information. This Web site provides a free mutual fund quote service that includes market commentaries, mutual fund charts, portfolio tracking, discussion forums, and a strong mutual fund and sector rating tool. It has links to many mutual-fund–related Web sites.

✔ **GLOBEfund (**`www.globefund.com`**)** has lots of mutual fund data. Enter the ticker symbol for your mutual fund and GLOBEfund provides quotes, charts, and company snapshots of selected Canadian mutual fund firms. GLOBEfund provides links to financial sites, investment articles, market information, and online research sources.

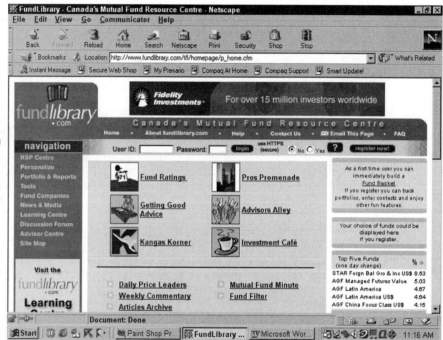

Figure 6-4:
Fund
Library.com
has loads of
information
and tools to
help you
navigate the
world of
Canadian
mutual
funds.

Understanding the real cost of sales fees

If you purchase a load fund, it costs the same amount whether you purchase it through a broker or directly from the mutual fund company. You really don't need to pay a "load" to get a great mutual fund. One of the advantages of no-load mutual funds is that you can purchase them directly from the mutual fund company and skip paying a sales commission. In the past, if you purchased a no-load fund through a broker, you were charged a brokerage fee. Now, many discount brokerages and large mutual fund companies offer no-load funds (and even some load funds) with no transaction fees. (Brokers receive a portion of the fund's annual expenses instead.)

For more information about one-stop shopping for your mutual funds, check out the following:

✔ **E*Trade Canada (**www.canada.etrade.com**)** offers many Canadian no-load mutual fund families. For online information about a fund, just click on any mutual fund "family" to see the details.

✔ **TD Waterhouse (**www.tdwaterhouse.com**),** shown in Figure 6-5, has more than 9,000 Canadian and U.S. mutual funds with no transaction fees for no-load funds, a combination of no-load and low-load funds with transaction fees, and load funds with transaction fees. TD Waterhouse is a public company that is affiliated with the TD Bank.

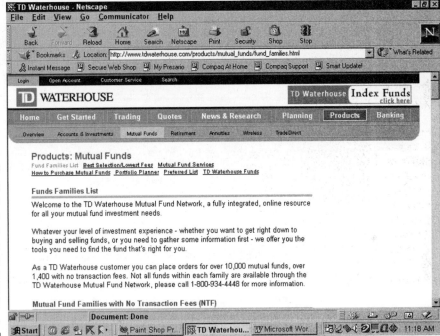

Figure 6-5:
TD
Waterhouse
lets you
choose from
its wide
selection
of no-load
mutual
funds.

Another way to reduce mutual fund management fees is to purchase several mutual funds from one firm. This approach would also help you track your investments more easily.

If you have to pay a commission fee for purchasing your mutual fund, deduct this amount from your return for the year. For example, if you pay a 5-percent commission fee on your $1,000 investment in mutual funds, the amount invested in the funds is actually only $950. If the fund increases by 10 percent in one year, you have a $1,045 investment. Your true yield is $95, or 9.5 percent ($95 ÷ $1,000) — not the full 10 percent.

A better way to buy mutual funds

Check out the E*Trade Canada site (www.canada.etrade.com) for details on a very efficient way to review, select, and purchase mutual funds. You can identify the historically best performers in a certain mutual fund category. You can then dig a little deeper as to their future potential. Next, you can buy several mutual funds in the same fund category and save time and effort because you don't have to call several mutual fund companies to open accounts and make your purchases.

If you are unhappy with one of the mutual funds, you can swap it with another mutual fund in the same family at little or no cost. At the end of the month, you receive only one statement that covers all your funds. E*Trade Canada also provides a similar concise, all-in-one statement for tax purposes. This makes calculating the tax you owe on your profits easier than usual. Anyone who helps make tax time a little easier gets a big stamp of approval in our book.

If you purchase a no-load mutual fund, however, your yield *is* a full 10 percent because you don't pay the commission fee. Assuming a 10-percent increase after one year, your original $1,000 investment in mutual funds is now worth $1,100 — $55 more than the fund with the sales fee.

Here are a few examples of firms that can sell you a mutual fund without a commission fee (or load):

- ✔ **E*Trade Canada** (www.canada.etrade.com) has mutual funds without any loads, but charges commission fees. A 1-percent fee is charged on the sale of all mutual funds held for less than 90 days. All funds are subject to minimum purchase and redemption amounts. Switch orders are permitted, but only within the same family of funds.

- ✔ **Scotia Discount Brokerage** (www.sdbi.com) has information about families of no-load funds, and segregated funds too. The site (see Figure 6-6) provides account access, brief overviews of fund performance, and application forms. If you want a prospectus, just ask for one at this Web site; Scotia Discount Brokerage mails one to you. Like TD Waterhouse, Scotia Discount Brokerage provides a family of back- and front-end load funds.

- ✔ **TD Waterhouse** (www.tdwaterhouse.com), which now also handles customers of the former CT Securities, provides plenty of information about its no-load funds. If you're a beginning investor, you'll appreciate the useful advice at this site. The site includes online prospectuses, charts to compare rates of return, and a list of the firm's financial services. TD Waterhouse offers no-load funds, but also has a family of back-end load and front-end load funds.

Figure 6-6:
The Scotia
Discount
Brokerage
Web site lets
you access
lots of useful
information
about
specific
mutual
funds.

Before you purchase a mutual fund, check out the fee and commission structure on the fund's Web site. You can also get this information from newspapers and books. Compare the fees to similar funds. That way, you're comparing apples to apples.

Opening a mutual fund account

Before you invest in a mutual fund, read the fund's prospectus so that you understand exactly what you're investing in. Next, fill out the online account application form for the mutual fund company. Canadian and U.S. regulations require your signature to open an account. Most sites indicate all the necessary steps for opening an account.

For specific details about opening an account, contact the fund company or broker. In general, you need to complete the following steps:

1. **Indicate your fund selections.**

2. **Mark what type of account you want: individual, joint, or trust.**

3. **Include your social insurance number.**

4. **Mark whether you want cheque-writing privileges.**

5. **Indicate whether you want direct or automatic deposits (when you sell or if you receive a dividend) from a chequing account or a paper cheque.**

6. **Mail your completed account application form and your cheque, made payable to the mutual fund.**

Starting Your Mutual Fund Account with as Little as $25

You don't need a great deal of money to buy a mutual fund. Before you start reading prospectuses, find out which mutual funds have *automatic investment plans* (AIPs). A mutual fund with an AIP often allows you to invest as little as $25 per month, after you meet the minimum investment amount.

The Internet provides information about which mutual funds offer AIPs. Here are a few examples of online mutual funds with automatic investment plans:

- **TD Waterhouse's Green Line Family of No-Load Mutual Funds** (www.tdwaterhouse.com) has a pre-authorized purchase plan of more than 30 funds to choose from. Invest quarterly, monthly, weekly, or even on your payday. Minimum initial and subsequent investments can be as low as $25. You can change your investment amount, frequency of purchase, and choice of funds at any time.

- **T. Rowe Price** (www.troweprice.com) has more than 20 American no-load funds in its automatic investment plan that allow monthly, bimonthly, quarterly, semiannual, and annual automatic payments. Minimum payments can be as little as $25 U.S.

After you select several mutual funds with AIPs, ask for the funds' prospectuses and application forms. You can request the forms online, by telephone, or by mail. Fill out the section marked automatic investments and complete the form. You are authorizing the mutual fund company to make regular electronic withdrawals from your chequing account. Many funds let you decide how much you want to invest. For example, you may decide to invest $50 per month (or $25 every payday). If you reinvest your fund's cash distribution, you'll enjoy the benefits of compounding and your capital gains could add up quickly.

The Winning Ways of Segregated Funds

Segregated funds are the insurance industry's version of mutual funds, and are popular with many Canadians. One reason for their popularity is that they have several distinct benefits that traditional mutual funds don't. For example, segregated funds

- ✔ Have a guaranteed return on death and maturity, where you determine the amount of money you will get back
- ✔ Cannot be legally claimed as collateral by creditors, because of their "insurance product" nature
- ✔ Provide protection from probate fees, as long as a beneficiary is named
- ✔ Usually have insurance protection of up to $60,000

A detailed discussion of segregated funds is beyond the scope of this book. However, if you want to access a ranked list of Canada's 850-plus segregated funds, check out Morningstar Canada's BellCharts feature at www.morningstar.ca, discussed earlier in this chapter. The BellCharts service costs $69 for a monthly subscription, $229 for a quarterly subscription, or $459 for an annual subscription, excluding taxes. This subscription provides you access to both segregated and mutual fund information.

You can also find an insurance company by using the Yahoo! (www.yahoo.ca) Web directory, or by using the Canada411 (canada411.com) phone directory and then calling the company for a brochure. Once you are at the insurance company's Web site, you can take a closer look at its segregated fund offerings.

Exchange-traded Funds: The ABCs to XYZs

A super-cool new financial product has taken its place in the investment world, and it's generating a lot of investor interest. The mystery product is called an *exchange-traded fund*, or *ETF*. The reason that investors have so far given ETFs a warm reception is because ETFs are simple to understand, cheap to buy, easy to trade, and perhaps better structured and better performing than mutual funds. Canadians may consider giving ETFs a home — or at least a room — in their investment portfolios.

What are ETFs?

Exchange-traded funds are essentially index investments. They provide you with the approximate return of a target stock index. Index investments have lower management expense ratios (MERS) than typical mutual funds. They also stand to outperform them over time.

ETFs can be traded on a stock exchange such as the Toronto Stock Exchange (TSE) or the Big Board — the New York Stock Exchange. While you must go through a bank or mutual fund company to obtain an index mutual fund, you obtain an ETF just the way you would a stock — cite the ticker symbol, indicate the number of shares you want, and voilà, your order is filled! Through a discount broker such as TD Waterhouse, you can get just about any ETF out there for as little as $40.

Exactly what do ETFs do?

Scores of Canadian, U.S., and other foreign global stock indexes are tracked by exchange-traded funds. *Tracking* means that the ETF (or other index fund) is structured essentially the same way as the underlying index. Among other things, ETFs can track indexes such as the Dow Jones Industrial Average or the TSE 60. Even other international stock markets, such as those represented by the German DAX or Japanese Nikkei indexes, can be mimicked.

Within an index, ETFs can also be fine-tuned to include only industry sectors, such as health-care or technology. Compared to index mutual funds, many more indexes are available through ETFs. This abundance of choice does, however, lead us to a potential challenge.

Choices, choices

In our opinion, there are too many exchange-traded funds to choose from, at least in the United States. Cherry-picking through the choices can be confusing and time-consuming. While Canadian ETFs are not as plentiful as U.S. ETFs, many new ETF products will be coming our way in the near future. To help you select one, consider the ETF's management expense ratio (MER). The lower the MER, the higher your return.

Consider also the index being tracked. ETFs often allow you to choose several differently structured indexes (TSE 35 versus TSE 300) that track the same general market (Canadian companies on the TSE). Also, ETFs should have broad market coverage to diversify your investment, as well as liquidity. The ETF must be liquid, because some funds may go a whole week without being traded once.

There are only a few ETFs in Canada at the moment: iUnits S&P/TSE 60 Index Participation Fund (XIU-TSE), from Barclays Global Investors; the SSgA Dow Jones Canada 40 Index Participation Fund (DJF-TSE), which is managed by rival State Street Global Advisors; and a handful of others. Both are large-cap funds with about 40 percent of their assets allocated to Nortel Networks Corp. The DJ40 has a 0.08-percent MER. The i60 weighs in at a 0.17-percent MER. A new ETF, called the i60C, is based on the S&P/TSE 60 Capped Index. It is expected to make an appearance sometime in late 2001. This fund will limit individual stocks to no more than 10 percent of the total holdings, which provides more risk diffusion within the fund. That way, if Nortel tanks again, you won't have to sell the shirt off your back to help pay for your retirement.

Canadians with Registered Retirement Savings Plans will soon be able to buy a U.S. S&P 500 ETF *without* a 30-percent foreign content restriction when placed inside an RRSP. (Canada Customs and Revenue Agency currently limits the amount of foreign investments you can hold in your RRSP to 30 percent.) Watch for news about product offerings in the newspapers, or ask your financial adviser about this.

Itsy, bitsy spiders

A *spider* (SPDR) is a type of exchange-traded fund that mimics and tracks the value of a particular index. Individual investors can buy or sell these open-ended funds on the market, just like a stock. They can be purchased from any broker for a commission. For example, you can buy a "spider" to track the S&P 500 Index with SPY—Amex, which is the street name for S&P Depositary Receipts. You can mimic the Dow with Diamonds (DIA—Amex), a popular ETF with a management expense ratio of 0.18 percent. The most popular, and perhaps most risky, ETF is called the Qube (QQQ—Amex). It lets you invest directly in the Nasdaq 100 index of the largest non-financial stocks listed on the Nasdaq National Market. The MER on this fund is 0.18 percent.

Performance: The proof is in the pudding

Over the ten-year period from 1991 to 2001, the average U.S. equity mutual fund posted an average annual gain of about 18 percent, while the S&P 500 made about 20 percent. Canadian figures are similar. Many investors rightly consider this gap to be a rip-off. In other words, mutual funds' lower returns relative to the stock market coupled with their high MERs make them increasingly less palatable to investors. That's why more investors are turning to index/ETF investing. Low fees relative to mutual funds make them attractive.

ETFs are also tax-smart. ETFs change their portfolio mixes only to reflect changes in their mimicked index, translating into fewer trades and taxable distributions of potential taxable gains.

ETFs offered by Barclays Global Investors and information about iShares (another ETF) can be found, respectively, at www.iunits.com and www.ishares.com. You can learn about HOLDRs — which are fixed baskets of stocks that are also exchange-traded on the AMEX index, and track any one of several industry sectors such as biotech, utilities, or pharmaceutical — at www.holdrs.com or www.amex.com. If it's spiders you want to know more about, check out www.spdrindex.com.

Wrap Accounts

A wrap account is the financial service industry's version of an all-inclusive vacation. A bunch of investment services are "wrapped" under one fee. The annual wrap fee covers a professionally managed portfolio, trade transactions, account administration, and more. Wrap accounts are designed for investors without the inclination or expertise to manage their own portfolio. Many brokerage firms, mutual fund companies, financial planners, and banks and trust companies sponsor wrap products. A primer on wrap accounts can be found at OnMoney (onmoney.lycos.com/Editorial/Guides/getting_started_investing/accounts_for_investing.html).

Traditional wrap accounts and mutual fund wrap accounts

There are two types of wrap products to choose from: a traditional wrap account and a mutual fund wrap account. *Traditional wrap accounts* provide a full range of securities and are customized according to your investment horizon, risk tolerance, and personal goals. *Mutual fund wrap accounts* contain only mutual funds. A younger investor with a greater risk tolerance may prefer a traditional wrap portfolio, which emphasizes equities. A nearly retired investor may prefer a mutual fund wrap portfolio that holds safer, income-generating holdings such as government or corporate bonds. Both types of wrap accounts can provide you with a portfolio that is modified to your risk tolerance.

Tell me more

Typical services offered by wrap accounts include consulting, asset allocation (keeping a mix of cash, stocks, and bonds to reduce risk), custodial services, transaction costs, and performance monitoring and reporting. Traditional wrap accounts offered by financial institutions usually require a minimum commitment of $100,000 or more. Many mutual fund companies offer wrap products with a minimum investment of $10,000. Some financial institutions now offer "mini" wrap accounts for investors with less investment capital.

Although management fees vary according to the type, complexity, and size of the account, they usually fall in the 2- to 4-percent range, based on asset values. Many mutual fund wrap accounts also charge commission fees, although their commission fees tend to be lower than those of traditional wrap accounts. Read the fine print to be sure that you know about all of the management fees involved, including close-out fees! The sponsor of the account can supply you with more information. That's a wrap!

Part II
Finding the Right Investments

The 5th Wave   By Rich Tennant

COACH SPAULDING AND HIS WIFE CHECK THE STOCK MARKET

"Get ready, Mona— I think I found a winner."

In this part . . .

You discover how to research fixed-income securities, stocks, and mutual funds. Find out how to use the Internet to rate existing bonds and to seek out new bond offerings. Search for company financial statements and annual reports online, and find out how to analyze this information. Dig deeper into individual stocks with fundamental and technical analyses. Let online resources show you where the economy or a certain industry may be heading. See how you can use the Internet to help you find a mutual fund that best meets your needs and investment profile. Check out what others are saying about companies and mutual funds on online discussion boards and newsletters.

Chapter 7

Checking Out Fixed-Income Investments

● ●

In This Chapter

▶ Finding new offerings online

▶ Watching the fixed-income markets

▶ Evaluating risk

▶ Discovering more exotic types of fixed-income investments

▶ Locating online information about fixed-income investments

● ●

*I*n Chapter 4, you got a basic overview of how each fixed-income investment option works. The purpose of this chapter is to show you how you can dig a little deeper — how you can find the right fixed-income investments by using the Internet as a tool to help you along. We dig deeper into a few of the Web resources — and fixed-income instruments — introduced in Chapter 4. We also take a look at a few new research-oriented Web sites. Resources to find both Canadian and U.S. bonds are presented.

Using the Internet to Find New Bond Offerings

New bond issues generally provide a slightly better yield than comparable issues of existing bonds offered on the secondary market. That's because bond issuers are eager to get the new bonds sold. Incentives are often provided. Following, we list some popular online sources for information about new bond offerings:

✔ **Bondcan.com** (`www.bondcan.com`), shown in Figure 7-1, is a Canadian investment Web site that specializes in fixed-income instruments, including new issues. Its Daily Commentary feature provides a summary of the day in the marketplace. That's also where you'll likely find information about recent offerings. In addition, daily quotes and end-of-session valuations are provided for existing issues. There is even a discussion forum on bonds! (And you thought that watching paint dry was fun!) As well, you can read the Bonds 101 primer, which introduces you to the fixed-income investment marketplace. A glossary lets you learn bond-market jargon. Links exist to bond-market–related articles, historical yields as published by the Bank of Canada, and Statistics Canada — which offers up information critical to any bond investor.

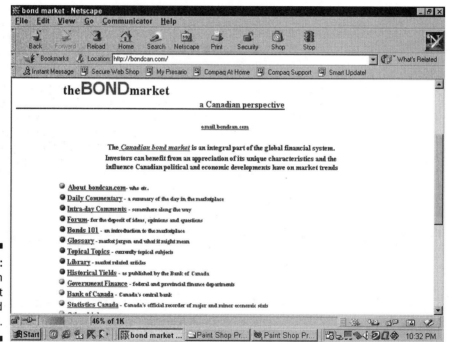

Figure 7-1:
Bondcan.com
is a good first
stop for bond
information.

✔ **Bondsonline** (`www.bondsonline.com`) is another good starting point for researching the bond market. Although this site focuses on U.S. bonds, you can research the specific type of bond that interests you — corporate, treasury, municipal, or savings. This Web site also includes new and daily offerings of corporate and municipal bonds.

✔ **E-Bond** (`www.ebond.ca`) provides rates for many different types of bonds. You can access live bid and ask prices and investor newsletters. This information can help you get the best price for a given bond. E-Bond covers all areas of the Canadian and U.S. bond markets, including federal government bonds, provincial and federal zero coupons, along with a selection of high-grade corporate debt. If you open an account, you can access it anytime. You can trade by phone or online. But be aware that commission rates are included in the price of the bonds and are not clearly spelled out. The company is registered to trade in some but not all provinces.

- **E*Trade Canada** (www.canada.etrade.com) provides pricing and yield information on exchange-traded Canadian and U.S. fixed-income securities. We take a much closer look at this Web site, and others like it, when we discuss trading in Chapter 15.

- **Investing in Bonds** (www.investinginbonds.com) is a bond supersite — offering practical and educational tools to help you find new bond offerings and learn more about bonds. This site has many useful bond-related links and provides quotes on virtually all classes of bonds. It has a comprehensive educational section that offers in-depth explanations of different types of bonds and a seven-step online educational program.

- **Salomon Smith Barney Municipal New Issues Calendar** (www.smithbarney.com/prod_svc/bonds/munical.html) provides a free listing of new American municipal free issues and bond issues that Smith Barney is involved in or intends to bid on its own, or as part of a syndicate. (A syndicate is a group of investment bankers that jointly share in the underwriting, distribution, selling, and management of a new issue.) The bonds listed on the Web site are updated weekly but are subject to prior sale (and may not be available).

Finding Bond Indexes and Historical Data Online

Bond indexes are designed to represent either the average yield to maturity or the average price on a portfolio of bonds that have certain similar characteristics. Historical data can also provide bond performance insights. The Internet offers several sources for these averages and historical data. In addition to Bondcan.com, there are a few other Web sites that provide historical performance data:

- **Bondsonline** (www.bondsonline.com) once again comes in handy. It provides charts and historical data that compare various bond market sectors and stock market indexes — for example, a comparison of the 30-year treasury bonds, 10-year treasury notes, and the Dow Jones Industrial Average. This site also offers a comparison of tax-free municipal yields as a percentage of U.S. treasury yields. It focuses on the U.S. market.

✔ **Moody's Investor Services** (www.moodys.com) gives long-term corporate bond yield averages based on bonds with maturities of 20 years and more. Corporate bond averages are sorted into average corporate, average industrial, and average public utility groups, and by bond ratings. This service covers the U.S. and Canadian fixed-income markets.

Risk and Stability

The Canadian Bond Rating Service (www.cbrs.com/cbrs), which has now merged with Standard & Poor's (www.standardpoor.com); the Dominion Bond Rating Service (www.dbrs.com) (see Figure 7-2); and Moody's Investor Services (www.moodys.com) are the best-known and most prominent Canadian and American credit-rating agencies. These companies assess the risk of bonds by studying all the bond's information and then assign the bond a rank that reflects the issuer's ability to meet the promised principal and interest payments. This rating may change during the life of the bond, and a change in the rating can dramatically change the value of the bond. All the credit-rating companies rate bonds in descending alphabetical order, but each company uses a somewhat different letter scheme.

Figure 7-2:
The Dominion Bond Rating Service evaluates Canadian fixed-income securities and gives them a grade to help you with your investment decisions.

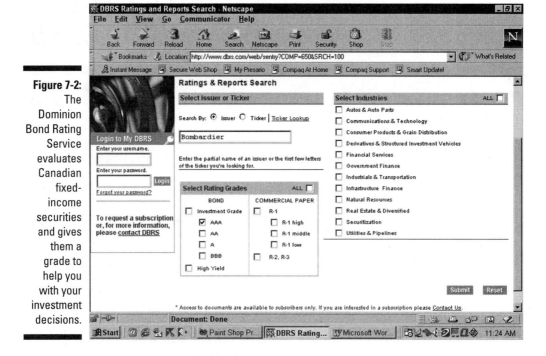

Ratings are not absolute measures of quality. Each rating takes into consideration factors such as the issuer's past earnings record and future earnings expectations, the financial condition of the issuer, the nature of the issuer's business, the backing for a particular issue, and the rating agency's appraisals of the issuer's management.

The rating agencies warn investors that a bond's rating isn't a "buy" recommendation. However, because of the risk–reward ratio, bonds with higher ratings offer lower yields; bonds with lower ratings, which represent a riskier investment, offer higher yields.

To minimize your investment risks, you should check out economic overviews, since the direction of the economy (and the health of industry sectors as well) influences the value of bonds and other fixed-income investments in a big way. Visit the Bank of Montreal's Economics page at `www.bmo.com/economic`. This site will help link you to economic and statistical commentaries and reports on the Canadian, U.S., and world economies. Check out the prospects for Canada's industries to 2004 and beyond! These forecasts are good to know and can help you build wealth right here in Canada. A look at the road ahead can help you better select the right investment for you.

How Small Investors Can Make Money with Fixed-income Investments and Bonds

Banks and credit unions across Canada have developed new ways of keeping customers happy. More than ever before, they offer a whole bunch of new investment plans that provide higher returns than traditional fixed-rate savings accounts. Credit unions allow their customers to invest in *commercial paper* (uninsured promissory notes to large business entities) instead of *certificates of deposit* (insured time deposits). This accommodating and innovative approach is a major departure from the conservative way banks used to operate.

The following shows three types of fixed-income and bond investments that are targeted for small investors seeking greater returns:

- ✓ **Guaranteed investment certificates (GICs):** Deposits do not require any minimum amount according to federal banking laws, but many banks have established a minimum requirement for deposits of $100 to $1,000. Maturities are generally 30 months and the interest paid is slightly below the 30-month treasury yield. Expect penalties for early withdrawals.

- ✓ **Short-term bond funds:** Purchasing short-term, no-load bond funds is one way investors can earn higher-than-passbook returns and still have lots of liquidity. Some bond funds even have limited cheque-writing privileges. (Writing a cheque is certainly more convenient and less expensive than placing a sell order to get at your cash.)

With short-term bond funds, small investors tend to pay more for bonds than professional bond fund managers (who keenly watch every movement of the bond market). However, these benefits aren't cost-free. Investors will incur an annual fund management fee that averages 0.2 percent.

✔ **Short-term money market certificates:** These U.S. financial instruments are available to Canadian investors. They come with hefty minimum deposits; a minimum deposit of $10,000 U.S. is typical. Yields are higher than short-term money market certificates. After you purchase the certificate, the rate is locked in until the certificate matures. When it does, you are free to reinvest your investment (this is also known as a rollover). If the current treasury security rate is higher, you'll make more money.

Investors can enjoy the type of liquidity that bond funds offer and not pay management fees by purchasing treasury securities directly from the government (see "The Basic Types of Government Bonds" next in this chapter for details). If you want to buy directly from the government but avoid doing the paperwork yourself, brokerages like EUTrade Canada and Schwab Canada can complete your transaction for about $75.

The Internet provides more information about fixed investments for investors. You can discover online what the benchmark rates are and which financial institutions have the best deals. The following are a few examples:

✔ **Bank Rate Monitor (**www.bankrate.com**)** shows the average rates for American money market accounts and certificates of deposit. Discover who has the best deals by checking the annual percentage yield for savings money market accounts, certificates of deposit, and treasury securities.

✔ **The Council for Canadian Unity (**www.ccu-cuc.ca/en/library/market.html**)** may have a name that has little to do with investing, but it's a storehouse of good information on the domestic and world investment front. In addition to information on Canadian, U.S., and world stock markets, it has loads of information about currencies, interest rates, bond yields, and economic indicators. It provides links to economic reports and several prominent business magazines including *The Economist, Report on Business, Money, Fortune,* and *Le Devoir.*

✔ **CANNEX (**www.cannex.com**)** compares interest rates on an array of fixed-income investment options — including term deposits and GICs — offered by banks, trust companies, credit unions, and other financial institutions. This service covers fixed-income investments offered in Canada, the U.S., and Australia.

✔ **Dun & Bradstreet Canada (**www.dnb.ca**)** has free market updates, information about the economy and certain industries, and consumer interest rates. It has a special section for Canadian investors, but you have to subscribe to access it.

The Basic Types of Government Bonds

Many organizations issue bonds, but the following government agencies issue the most bonds:

- ✔ **The Canadian federal government:** The Bank of Canada issues and administers treasury bills and Canada Savings Bonds.

- ✔ **Federal government agencies:** The Canada Mortgage and Housing Corporation (CMHC) is the main issuer of Canadian agency bonds.

- ✔ **Provincial and local government agencies:** Many of Canada's provinces, territories, regions, and municipalities issue a variety of bonds.

Treasury bills

Treasury bills are Canadian (and U.S.) government-backed fixed-income securities. They are a major source of government funds and a key investment for many consumers. They are very safe to boot, given that the Canadian government is highly unlikely to default on its treasury securities. But if it does, your dollar is also probably worthless anyway, so your investment is, essentially, risk-free.

The disadvantage of the risk-free rate of treasury securities is that it's generally considered to be the bottom of the yield pile — the lowest return on your hard-earned buck that you can get. With any investment, as the level of risk gets greater, your reward also increases. You can purchase treasury securities without a broker, directly from a Canadian bank. You can also buy them online. (We discuss buying fixed-income securities in Chapter 15.)

For more information on treasury securities, see the following Web sites:

- ✔ **Investor Learning Centre of Canada (**www.investorlearning.ca/ilcdev**)** provides "briefings" on how the treasury and non-treasury market operates in Canada. Click the Investor Learning Centre icon to get there.

- ✔ **Kirlin: About Investments (**www.kirlin.com**)** provides a good overview of U.S. treasury securities. This tutorial includes information on safety and availability.

Canada Savings Bonds: The easiest way to save

A popular fixed-income choice for beginning or risk-averse investors, Canada Savings Bonds are easy to buy. You can purchase them at any Canadian bank.

Your employer may have automatic savings bond investment programs. As an employee you can have an amount of money deducted regularly from their paycheques, and that money is used to purchase Canada Savings Bonds. For some people, this kind of investment program is the easiest and only way they can save money.

The full faith and credit of Canada is what backs Canada Savings Bonds. (You can find a complete description of these bonds in Chapter 4.) Figure 7-3 shows you where you can get information concerning Canada Savings Bonds. This Web page features lots of information about existing and new issues to help you invest wisely. Go to www.csb.gc.ca.

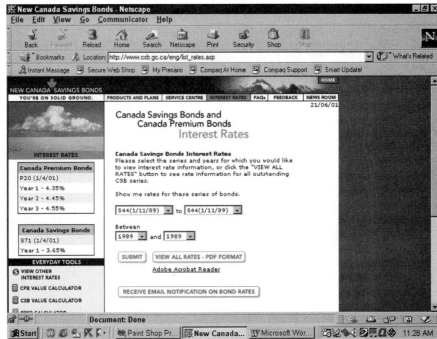

Figure 7-3: This government Web page gives you the scoop on Canada Savings Bond interest rates, maturity dates, and more.

Federal government agency bonds

From time to time, a Canadian federal agency such as the Canada Mortgage and Housing Corporation issues bonds to support housing programs. *Agency bonds,* such as those issued by the CMHC, offer slightly higher risk and marginally better returns. Many investors are willing to take on this additional risk because they are betting that if the agency becomes insolvent, the federal government would bail the agency — and the investors themselves — out of a mess.

Not all government agency bonds provide the same interest rates. Factors such as the agency's creditworthiness and the date the bond was issued affect agency bond returns. The Internet gives more information on specific types of government agency bonds. The following are two examples:

✓ **Canada Mortgage and Housing Corporation Bonds** (www.cmhc.ca) provides investors with background information about the mortgage-backed securities that the CMHC issues. In the Search box, type in NHA mortgage-backed securities. A list of issues appears.

✓ **Fitch IBCA** (www.fitchibca.com) covers the government agency bond market for Canada, the U.S., and 48 other countries! That's because Fitch IBCA is an international bond-rating agency. It also has well-organized research, bond news, and many useful links.

Municipal bonds

Canadian towns, cities, and regional municipalities issue municipal bonds. In fact, because of the recent amalgamation of a few Canadian municipalities, you can even find bonds issued by municipalities that no longer exist. They are true collector's items!

Municipal bonds usually have lower interest rates than comparably rated corporate bonds and treasury bills. The minimum amount required for investment in municipal bonds is usually about $5,000, and municipal bonds can be issued at a discount to face value of anywhere between 4 and 10 percent, depending on the creditworthiness of the municipality. Three primary types of municipal bonds exist. Each bond type has special features:

✓ **General obligation bonds** are backed by the full faith and credit of the issuing agency. For municipal bonds, full faith and credit also means the taxing power of the issuing municipality. Most Canadian municipal bonds fall into this category.

✓ **Industrial development bonds (IDBs)** are used to finance the purchase or construction of large public buildings, facilities, and your everyday white elephant! Ever wondered who paid for an Olympic village? It might have been you! Leasing and attendance fees associated with the buildings are used to meet construction expenses and the repayment requirements of the bonds. IDBs are most commonly found in the U.S.

✓ **Revenue bonds** are backed by the funds from a designated tax or the revenues from a specific project, authority, or agency. Proceed with caution here; revenue bonds are only as good (and as creditworthy) as the ventures they support. For example, Denver's new airport was financed by revenue bonds. Unfortunately for investors, revenues for the airport were dismal and investors lost money. Revenue bonds are primarily found in the U.S.

Several online resources exist to provide a variety of municipal bond information, such as frequently updated offerings for individual investors, bond market indexes, and more. Plan carefully, though — the securities listed by these firms are subject to changes in price and availability. To help you navigate the uncharted world of government bonds, check out these two trustworthy sites:

- **CIBC World Markets** (www.cibcwg.com/bigar/bigarrpt.shtml) provides information on many types of domestic bonds, including provincial, municipal, federal agency, corporate, and federal instruments (see Figure 7-4). This Web site has a comprehensive Broad Investment Grade Analysis of Return index (BIGAR), which tracks historical rates of return on all broad bond categories, including municipals.

- **E-Muni** (www.emuni.com) is a financial Web site for investors interested in the U.S. and Canadian municipal bond markets. It provides tables and charts of investment-grade municipal bond yields. Wire services as well as in-house sources feed its news section. It includes a list of new issues as well as a library containing information about older bonds.

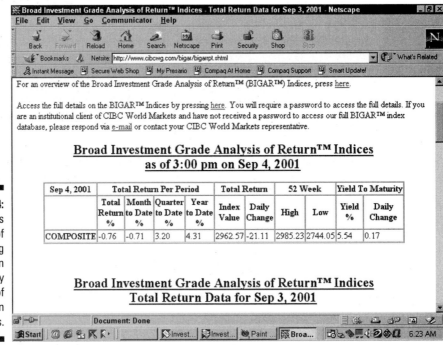

Figure 7-4: CIBC has lots of pricing information about many types of Canadian bonds.

For an overview of the Broad Investment Grade Analysis of Return™ (BIGAR™) Indices, press here.

Access the full details on the BIGAR™ Indices by pressing here. You will require a password to access the full details. If you are an institutional client of CIBC World Markets and have not received a password to access our full BIGAR™ index database, please respond via e-mail or contact your CIBC World Markets representative.

Broad Investment Grade Analysis of Return™ Indices
as of 3:00 pm on Sep 4, 2001

Sep 4, 2001	Total Return Per Period				Total Return		52 Week		Yield To Maturity	
	Total Return %	Month to Date %	Quarter to Date %	Year to Date %	Index Value	Daily Change	High	Low	Yield %	Daily Change
COMPOSITE	-0.76	-0.71	3.20	4.31	2962.57	-21.11	2985.23	2744.05	5.54	0.17

Broad Investment Grade Analysis of Return™ Indices
Total Return Data for Sep 3, 2001

Floating with Corporate Bonds

Corporate bonds are a major source of corporate borrowing. When corporations make corporate bonds, they *float* a bond issue. Such bond issues take the form of either *debentures* (unsecured corporate bonds backed by the general credit of the corporation) or *asset-backed* bonds (backed by specific corporate assets like property or equipment). Income from these bonds is taxable. However, top-rated corporate bonds are often almost risk-free and have a higher return than treasury securities. Corporate bonds are generally considered safer than stocks because of two factors:

✔ **The bonds state exactly how much the corporation will pay the bondholder.** Shareholders are entitled to cash dividends, but payment and the amount of the dividend is at the discretion of the corporation.

✔ **Bondholders are creditors.** They receive payment before the corporation can distribute any cash dividends to shareholders, which means that bondholders have greater protection in getting at least some return on their investment. (According to Canadian bankruptcy law, bondholders are paid from corporate assets before common shareholders. The same is true in the U.S.)

Some risk of default always exists. In the 1980s, many companies used junk bonds to finance highly leveraged takeovers of rival companies. Their bonds were rated non-investment-grade and speculative by the bond-rating agencies. Due to the additional risk, these bonds paid above-average interest rates. For some bondholders, these bonds were a windfall. For those bondholders who invested in the corporate bonds of companies that failed, their bonds went into default and became worthless junk.

Some professional money managers are required by law to purchase investment-grade securities so that they can't purchase junk bonds. These organizations generally limit their corporate bond purchases to issues rated B or higher by Moody's Investors Service.

More Internet Resources for Selecting Bonds

Just when you thought it was safe to turn off your computer because you've learned all you can about picking winning bonds, we have a few more tempting choices for you. These Web sites include search engines that sort through thousands of bond offerings while looking for bonds that meet your criteria. Their services are free, but look out for the sales pitch. Check out these popular bond sites:

✔ **Bondtrac** (`www.bondtrac.com`) is a company that provides software to security dealers and individual investors, to help them track bonds. Use of this Web site requires you to register (but it's free). Bondtrac provides a partial list of its services to demonstrate the use of its data and its software. The free services don't show offer, concession, price, yield, or dealer information; these types of data are considered restricted information for licensed security brokers. Once you're registered, you can look up corporate bonds, municipal bonds, and government agency bonds by using a variety of search criteria. Your screen results include information about bond amount, minimum purchase amount, rating, symbol, description, coupon, and maturity date. This mostly U.S. Web site also handles Canadian bond information.

✔ **The Standard & Poor's Blue List** (`www.bluelist.com`) shows current municipal and corporate bond offerings. This U.S. Web site has a static demo scan of their "Blue List Offerings" available to individual investors. The demo scans a maximum of 14 items and is designed to demonstrate the company's software. You can search the database for state issuers, maturity dates, lot size of the issue, coupon, and CUSIP. (CUSIP is the Committee on Uniform Securities Identification Procedures — the committee that assigns numbers to securities for identification.)

CUSIP is a numbering system endorsed by major segments of the financial community. See the CUSIP service bureau operated by Standard & Poor's for the American Bankers Association at `www.cusip.com` for more information about CUSIP numbering.

Two Alternative Types of Bonds

These relatively new types of bonds may be of interest to online investors:

✔ **Zero coupon bonds:** Zero coupon bonds offer no interest payments but are put on the market at prices substantially below their face values. The return to the investor is the difference between the investor's cost and the face value received at the end of the life of the bond. If you don't rely on interest payment income, zero coupon bonds may be one way to go for your non-taxable retirement plan (such as a Registered Retirement Savings Plan or Registered Retirement Income Fund). Canada Customs and Revenue Agency taxes Canadian and U.S. zero coupon bonds as if investors received regular interest payments. This tax is based on amortizing the built-in gain over the life of the bond. In other words, for taxable accounts investors have to pay taxes on income they haven't received, but for non-taxable accounts it can be a great investment choice. Call the CCRA or your tax adviser for the exact details on how these investments are taxed.

Some brokerages offer *treasury strips*. Large companies purchase 30-year treasury securities and clip the interest-bearing coupons. The brokers then sell these treasury coupons like zero coupon bonds. You purchase the treasury strip at a discount (say, $4,300) and redeem the coupon at face value ($5,000). Treasury strips are like zero coupon bonds because no interest is paid during the maturity term. They are mostly found in the U.S.

✔ **Eurobonds:** Investments in foreign securities typically involve many government restrictions. Eurobonds are bonds offered outside the country of the borrower and usually outside the country in whose currency the securities are denominated. For example, a Eurobond may be issued by a Canadian corporation, denominated in American dollars, and sold in Japan and Switzerland.

•For additional information about Eurobonds, see the following sites:

- **Bradynet CyberExchange** (`www.bradynet.com`) provides bond prices, analysis, research, ratings, news, information about new issues, forums, and more. Enter Eurobonds in the Search engine on the home page and select Search Bradynet. You get a page that includes a demonstration program that searches for specific Eurobond issues. You can also get information about Third World debt instruments.

- **Petercam Eurobonds** (`www.petercam.be`) provides valuation techniques for Eurobonds, benchmarks, and information about Eurobond primary and secondary markets. At the home page, click Eurobond Desk.

J.P. Morgan & Company, Inc. (`www.jpmorgan.com`) provides a government bond index that is a widely used benchmark for assessing and quantifying risk across international fixed-income bond markets. If you're looking for benchmarks, go to the J.P. Morgan home page and click Index. The indexes measure the total, principal, and interest returns in each market and can be reported in 19 currencies, including the Canadian dollar. You can compare Eurobonds to the index to provide a realistic measure of market performance.

Chapter 8

Taking Stock of Companies

● ●

In This Chapter
▶ Finding annual reports online
▶ Downloading, printing, and saving annual reports
▶ Analyzing annual reports
▶ Using annual reports to make your investment decisions

● ●

*I*n the past, only large financial institutions had access to high-quality financial data. Clients had nowhere else to go for stock advice, which meant that brokerage houses and their minions charged hefty commissions for their research. Many of these quality data are now available on the Internet. Some of the databases are free, while others are fee-based. Databases that charge fees require subscription fees — payment by the month, by database, or by document.

Even with free or low-cost information, researching stocks is still hard work. Doing so requires good judgment, the ability to fit all the bits and pieces of information together, lack of emotion, and decisiveness. If you're thinking about investing in stocks, you need to research the following specific and "big picture" information:

✔ **Companies:** Profiles, management, financial health, insider trading, potential mergers and acquisitions

✔ **Industries:** Industrial markets, industrial standards, and trends

✔ **Economic indicators:** The national, regional, and local economics

✔ **Other factors:** New legislation, technological breakthroughs, and new stock offerings

Researching deeper into a company, and wider into an industry or the economy, is the topic of most of Chapter 9. In this chapter, we focus on more of the company-specific things you need to know — that is, we lay a foundation for researching stocks online.

Often the best starting point for researching the stock of a certain company is the annual report. The best place to find annual reports is on the Internet. This chapter shows you how to locate annual reports by using a search engine, special company locator sites, investor supersites, and securities regulator databases — SEDAR (for Canada) and EDGAR (for the United States).

Canadian publicly traded companies are required to file annual and quarterly reports with provincial securities regulators such as the British Columbia Securities Commission (www.bcsc.bc.ca) and the Ontario Securities Commission (www.osc.gov.on.ca). American companies file with the Securities and Exchange Commission (www.sec.gov). These reports provide updates of a company's activities since it filed its last report. If the company is going through a momentous change (such as a merger or acquisition), it's required to file more often. This filing is usually called a "notice of material change."

You can find important information about a company in its annual report, but annual reports require careful reading. This chapter shows you how to download an annual report (and other information that a company is required by law to publicly disclose) and analyze any publicly traded company. After all, reading a company's annual report is a little like kicking the tires of a used car. You want to see what you're getting.

Finding Financial Statements Online

If you're a shareholder, you automatically receive the company's annual report. Annual reports are free for the asking to anyone else. All you have to do is call the firm's investor relations department and request that they mail you a copy.

For online investors, getting annual reports is even easier. The Internet provides four sources for annual reports:

- ✔ **Annual report Web sites:** These Web sites are designed for investors, shareholders, and money managers who want instant access to company annual reports. Many sites also include company quarterlies, fact books, and press releases.

- ✔ **Company Web sites:** Many companies have sites on the Internet that let you download their annual reports. You can use commercial search engines and directories to find them.

- ✔ **Investor compilation sites:** These Internet investor supersites often include annual reports, company news, earnings forecasts, and other useful information.

> ✔ **Securities regulator filings:** Securities regulators in Canada and the U.S. do a great job of making timely, electronically filed company reports available online to the public.

In the following sections, we show you how to find annual reports using these sources.

Accessing Web sites that specialize in annual reports

The Internet features Web sites that focus on the individual investor's need for company information. These sites deliver annual reports in a variety of ways. For example, you can order hard copies of the original reports, immediately access online versions, or view annual reports in their original formats using free Internet plug-ins (such as Adobe Acrobat Reader, available at `www.adobe.com`). The following are a few examples of information services on the Internet:

✔ **The Annual Reports Library** (`www.zpub.com/sf/arl/index.html`): Founded in 1983, the Annual Reports Library includes more than 1.6 million original annual reports from corporations, foundations, banks, mutual funds, and public institutions located throughout the world. If you're an antique collector as well as an online investor, this site is ideal for you!

✔ **Disclosure** (`www.disclosure-investor.com`): This site, shown in Figure 8-1 on the next page, provides securities regulator filings, financial information on Canadian, U.S., and over 13,000 global companies, and company press releases. The securities regulator information, corporate snapshots, and company PRNewswire press releases are free. Profile and investment tearsheets are $3 U.S. each. (*Tearsheets* are one-page profile reports that consolidate company financial information.)

✔ **Investor Relations Information Network** (`www.irin.com`): The Network offers over 2,500 free company annual reports in their original formats, with photographs, graphs, and text. You use the Adobe Acrobat pdf format to read the information. (Reports are readable on Windows, Macintosh, DOS, and Unix operating systems.)

✔ **Public Register's Annual Report Service** (`www.prars.com`): This service is free and provides both online annual reports and hard copies of company annual reports. Some annual reports are in Adobe Acrobat format. You can download a free copy of the Adobe Acrobat Reader at the Web site.

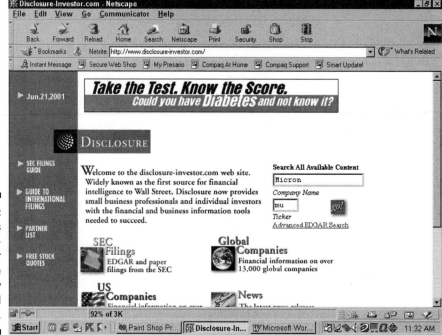

Figure 8-1:
Disclosure is
an easy-to-
use provider
of online
company
annual
reports.

Using a search engine or special directory to find an annual report

Almost all publicly traded companies now have Web sites on the Internet. These sites often include the company's annual report as part of the firm's public relations and investor services.

To find these annual reports, you can start with a commercial *search engine* (a Web-based tool that enables you to hunt for Web sites on topics that you specify), such as Google (www.google.com), AltaVista (www.altavista.ca), or Yahoo! (finance.yahoo.com). After you access one of these search engines, you simply enter words or phrases that describe the information you want to find, and then you click the Search button. To find a company report, you enter the company name, a plus sign (+), and the words *annual report* in quotation marks, as in the following example:

```
Microsoft + "annual report"
```

You may get hundreds of search results. To help you manage this pile of data, use search engines that rank results. Although most search engines do have some sort of ranking scheme, Lycos (www.lycos.com) and AltaVista do the best job of supplying a useful and manageable list of search results.

Many Web sites provide a directory of links to the home pages of large businesses. Here are two examples of these sites:

- ✔ **Global Securities Information, Inc.** (www.gsionline.com): This site provides links to the home pages of large corporations.

- ✔ **Web100** (www.w100.com): This site provides links to the 100 largest U.S. and international businesses on the Internet. You can sort the database by industry and Fortune 500 rankings.

Finding annual reports online: Investor supersites

If a commercial search engine or a business Web site locator doesn't lead you to the annual report you want, try one of these investor supersites:

- ✔ **Raging Bull** (www.ragingbull.lycos.com): This site, shown in Figure 8-2, provides "raging links" to annual reports for many Canadian and U.S. companies. Whereas many supersites are thin on Canadian company content, Raging Bull, a relatively new site, has bested its peers on this count.

Figure 8-2:
Raging Bull has lots of information about Canadian companies, including annual report links, company profiles, and free real-time quotes.

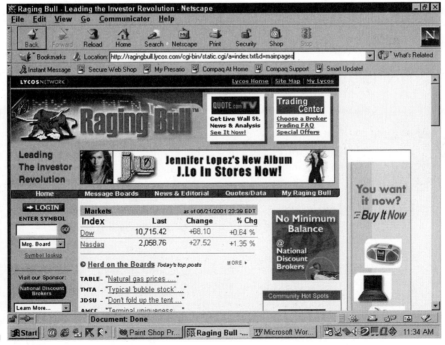

✔ **Hoover's Online Company Profiles** (`www.hoovers.com`): This site includes company profiles and annual report information on more than 25,000 publicly traded, private, and international firms, including Canadian public companies. You can get capsule information for free; you pay a fee for access to the entire database and to search for companies by industry, location, or sales. You can even find out which companies plan to go public.

✔ **Zacks Investment Research** (`www.zacks.com`): Zacks Investment Research's database includes more than 7,500 U.S. and Canadian companies. The site also tracks about 200 industry groups.

We look at several of these sites, and other similar sites, in more detail throughout the book.

Researching and downloading SEDAR submissions

In Canada, publicly traded companies are required to file business and financial information with provincial securities regulators. These reports are entered into a government-sponsored database called SEDAR — the System for Electronic Data Analysis and Retrieval (`www.sedar.com`). Currently, there are over 110,000 documents in the SEDAR database, with more added each day. Securities documents have been filed through SEDAR since it was launched in 1997. You can access profiles of more than 6,500 companies and mutual funds.

In the U.S., the peer site to SEDAR is called FreeEDGAR (`www.freeedgar.com`). The FreeEDGAR service provides registered users with an e-mail alert every time a certain firm files a document, and then links you to that document. (SEDAR does not have this service — but look out for it to arrive.) Downloadable data from both Web sites can be accessed by individual investors. You also can save SEDAR- and EDGAR-obtained reports on a disk and read them later.

Be aware of the fact that annual reports may include more than 50 pages and often exceed 100 pages. For example, Canadian and U.S. annual reports include financial statements, notes to financial statements, supplementary data, wordy management discussions of financial conditions and results of operations, descriptions of the business, legal proceedings, shareholder voting matters, insider transactions, executive compensation, and leasing agreements. Fun stuff! So be selective about how much information you want — and need — to download.

When you search the SEDAR and EDGAR databases, you're asked (via a drop-down screen or report number) for the document you want. The reports are organized in the following manner:

✔ **Annual reports (*10-K Reports* in EDGAR):** Annual reports that include shareholder information covering the firm's fiscal year

✔ **Quarterly reports (*10-Q Reports* in EDGAR):** Quarterly reports that include shareholder information for the company's last quarter

✔ **Notice of material changes (*8-K Report* in EDGAR):** Special reports that are the result of a significant contract, lawsuit, or other material event

✔ **EDGAR S-1 registrations:** Forms required for businesses that want to offer stock to the public; often used for initial public offerings (IPOs), an S-3 registration is used for a secondary offering of stock to the public after an initial public offering

✔ **Notice of annual or special meetings (*14-A Form* in EDGAR):** Information about annual general meetings (AGMs) and voting matters such as candidates seeking election to the board of directors, approval of increase in authorized capital stock, and/or approval of merger or acquisition

After you find the report you want, and after it is opened in Adobe Acrobat Reader or similar format, you can save the data in just three clicks:

1. **Click the File menu at the top-left corner of your Internet browser screen.**

2. **Click Save.**

   Your browser displays a dialogue box asking you which drive you want to save the data on and which name you want to file it under.

3. **Enter a filename and specify where you want to save the file.**

   Use the company's name, initials, or ticker symbol for the filename and a file extension of .pdf.

4. **Click Save.**

   You've finished downloading a 50-page document from the Internet!

To read the file, just access it through Windows Explorer (or similar file list) and open the file by double-clicking it.

Analyzing a Financial Statement

Companies often use their annual reports to attract new investors; you can guess that these reports contain some marketing fluff and exaggerations. Most of this embellishment is self-evident. Analyzing a company with a calculator, paper, and pencil will take you about an hour, and the results of this examination can help online investors make informed investment decisions. Buying stock in a company without reading the annual report is like buying a house without seeing it. Here's a checklist of the information you need to consider while you review a company's annual report:

- **Profitability:** How much money did the company make last year?

- **Survivability:** How is the company coping with its competition? Is there any ongoing competitive threat?

- **Growth:** Is the company expanding? Is the industry it operates in expanding?

- **Stability:** Is the company subject to radical changes from year to year? Does it handle these changes well?

- **Dividends (if any):** Is dividend growth constant? How does it compare to industry averages? Is money not paid out in dividends reinvested to fund research, expansion, or other strategic initiatives?

- **Problems:** Does the company have any pending lawsuits? Are there any other problems?

- **Risks:** Is the company subject to any environmental, legislative, financial, competitive, or business risks?

- **Other factors:** Is the management team experienced? Does the company need more executive talent?

Adviceforinvestors.com (`www.adviceforinvestors.com`), formerly known as Carlson Online, provides many information services, including Canadian regulatory filing information and detailed company profiles. Free services include access to the SEDAR database, press releases from Canadian Corporate News and Canada NewsWire, instant access to research reports on over 600 companies, access to discussion forums, quotes, and charts for over 1,700 companies. You can download annual reports, financial statements, and prospectuses. Adviceforinvestors.com lets you search by company name, ticker symbol, industry, or a combination of these. Its subscription service ($10 per month) gives you unlimited access to data from Globe Information Services, insider trading data, short position reports, stock screening (discussed in Chapter 12), and ratio analyses (the evaluation of a company's financial strength by applying standard measures of profitability, liquidity, and leverage).

Adviceforinvestors.com's enhanced subscription services (check out their Web site for their escalating rates) offer real-time text retrieval and the ability to export reports to word-processing programs and financial data to Lotus or Excel spreadsheet programs (something that SEDAR and FreeEDGAR can't do). In addition, Adviceforinvestors.com allows you to review executive salaries, stock options, corporate board memberships, and individual insider trading. (You may want to know whether the company CEO gave himself a big salary increase as sales revenues dropped and profits dwindled. It happens all the time!)

Dissecting an Annual Report

Despite their glossiness, annual reports often present many unglamorous but truthful statements about a company. Corporate challenges are often treated with amazing frankness.

TIP

The National Association of Investors Corporation (NAIC) (www.better-investing.org) is a non-profit educational organization that supports individual investors and investment clubs. The association offers downloadable demos of its investment analysis, stock screening, and portfolio management software programs. (See Chapter 2 to discover how you can easily download software.) The programs are designed for computer novices. If you are math-averse, using these demos is a good way to approach the ratio-analysis tasks described in this section.

In general, annual reports consist of nine sections:

- Letter to the shareholders with the year's highlights
- Company overview
- Multi-year figures, charts, and graphs of financial and other measures
- Management discussion and analysis of operations
- Independent auditor's report on financial statements
- Financial statements and notes
- Stock price history
- Subsidiary, brand, and contact information
- List of directors and officers

As you start analyzing annual reports, you'll probably notice that each company has its own style and approach. As you read, you may see that some sections are clear and straightforward; others are not very accessible and require your close attention. Some sections may be lengthy and others brief. These inconsistencies are the result of different company departments and individuals writing different sections. Often, the annual report is an ongoing company project and not just something that is written at the end of the fiscal year. Some are great reads. Others will put anyone, except a lawyer or accountant, to sleep.

Reading the letter to the shareholders

Although the letter to the shareholders is usually at the beginning of the annual report, save reading it until the end, when you can compare it to the facts you uncover about the company. Ask yourself, Is the CEO being truthful with the shareholders? What is the CEO's view of the company's operations? What does this letter say about the character of the CEO? Does the letter smack of "hype," or does it seem factual? Never accept what you read at face value, and consider the following questions as well:

- What changed in the past year?
- Are conditions continuing to change?
- Which goals were not achieved?
- What made the company miss the mark?
- What are the company's goals for next year?
- Are these goals realistic, given current economic conditions and the company's resources?
- What is the time schedule for specific actions?
- Does the letter apologize for anything?

Examining the company overview

Following the letter to the shareholders, the annual report usually presents an overview of the company, which includes a description of the company's products and its channels of distribution. This section should answer the following questions:

- What product or service does the company sell?
- Is the company introducing any new lines of business?
- How, where, or when does the company sell its products or services?
- Where (in what geographic region) does the company make most of its money?
- Does the company divide its various lines of business into logical groupings, such as global sales, continental sales, national sales, and regional sales (or electronics, computers, and software sales)?

Making sense of the multi-year figures, charts, and graphs

Companies often provide selected financial and non-financial data. The ten-year summary of financial figures should show the steady growth of the company (if there was steady growth). As you review the annual report, ask yourself the following questions:

✔ Are the financial data on steady growth included?

✔ Are non-financial data relevant to your investment decision?

✔ What's the growth in profits? Often, the year-to-year percentage of growth is calculated for you.

✔ What's the growth in operating income? The company may have calculated this number for you. If not, you'll have to download the data to your spreadsheet program and do the analysis yourself.

Microsoft's Investor Relations (`microsoft.com/msft/tools.htm`) provides annual reports, earnings reports, stock information, SEC filings, and investment and acquisition data, in addition to many online annual report analysis tools. These tools allow you to download several spreadsheets with macros that help you analyze specific company data. For example, you can click on a hyperlink, and the company's financial history from 1985 to the current report appears in a special free Excel program that allows you to manipulate the numbers. A second analysis tool lets you look at the sources of revenue by sales area or product group (for example, you can look up sales revenue in Europe). A third financial model allows you to perform a "what if" analysis, which lets you forecast various company income statements in a free Microsoft Excel Viewer.

Reviewing the management discussion and analysis of operations

The management discussion, which is one of the most significant sections of the annual report, usually focuses on corporate operations. This section is like an "armchair discussion" among the members of the company's management team — and you. It addresses such issues as the impact of technology on the company, the effects of the competition, the risks facing the company, and management's expectations for the next year. Consider the following questions when you review this part of the annual report:

✔ Does the management discussion offer a clear analysis of significant financial trends over the past two years?

✔ Is the discussion candid and accurate?

✔ Has the company sold any parts of its business?

✔ Have any products been discontinued?

Scrutinizing the auditor's report

Toward the back of the annual report, you generally find an opinion letter with a title like *Auditor's Report* or *Report of Independent Auditor*. Keep in mind that the company pays the auditor, a fact that can lead to a biased opinion. CA firms are sued from time to time, as evidenced in many Canadian dailies. Sometimes, the lawsuit alleges bias. (During the recent Bre-X and YBM scandals, for example, the annual reports and notes to financial statements didn't reveal shaky financial situations that were the underlying reality.)

The first part of the auditor's opinion is standard. The keywords to look for are "in our opinion, the financial position stated in the annual report has been fairly stated in all material aspects and in conformity with Canadian or American generally accepted accounting principles," or something to this effect. If this statement isn't used, a material problem may exist. As you read the independent auditor's report, ask yourself the following questions:

- ✔ What are the qualifications of the public accounting firm? (Is this a Big Five accounting firm, like PricewaterhouseCoopers or Deloitte & Touche, or is it a firm you've never heard of?)

- ✔ Are the firm's accounting procedures standard for the industry?

Examining financial statements and notes

Many companies are part of conglomerates that operate in several industries and countries. In these cases, it isn't possible to compare company performance to an industry average. The only way you can judge the company's performance is to compare current financial ratios to previous ratios.

The notes to the financial statements are often the most revealing part of a financial statement. They represent the "fine print" of a financial statement package. Notes define accounting policies and disclose any "material" development that could influence the market price of a security. For example, lawsuits involving significant — or material — amounts of money should be noted in the financial statements. The company's financial statements consist of four documents:

- ✔ **Balance sheet:** A snapshot of the company's assets and liabilities

- ✔ **Income statement:** The results of operations for the past year

- ✔ **Statement of cash flows:** An analysis of how the company made its money and spent its cash

- ✔ **Statement of retained earnings:** An analysis of how company profits were distributed to shareholders

Canadian GAAP — generally accepted accounting principles — are almost the same as U.S. GAAP. So you don't have to worry too much about the risk of comparing Canadian apples with U.S. oranges!

When analyzing financial statements and financial ratios, you should note the following information:

- **Growth in sales:** Are sales increasing or decreasing?
- **Growth in profits:** Are profits growing as fast as sales? Are high interest payments eating away at profits? Do company expenses "burn" through cash reserves too quickly?
- **Profits:** Have earnings per share increased every year? If not, why not? There may be a logical answer. For example, a nickel company's profits may not rise every year because the commodity price of nickel fluctuates. Also, non-cash charges, such as amortization expenses, may decrease profits but not impair cash flow.
- **Research and development spending:** Does the company spend the same amount on research and development as similar firms?
- **Inventory:** Are inventories going up or down because of a change in accounting procedures? Are inventories building up because competition is fierce and sales are lagging?
- **Debt:** Are debts increasing?
- **Assets:** Are most of the company's assets leased?
- **Litigation:** Is there any pending litigation (lawsuits)?
- **Pension plan:** Is the pension plan in bad shape?
- **Changes in procedures:** Is the company altering its accounting procedures in a way that may inflate earnings?

You may want to calculate several ratios that you can then compare to the company's previous ratios and to industry averages. Industry averages provide a benchmark for your analysis.

Investor ratios include the following:

- Last closing stock price (price per share)
- P/E ratio (current price per share divided by annual earnings per share)
- Dividend yield (annual dividend divided by price)
- Return on equity ratio (net income available to common shareholders divided by common equity)

- ✔ Debt to equity ratio (total debt divided by common equity)

- ✔ Percentage change in EPS (earnings per share) from the last quarter (current EPS divided by last quarter's EPS less 1.00)

- ✔ Earnings growth rate (net income from this year divided by last year's net income less 1.00)

Company solvency ratios include the following:

- ✔ Current ratio (current assets divided by current liabilities)

- ✔ Quick ratio (current assets minus inventory, divided by current liabilities)

- ✔ Times interest earned ratio (the number of times interest expense is covered by operating income)

- ✔ Debt ratio (total debt divided by total assets)

Investigating the stock price history

Evaluating a company's stock price history may give you some useful insights. For example, you can find out if the current stock price is the highest in the history of the company. This section of the annual report should answer the following questions:

- ✔ What are the company's general stock price trends over time?

- ✔ On which exchange is the company traded?

- ✔ What's the company's stock symbol?

- ✔ What's the company's dividend history?

- ✔ Has the company had any stock splits?

You don't have to be a math whiz to calculate ratios

Check out the Baker Library listing at `library. hbs.edu/ratio.htm` for more information about financial and operating ratios. This listing — which applies to any company, regardless of geographic location — shows sources for comparative industry ratios, ratios for specific industries, competitive company ratios, and customized online searches. It's particularly handy if you're trying to evaluate a company in the high-tech field. That's because the area of high-technology company ratio analysis is still a relatively new discipline. In fact, a book about it probably hasn't been published yet!

Using Prepared Online Ratio Analyses

Many organizations provide online annual reports that include ratio analyses, performance statistics, accounting notes, and other relevant information. You can download, print, and save all these reports. Many of the downloaded data are ready for your spreadsheet program and the application of your analytical skills. However, you may need to reformat some data, and some types of data do not convert to a spreadsheet.

In the following list, we describe two sources of prepared online ratio analysis and company information:

✔ **Multex Investor** (www.multexinvestor.com), shown in Figure 8-3, provides information about stocks, mutual funds, and more. You can read company information, see what analysts are saying about a company, and access online analytical tools. Company and analyst information includes the latest company press release or news, key ratios, overall company profiles, special reports, and earnings estimates. Online tools include a stock screen to help you find companies that meet your criteria.

Figure 8-3: Multex Investor will help you keep track of where the markets have been, and where they may be headed.

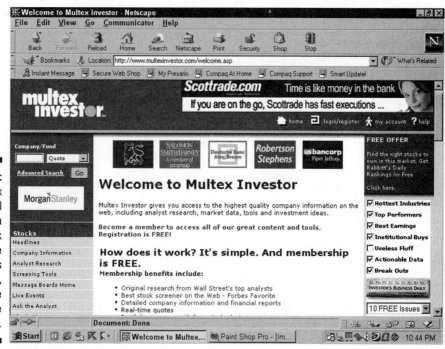

✔ **Thomson Investor Net** (www.thomsoninvest.net) provides more than 7,500 in-depth Canadian and U.S. company reports updated twice a month. For stock research, the company provides stock quotes, company information, stock screening, a list of the month's top performers, and more. Company reports include comparison of the firm's ratios to industry averages, though you can't download the reports to your spreadsheet. Monthly subscriptions are $9.95 U.S. and include 25 in-depth company reports and 25 mutual fund reports. Additional company reports are $2.50 U.S.

Financial statement analysis does not just involve examining the company's annual report and ratio analysis. Looking beyond the firm's numbers and evaluating changes in accounting procedures that may hide serious problems is also important. For example, the ways firms account for depreciation and the value of inventory can be quite different within the same industry. The result can be earnings per share (EPS) that aren't truly representative of a firm's performance, especially when compared to previous EPS and the industry standard. An inaccurate EPS number can lead to big surprises toward the end of the year when the company doesn't perform as expected.

Chapter 9

Digging Deep: Researching Investments

••

In This Chapter

▶ Turning your hunches into investment strategies

▶ Getting hard data on the economy

▶ Researching stocks online with facts

▶ Paying the right price for stocks

••

*Y*ou may use an online stock screen (see Chapter 12) to whittle down the number of common stock investment candidates you're considering. Or you may select a few companies because you know something about the products they sell. Maybe you work in the industry or have used the company's products or services over a long period of time.

After you find a few investment candidates, you can use online tools to download the annual reports of the companies that interest you (see Chapter 8). You can read the financial statements and calculate key ratios. You can select a candidate that you think will meet your investment objectives. You may think that you're done — and before the Internet you may indeed have been done — but you need to do a little more research before you contact your online broker. Why? To be blunt — because you can! The Internet lets you access powerful tools that enable you to dig deeper to understand in detail how your investment candidate operates. You also want to dig wide, to better understand the broad economic environment in which the company operates.

In this chapter, we help you locate the online sources that you can use to determine where the company stands in its industry and what type of marketing techniques it's using to maintain and increase revenues. We show you where to find out what the experts are saying about your stock pick and where to go online to find analyst earning estimates. We point out where you can get historical stock price information. We also show you where you can get industry and economic information to help you develop and frame a "big picture." After you have all of these details and broad facts, you can make your investment decision.

Many investors do not have the confidence to select their own stocks. This chapter shows how you yourself can conduct even more in-depth online research to find winning investments. Many of the sources we list in this chapter are the same sources that full-service brokers use in their stock analyses.

Exercising Due Diligence

Every online investor has his or her own research system for investigating investment candidates. What makes any system work is that it's repeatable and that it ensures that you don't make investment decisions based on emotional factors. The following guidelines can assist you in turning your hunches into investment strategies. This process is often referred to as "due diligence." You can begin your due diligence process as follows:

1. **Find the candidates that you want to research.**

   Match your hunches about stocks that are positioned to be top performers to your investor profile and use a stock screen or some other method to identify investment candidates. (For more information about researching individual stocks, see Chapter 8. For in-depth coverage of Internet stock screens, refer to Chapter 12.)

2. **Trim your list of candidates.**

   Locate the online annual reports for your short list of stock candidates by using the online and manual techniques we outline in Chapter 8. Conduct your analysis and reduce the list to several companies.

3. **Find out more about each company.**

   Use this background information to put each company into a broader context using the sources we detail in this chapter. For example, is the company a market leader?

   The good news is that the Internet has tonnes of this type of information, and most of it is free. Here are some examples of sources for this information (we list Internet resources for the following categories of information later in the chapter):

   - **News:** Read the company's press releases and keep current with breaking news. Try to connect isolated news articles to spot trends.

   - **Industry:** Read news articles and industry trade journals to spot patterns that may indicate technological breakthroughs or new products. Does the industry have problems with oversupply, and, if so, how does this situation affect the profits of the company you're researching?

- **Economics:** Note how changes in the national, regional, and local economies affect your investment candidates. Will a rising dollar lower corporate returns? What do the Bay Street and Wall Street economists say?

- **Market:** What's happening in the stock market? Are prices and trading volume increasing? Are insiders purchasing stock?

- **Analysts' evaluations:** Bay Street and Wall Street analysts often provide opinions on most publicly traded companies. Study what the analysts are saying about the company. While you can't always rely on what analysts say, their comments may provide you with leads for additional research.

- **Earnings estimates:** Keep current with the earnings estimates of professionals. Are the estimates going up or down?

- **Historical prices:** Sometimes you can tell where a company is going by seeing where it has been. Evaluating a company's past stock prices may provide you with new insights. It's hard to buy low and sell high without this information at hand.

4. **Decide whether the company is a low-priced, high-quality stock, or a loser.**

   When you put all the facts together, you gain a good understanding of what causes the company's stock price to rise or fall. As well, you know what's a normal situation for the company.

5. **Ask yourself, "What if?"**

   For example, what if sales drop by 10 percent, like they may have done many years ago? What if the material the company uses to manufacture its product becomes scarce — would this scarcity cause lost sales, or cause the cost of goods to increase? Would such a change reduce profits so much that the company couldn't pay its interest expense? Would the company be forced into bankruptcy?

6. **To complete your investment strategy, determine how risky the stock is.**

   Could you lose your entire investment? If so, you need to add a *risk premium* to your required rate of return. A risk premium compensates you for the additional risk of your investment. Should the return be 10 times your investment or maybe even 30 times your initial investment? Making this decision can be difficult, because everyone defines risk differently and everyone has a different risk-tolerance level. Still, it can help you decide whether or not to invest.

Conquering Uncertainty with Precise Online Research

You can use the Internet to get background company information by accessing one of the many free and fee-based databases, where you can dig up all kinds of facts and opinions about a company. Some of this information can provide you with new insights, ideas, and leads about additional research. Overall, this information can provide you with an understanding of how a company works within the economy, how it copes with the competition, and how it ranks within its industry. This information is often critical to your investment decision.

With millions of Web pages on the Internet, finding exactly what you're looking for can be a challenge. However, uncovering one small fact can make the difference between purchasing a mediocre stock and buying a stock that can bring you exceptional returns. As you surf the Internet, you may encounter sites that discuss stocks, markets, online trading, and more. In the following sections, we help you locate the right online sources that can assist you in finding the background information you need to complete your company research.

Gaining new investor insights with breaking news

Daily news and press releases can assist you in keeping current with your investments or investment candidates. These sources often provide the first glimpse of why a stock price is rapidly increasing or falling like a stone. One of the advantages of these online sources is that they have *archives,* where you can check past company events that made news. Most press releases also give a brief and current profile about what the company does. It's a quick way to get a "first impression" of a company.

Here are a few Internet resources for finding press releases and breaking news:

- ✔ **Bloomberg Online (**www.bloomberg.com**):** This site has edited online columns, audio clips about current market performance, and other information about stocks, bonds, markets, and industry. The site is well organized and provides access to current market statistics, business and financial news, major Canadian and U.S. investment stories, and financial analysis tools. (Bloomberg charges a fee for subscribing to its magazine, but you can browse its Web site for free.)

- ✔ **National Post Online (**www.nationalpost.com**):** This interactive site contains recent news, business, and market columns from the *National Post.* Articles have links to charts, graphs, and tables. Daily news is continually updated. The *Financial Post* part of this Web site includes closing index values, stock quotes, and a summary of each day's activities.

There is no fee to subscribe to the National Post Online — this paper's priority is to build its paid print readership. More good news — the National Post Online has plenty of information from the print version, plus some extras such as excerpts from conference calls and other items that are too lengthy for print. They plan to introduce audio and video media to their site.

✔ **WSRN (`www.wsrn.com`):** This site provides a good starting place for your search for global company information. WSRN has more than 500,000 links to Internet financial sources to help professional and individual investors alike. The site is divided into eight sections: company information, economic research, market news, news, research publications, mutual funds, broker services, and what's new.

You can start at the Research a Company page and use the links to get Securities and Exchange Commission (SEC) filings, quotes, graphs or charts, news, earnings estimates, research reports, and summaries.

✔ **Yahoo! Finance (`finance.yahoo.com`):** This Internet portal, shown in Figure 9-1, has a very thorough collection of news and company press releases from an array of news providers. Simply call up the Canadian or U.S. company by stock ticker symbol, by an alphabetic index, or by a search, and a list of recent news stories and press releases is displayed. Yahoo! also lets you access archives of older news releases. These services are free.

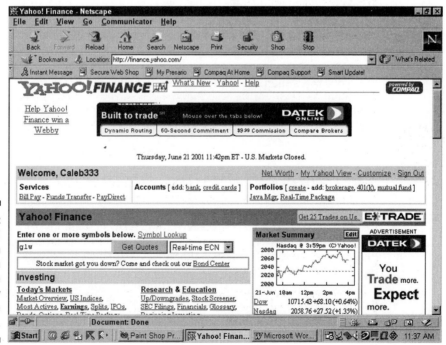

Figure 9-1:
Yahoo! Finance can provide you with the company news you're looking for.

Locating company profiles and related data

In much the same way as the literary world includes biographies of famous people, the world of finance has *company profiles*. Company profiles include all the events that make a company what it is today. You can keep all of a company's pertinent facts handy by obtaining a company profile. Company profiles are often designed for investors and highlight investor-related information.

Here are two online sources for obtaining company profiles:

- ✔ **Adviceforinvestors.com** (www.adviceforinvestors.com): Formerly known as Carlson Online, this site has free information on over 4,000 Canadian companies. Company profiles include the firm's address, phone numbers, executive roster, recent sales figures, and company status. The site also has links to Canadian regulatory financial data. You can download annual reports, financial statements, and prospectuses. Its subscription service ($10 per month) gives you unlimited access to even more detailed profile information, such as insider trading data, consensus estimates on more than 1,000 Canadian companies, brokerage recommendations, short position reports, and key ratio analyses. An enhanced service that costs even more provides you with a portfolio-tracking tool and access to advice on Canadian stocks from the site's writers. You can also download brokerage research reports for many of the tracked companies by paying a fee for each report, or by paying an additional subscription fee for wider access.

- ✔ **Company Sleuth** (www.companysleuth.com): This Web site features a free service that provides daily e-mail updates on your Canadian and U.S. stocks, as well as scoops on their competitors and clients. Follow your investments' activities to know the next move to make. It also includes information on patents, trademarks, and insider trading, plus analysts' reports, an assortment of discussion forums, SEC filings, stock quotes, and breaking corporate news.

Checking out analyst evaluations

Often stock prices move on the strength of an analyst's critique — up or down, depending on what she had to say. Although these opinions are supposed to be "informed," they're still opinions and shouldn't overshadow your good judgment. For example, assume that an analyst suggests buying a stock and forecasts the price to increase to a record high. Over the year, the stock reaches the mark, and then the analyst places a hold on the stock. (A *hold* is a suggestion to investors that they neither sell nor buy the stock.) This hold may look like an unfavourable mark against the stock, but the stock performed just as expected and is currently a good investment.

Analyst opinions are also supposed to be timely, but quite often are late. During the recent technology stock correction, far too many stocks earned sell recommendations — after they had already dropped 90 percent in value from their 52-week highs! An individual investor can be excused for expecting the "strong buy" recommendations to arrive only once new highs are reached.

The Internet lets you access most analyst reports sorted by individual Bay Street and Wall Street brokerage houses, or groups of analysts who study a particular stock. However, brokerage houses sometimes participate in or lead the financing of the companies they're analyzing. Consequently, you rarely see a "sell" recommendation. They may be biased. As well, you may see that analysts' opinions vary. Feel free to disagree with their conclusions, but know what the professionals are saying about a company that interests you. It may lead you to consider something you might not have thought of.

CCN Newswire (www.ccnnewswire.com) is a comprehensive Canadian business news service that reports analyst recommendations by date and by company name. Of course, being a news service, it reports corporate press releases and media news stories as well. It's free.

For about $5, Standard & Poor's (www.standardpoor.com) has basic stock reports, industry reports, news stories, and *Wall Street Consensus Reports*. The *Wall Street Consensus Reports* include analyst earnings estimates. Standard & Poor's covers mostly American companies, but also has information on some of the larger Canadian companies.

A new service called ProTrader Alert (www.protrader.com) aims to deliver hot fund managers' top stock picks to individual investors — just shortly after the fund managers have made the big trade. Subscribers receive the notification by e-mail, and can access it with a Palm Pilot or RIM Blackberry device. The ProTrader service attempts to isolate the top trades made, based on very recent fund manager performance. In other words, it links you to the hottest managers at a given point in time. Because a large volume of stock transactions can move prices significantly, subscribers can potentially benefit from the price momentum inherent in large trades and an institutional following.

Tracking down earnings estimates

The price you pay for a stock is based on its future income stream. If earnings estimates indicate that the earnings per share (EPS) is dropping, the stock price you pay today may be too high for the true value of the stock.

Here are several Internet sources for earnings estimates:

- **First Call** (www1.firstcall.com): The First Call database follows more than 35,000 companies, including Canadian and U.S. listings, and also tracks more than 100 industry groups, several commodities and economic indicators, plus major market indexes. Products and subscription prices vary. For example, a *First Call Reports* subscription costs $20 U.S. per month, or $199 per year. The first 30 days are free. Other products, such as individual consensus estimate reports by company, are also available. See the Web site for details.

- ✔ **Stock Smart** (www.stocksmart.com): This site provides earnings estimates for a price. Stock Smart includes a professional portfolio manager, earnings calendar, unlimited stock quotes and graphing, shareholder data, comprehensive research, stock screening, week in review, industry roll-ups, mutual funds, and market information. Subscriptions to the basic service are $12.95 U.S. per month and include a free ten-day test drive. Enhanced services, including real-time quotes and wireless alerts, cost more. Because this service is pricey, it is best suited for Canadians who are interested only in U.S. stocks. Not all Canadian stocks are covered.

- ✔ **Yahoo! Finance** (finance.yahoo.com): A free summary of all recent analyst recommendations is available here. After you enter the stock ticker symbol of a Canadian company, click the Research icon.

- ✔ **Zacks Investment Research** (www.zacks.com): This site provides estimated earnings reports based on analyst opinions. The site includes a listing of current earnings surprises, recommendations, and the company's annual balance sheet and income statement. Although this is an American information service provider, it covers many Canadian public companies.

Researching historical performance

Seeing where a company has been is always important in order to get a feel for where it's headed. Here are a few Internet sources for checking up on a company's stock price — past and present — which will help you decide whether *you* invest in it in the future.

- ✔ **Standard & Poor's Stock Screens** (www.standardpoor.com): The *Historical & Projected Industry P/E Ratios Report* is a very useful page for online investors. The report includes price-to-earnings (P/E) ratios for all the major industries from 1995 to the present.

- ✔ **ValueLine** (valueline.com): Provides comprehensive coverage of 3,600 U.S.-listed companies including ratings, analyst research reports, and opinions.

- ✔ **Quote.com** (www.quote.com): This well-known site provides historical data files as an additional service ($2 U.S.) for current subscribers. Four types of historical data are available:

  - U.S. stocks — daily history from October 1988 to the present

  - Canadian stocks — daily history from April 1994 to the present

- Commodity futures — daily history from April 1994 to the present
- Indexes and indicators — daily history from October 1988 to the present

Researching Industries

After you have learned more about a specific company, you need to gain an understanding of the industry and economy (or economies) that the company operates in. Web sites help you out with this.

Finding industry and statistical information

Annual reports often provide good insights into the forces that drive certain industries. However, this information may not be enough to answer your questions. Here are some online sources for industry and statistical information:

✔ **Strategis (**strategis.ic.gc.ca**):** Shown in Figure 9-2, this Industry Canada Web site is very comprehensive. After you click the Business Information by Sector icon from the home page, you can conduct information

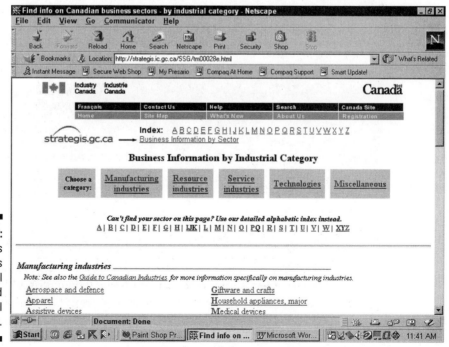

Figure 9-2:
Strategis
provides
useful
industry and
statistical
information.

searches by industry to find information about trends and comparative analyses to U.S. industries. Detailed overviews of particular industries are accessible at this site.

✔ **LexisNexis** (www.lexis-nexis.com)**:** Shown in Figure 9-3, this site has a wide variety of business and legal databases. The site recently added a new database of 10- to 20-page market summaries of industry sectors or demographic markets. Pricing for different types of usage varies — if you're interested in this service, contact it for a firm price quote. LexisNexis accesses both Canadian and U.S. databases.

✔ **TechnoMetrica Market Intelligence** (www.technometrica.com)**:** Among other things, TechnoMetrica provides business research that includes industry and market features and trends, market share analysis, market potential analysis, and strategic planning.

Figure 9-3: LexisNexis has a huge database of detailed company information.

Gathering economic and related data

Many individuals try to predict economic trends, but few (if any) are successful. However, having a good understanding of current economic conditions and where they're headed is vital to your comprehension of the company in its broader context. After all, many companies are sensitive to changes in the economy.

The Internet has many sources for economic information. Here are a few examples:

✔ **Statistics Canada (`www.statcan.ca`):** Shown in Figure 9-4, Statistics Canada maintains hundreds of databases of statistical information provided to the public. This site includes many reports in either full text or abstract forms. Most are free, but some have to be purchased. Most information resources are well organized and searchable. You can access information about industries, geographic locations, population densities, housing, employment, and more.

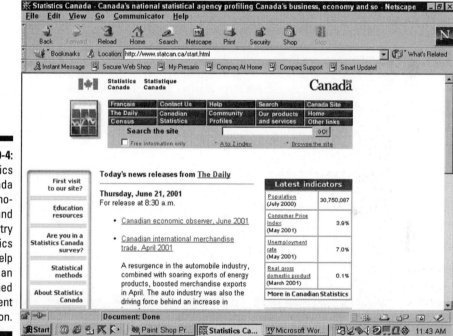

Figure 9-4:
Statistics Canada has demographic and industry statistics that can help you make an informed investment decision.

✔ **Census Bureau (`www.census.gov`):** The Census Bureau is the American equivalent of Statistics Canada, and provides much of the same information as described above. Of special note is the *Today's Economic Indicator Report,* which provides information about government and related entities releasing economic reports on industrial production, consumer sentiment, and so on. This type of information often moves the U.S., and even the Canadian, stock market.

✔ **Internet Federal Reserve site (`www.federalreserve.gov`):** This site provides links to all the Federal Reserve (the Fed) home pages. Publications by this organization include high-quality statistics, analyses, and forecasts of regional, national, and international economic and financial conditions. Because whatever the Fed does also affects Canada, you should know about this site.

Collecting market information

Understanding the current market environment can help you select a stock with the return you want. You need to know how a company markets its products or services (catalogue sales, face-to-face meetings, and so on), and the share of the total market the company commands. This information can give you a better understanding of what drives the company's stock price.

Here are some online sources for market information:

✔ **Quote.com** (`www.quote.com`): Shown in Figure 9-5, this site provides free unlimited delayed security quotes from U.S. and Canadian exchanges; limited balance-sheet data; some company profile information; an unlimited number of updates for a portfolio of up to seven securities; daily, weekly, and/or monthly stock price charts; daily market index charts; daily information for major industry groups; and foreign exchange rates.

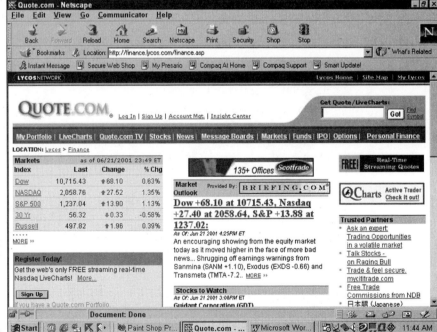

Figure 9-5: Quote.com is one Web site where you can get prices of both Canadian and U.S. stocks.

✔ **E-Line (**`www.financials.com`**):** This site provides U.S. and Canadian stock ratings and market data. Canadian data can be accessed through the Market Vision "World Markets at a Glance" link. This link takes you to data about foreign exchange, foreign indexes, and more.

✔ **Holt Stock Report (**`metro.turnpike.net/holt/holt_rpt.htm`**):** This online resource provides indexes, averages, and information about Canadian, U.S., and other foreign markets; issues information on trades, new highs and lows, currency, gold, and interest rates; and covers most active issues on major stock exchanges.

✔ **Thomas Register (**`www.thomasregister.com`**):** This site includes buying information for the products and services of more than 160,000 domestic and international companies. Information is divided into over 55,000 categories. After you register, use of the online catalogue is free. This site is an excellent source for discovering more about a company's chief competitors.

The Price Is Right — with Research

There's no secret to making money in the stock market. All you have to do is buy low and sell high. The tricky part is deciding when to execute purchases and sales! That little bit of extra research and analysis on your part is what you really need to keep you ahead of the pack. There are three types of analysis you can do — fundamental, technical, and quantitative.

✔ **Fundamental analysis** requires a review of several factors, such as earnings, assets, cash flow, liquidity, markets, competition, management strength, and other factors.

✔ **Technical analysis** involves checking out the security itself. It also includes the study of the indexes that measure market performance, such as the Nasdaq, which measures mostly high-tech industry performance. Patterns of historical price movements and momentum help technical analysts spot turning points and predict price changes.

✔ **Quantitative analysis** uses both fundamental and technical models. It uses computer spreadsheets to crunch lots of numbers. It's a favourite tool for investors who try to time the market. (In this book, we deal with fundamental and technical analysis in greater depth, since quantitative analysis is essentially a hybrid of the others.)

Getting down to fundamentals

Fundamental analysis focuses on the underlying economics of the company being researched. Analysts try to forecast sales, earnings, and expenses, which in turn are used to forecast the company's stock price or returns.

Fundamental analysis relies on forecasts of the economy, the industry, and the company's commercial prospects. Analysts use this type of analysis to determine the intrinsic value or fair value of a stock. The fair value is compared to market values to determine whether the stock is underpriced or overpriced. In other words, the purpose of fundamental analysis is to locate mispriced stocks, or undervalued stocks that you can buy. It is the approach most often used for common stock valuations.

If the stock has higher risk than usual (because of past volatility, political turmoil, or other factors), then the investors include a *risk premium* in the required rate of return. This risk premium serves to compensate the investor for the higher than normal risk.

Money.com's Portfolio Forecaster tool (shown in Figure 9-6) lets you see how much your portfolio may be worth in the future, under certain assumptions. You can assess how risky your portfolio is, and see whether you'll be able to achieve your investment goals. The Portfolio Forecaster tool simulates thousands of different economic scenarios involving interest rates, inflation, and returns on various investments. You can analyze your existing portfolio, or a hypothetical one, as well. Go to (www.money.com/money/depts/investing/financialengines/pt.html).

Figure 9-6:
The Portfolio Forecaster can help you see how well your portfolio may do.

Proceed with caution

After crunching all the numbers, it's time for a reality check. The fundamental analysis method is limited because it often assumes that the investor is going to hold on to the stock until the company folds, or simply ceases to be. If the investor holds on to the stock for a short period of time (and let's face it, most of us will probably sell it before we pay off the mortgage, or even the car), he may not get all the expected returns. As well, investors and analysts can make errors in dividend projections or may ignore relevant external factors that can result in their not valuing the stock correctly. Before you log on to your broker or another online investment resource, you need to review your analysis and the data you collected. This is your money and your investment decision. Trust your own common sense to evaluate what you think is going to happen to this company in the future.

Shop for value

If you're a bargain shopper, you understand how difficult it is to separate the treasure from the trash. This search for value extends to investors who are seeking securities that seem underpriced relative to the fair value or financial prospects. Experts have a variety of opinions about how to decide whether a stock is undervalued (and unloved) or just a loser.

The Leuthold Group at T. Rowe Price (`www.troweprice.com`) has developed one approach. At the T. Rowe Price home page, enter "value investing" in the Search function box and click Go. At the search results screen, click Value Investing.

Table 9-1 shows a snapshot of this methodology. The Leuthold Group suggests that investment candidates meet at least six of the following factors. This is one way of separating the winners from the losers.

Table 9-1	Value Investing (Spotting the True Bargains)
Factor	*Analysis*
Price-to-book-value ratio (1)	Never over 2.0X
Price-to-earnings ratio (2)	Using 5-year average earnings never over 12X
Ratio of cash flow per share to price per share (3)	At least 10%
Dividend yield	(Dividend yield is equal to the annual dividend divided by the market price.) Dividend yield should never be below 3%
Price to cash flow	80% or less of the S&P 500 cash-flow ratio

(continued)

Table 9-1 *(continued)*

Factor	Analysis
Ratio of long-term debt (plus unfunded pension liabilities) to total capital	The debt equity ratio should be under 50% (include unfunded pension liabilities in the debt)
Financial strength	Creditworthiness should be at least equal to the industry average. The analyst rating should be at least B-minus.

Following are explanations of the terms used in Table 9-1. (For more information on many of these terms, see Chapter 8.)

Price-to-book-value (P/BV) ratio (1): Expresses the current selling price divided by book value. If the current selling price of the stock is below this amount, the stock is underpriced. Then again, the company may be on the verge of bankruptcy and that may be why the stock price is depressed.

The price-to-earnings (P/E) ratio (2): Reflects how many years of current earning must be earned to purchase one share of stock. For example, if annual earnings are $2 and the stock is selling at $30, the P/E ratio is 15 ($\frac{30}{2}$). Many investors believe that the higher the P/E ratio, the better. If investors expect earnings to decrease, the P/E ratio will decrease to below the industry average.

Cash flow per share (3): Expresses the firm's net income plus non-cash expenses minus non-cash gains, divided by the number of outstanding shares.

Many software programs can assist you with your fundamental analysis. One example is PowerTrader (www.powertrader.com/products.htm). This software program is designed to analyze common stocks using a combination of fundamental, technical, and quantitative analysis tools to help investors determine the fair value of common stocks, while identifying stocks that are over- or underpriced. The cost depends on the software package selected. Check out this company's Web site for product and pricing details.

Getting technical

Technical analysis focuses on stock data analysis and stock market statistics. Analysts search for early indicators of pattern changes. As soon as analysts identify the beginnings of a change in a pattern, they use it to predict the future. However, this method fails to recognize that stock prices change when the investment community's opinion concerning the value of the stock changes.

Technical analysis values a stock by tracking price trends of stocks, bonds, commodities, and the market. It assumes three things:

- The past action of the stock market is the best indicator of future performance.

- The stock's performance is viewed as mostly outside the company's control, with the balance of stock performance attributed to internal company factors.

- The stock market is based on 85 percent psychology and 15 percent economics.

Although technical analysis consists of many approaches, the most popular approach is the Dow theory. The *Dow theory* is based on *Wall Street Journal* founder Charles H. Dow's methodology for identifying signals of bull and bear markets. The theory suggests that as soon as the market heads in one direction, it stays that course until cancelled (stopped) by both the Dow Jones Industrial Average (DJIA) and the Dow Jones Transportation Average (DJTA). (It takes both averages to indicate that the market has changed its course.)

Technical analysis uses the Dow theory to analyze individual stocks. However, Dow developed this methodology to predict changes in the general market. He did not expect his theory to be applied to individual stocks. See E-Analytics at www.e-analytics.com/f13.htm for more on the Dow theory.

Check out Decision Point at decisionpoint.com/TAcourse/TAcourseMenu.html for a more detailed explanation of technical analysis techniques in general.

Technical analysis requires a large amount of information (usually historical price and volume data) that can be manipulated with technical analysis software programs. Some programs are designed for certain types of securities and for specific indicators and markets. Some programs are designed for beginners and others for professionals. Following is a list of some of the available programs:

- **ChartSmart 2000** (www.chartsmart.com): This program is a comprehensive tool for researching securities on U.S. and Canadian exchanges. You can get a downloadable demo at the Web site.

- **Equis International** (www.equis.com): This Web site houses MetaStock Professional, which analysts sometimes refer to as the granddaddy of technical analysis software. MetaStock Professional costs $350 U.S. Other features are free. The Web site also includes back issues of the Equis newsletter, files of tips, system tests, and custom formulas for use with the software. A downloadable demo is available.

✔ **VectorVest** (www.vectorvest.com)**:** This program uses fundamental valuation and technical analysis to rank over 7,000 stocks each day. Go to the Web site and sample the service. Just enter the ticker symbol of the company you're analyzing. Subscribers can get a five-week trial for $30 U.S. Non-subscribers get three free analyses per day, up to a maximum of 100. Check out the site for more product and pricing details.

Stocks and Commodities (www.traders.com/documentation/survey/98softwr.html) offers reviews of technical analysis software. You can view a survey of the program's features by clicking the name of the software product.

Chapter 10

Online Research and Analysis of Mutual Funds

*W*hen selecting a mutual fund, investors often look for relative performance over the past ten years, five years, and three years to see how the fund reacts to different economic conditions and stock market environments. Other factors in selecting a mutual fund include evaluating the fund manager's experience and record, the fund's level of consistency, and the fund's major investment holdings.

In this chapter, we show how you can match your financial objectives and risk-tolerance level to the right mutual funds. As a result, you can decide how much you should invest in a particular type of fund. We also describe how you can use online mutual fund rating tools to assist you in selecting the very best mutual funds for your personal portfolio. To conclude, we show you how to find detailed facts and figures about Canadian (and U.S.) mutual funds online.

Going Online with Mutual Funds

Chapter 6 tells you why mutual funds are great for investors who lack capital, technical knowledge, and the time to establish and maintain a diversified stock or bond portfolio. The advantages of mutual funds include easy access to your assets, the ability to sell the funds if you need to, and professional investment management.

With so many mutual funds available, no two are exactly alike. Many large mutual fund companies manage *families* of funds. A mutual fund family is a group of mutual funds all under the same management. Today, you can select from thousands of different Canadian and U.S. mutual funds in over 750 fund families. One of these funds is bound to fit your bill — meeting your personal goals and risk-tolerance level. If you aren't satisfied with the fund you select, you can always switch to another in the same fund family (often without any extra exchange costs).

You can find information about a fund's goals, strategies, performance, management, and fee structures in its prospectus. Prospectuses are often located at the fund's Web site (for example, Altamira's site is at `www.altamira.com`), and they're also filed at SEDAR (`www.sedar.com`).

Mutual funds fall into two main categories: *open-end funds* and *closed-end funds.* Different funds have different fees. Some funds have *front-end loads* or *back-end loads,* and some funds have *no loads.*

All funds have fees and expenses, but the amounts vary. As well as sales and redemption fees, the mutual fund's prospectus indicates the fund's management and administration expenses. The fund's manager generally receives 0.5 to 1.0 percent of the fund's average daily net assets. Administrative expenses include legal, auditing, and accounting costs, along with the fees for directors and the costs of preparing the annual report and proxy statements. These administrative expenses are added to the investment advisory fee.

Total mutual fund costs often average between 0.75 percent and 1.25 percent of fund assets. Veteran mutual fund investors are wary of funds that charge more than 1.25 percent. Stay away altogether from mutual funds that charge 1.5 percent or more. Opt instead for a better-priced fund.

Finding the Right Mix of Investments

Before you can apply online research techniques to selecting a mutual fund, you first need to figure out your asset allocation objectives. *Asset allocation* is the specific amount of money that you spend for each type of investment. In Bay Street–speak, the term describes how you diversify your financial assets (stocks, bonds, and cash) by amounts that you determine. Asset allocation also means trying to squeeze every bit of return out of each asset type, given the level of risk. Overall, the right asset allocation approach is the one that works best for you. There is no one "right" asset mix. Your asset allocation should take into consideration your age, the amount of time you can spare to manage your money, your financial goals, your risk-tolerance level, and the impact of taxes on your investment decisions.

Table 10-1 shows the ingredients for finding the combination of assets that may be just right for you. There is no definitive asset allocation model. The table below is one of several possible models, and is used for illustration purposes only. It shows definitions of nine investor types, and is typical of most guidelines. The types are categorized as conservative, moderate, and aggressive. The investment time frame fills out the picture. The investment period can be short-term, medium-term, or long-term. The asset allocations are by percentage.

Table 10-1	Mutual Fund Asset Allocations (%) Based on Investor Risk-Tolerance Levels		
Risk	**Time Frame**		
	Short-term **(0 to 2 years)**	**Medium-term** **(3 to 5 years)**	**Long-term** **(6 years +)**
Conservative	**#1**	**#2**	**#3**
Stocks	5	35	50
Bonds	5	20	50
Cash	90	45	0
Moderate	**#4**	**#5**	**#6**
Stocks	15	60	65
Bonds	35	35	35
Cash	50	5	0
Aggressive	**#7**	**#8**	**#9**
Stocks	35	75	100
Bonds	35	25	0
Cash	30	0	0

Many Canadian and U.S. mutual funds match the asset allocation table shown in Table 10-1. You can start with one mutual fund or you can purchase a mutual fund for each allocation. If you purchase several mutual funds, you can diversify your risk even more. For example, to complete your portfolio, you may want to buy a money market fund, a stock mutual fund, and a fixed-asset (bond) mutual fund. It's your money and your choice.

Matching Mutual Funds to Your Financial Objectives

Table 10-2 shows how you can match mutual fund categories to your financial objectives and risk-tolerance level. After you read Table 10-1, decide which of the nine investor types most closely matches your personal financial plan and risk-tolerance profile. Table 10-2 shows what categories of mutual funds are right for your investor type. The percentages listed below match the recommended allocations shown in Table 10-1. (For details about fund types, see Chapter 6.)

Table 10-2 Suggested Mutual Funds for Nine Types of Investors

Investor Type	Cash	Stocks	Bonds
1	(100%) Money market fund	(0%)	(0%)
2	(45%) Money market fund	(30%) General equity funds	(25%) Intermediate fixed-income partial equity funds (asset allocation); tax-free fixed-income funds (municipal bonds)
3	(0%)	(50%) General equity funds (income, growth)	(50%) Taxable fixed-income funds (government agency, income); fixed-mortgage income, partial equity funds (asset allocation)
4	(10%) Money market fund	(30%) General equity funds (income)	(60%) Short-term fixed-income funds (diversified); fixed-income partial equity funds (asset allocation, balanced)
5	(10%) Money market fund	(55%) General equity funds (growth, income)	(35%) Intermediate fixed-income funds (diversified); intermediate fixed-income partial equity funds (balanced); tax-free fixed-income funds (municipal bonds)

Investor Type	Cash	Stocks	Bonds
6	(0%)	(65%) General equity funds (growth, growth and equity)	(35%) Fixed-income bonds (diversified, corporate); fixed-income partial equity funds (balanced); tax-free fixed-income funds (municipal bonds)
7	(40%) Money market fund	(30%) General equity funds (aggressive growth, small-cap)	(30%) Short-term fixed-income funds (corporate, high-yield); short-term fixed-income partial equity funds (convertible)
8	(0%)	(70%) General equity funds (aggressive growth, small-cap); specialty equity (technology, other)	(30%) Intermediate fixed-income (corporate high yield); intermediate fixed-income partial equity funds (flexible); tax-free fixed-income funds (municipal bonds)
9	(0%)	(100%) General equity funds; small-cap equity funds; specialty equity; international equity	

Interested in finding specific mutual funds in the categories that match your personal financial profile? The Fund Library's (www.fundlibrary.com) **Fund Filter** tool can help you find the mutual fund that's right for you. You can tailor your Fund Filter to pull up only those mutual funds that meet your risk, fund category, performance, and other criteria. When you reach the Fund Library home page, you'll see that it offers free services such as price charts, press releases, simple fund ratings, a learning centre, and much more. The services found on this site are free because this fairly independent Web site is financially sustained through the support of its member companies and advertising revenue.

Using the Internet to Help You Choose the Best Funds in Each Class

Past performance doesn't guarantee future performance. However, annualized returns are often used to compare funds. The Internet offers tables of fund comparisons for each month and for periods ranging from a month to ten years or more. For example, CANOE (www.canoe.ca) has a mutual funds section that provides listings of the returns for the best funds, the worst funds, and so on. An even more comprehensive site that does this sort of comparison is Morningstar Canada (www.morningstar.ca). Morningstar specializes in mutual funds and has some of the most powerful online tools on the Web for the individual mutual fund investor (see Figure 10-1).

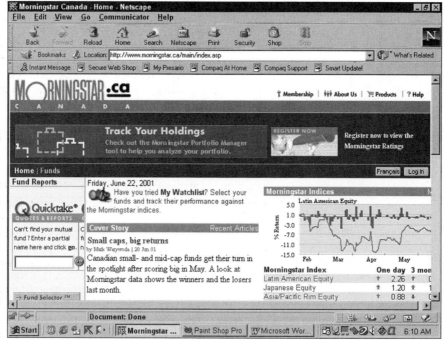

Figure 10-1: Morningstar Canada has mutual fund industry information, fund profiles, articles, comprehensive fund ratings, and a glossary.

Comparing a fund to similar funds is a good way to examine its performance. Web sites such as GLOBEfund (www.globefund.com) have mutual fund tables that make comparisons easy by grouping fund classes (see Chapter 6 for details about fund classes) and including the statistics for each category. A fund's capability to outperform similar funds consistently is one sign of good quality. In contrast, funds that have consistently underperformed their peers for three years or more are not high quality and you should avoid them.

Make certain that the funds you're comparing are similar. A big difference exists between an aggressive growth fund and a growth fund, for example. To verify your analyses, check the prospectus of each fund. The fund's investment objectives are usually listed in the first paragraph. You may discover that the fund that looked so attractive at first is a little too risky for you.

A mutual fund checklist

As you select your first mutual fund, consider this checklist:

- **The fund manager:** Often a fund is only as good as its management. In all too many cases, mutual fund managers are inexperienced, overpaid, and under-performing rookies. Don't get stuck with a rookie! If a fund manager has shown great performance in the past, future performance is likely, but not guaranteed, to be above average. More often than not, it's the markets in general that drive fund performance — not the manager. A fund manager's true role is simply to not "drop the ball." In other words, she should buy stocks at the beginning of a bull market, and buy defensive investments at the beginning of a bear market. If the fund manager has been replaced, past performance becomes less meaningful and may even be worthless. A poorly performing fund that gets a new fund manager may turn around and become a top performer.

- **The stability of the fund's philosophy:** If the fund seems unclear about its financial goals and is switching investment methods, it may be in trouble. Avoid rudderless ships!

- **The size of the fund:** Good fund candidates should have at least $25 million under management and be large enough to keep up with institutional investors. At the other end of the spectrum, Canadian funds with more than $5 billion (and U.S. funds with more than $50 billion) can be too large. They become so diversified that their values do not change significantly. Also, when they buy or sell a holding, it often causes a sharp change in the underlying security's price, which can distort returns.

- **The objectives of the fund:** Some funds focus on particular sectors (health-care, technology, and so on) and may offer great returns. However, they aren't good funds for the online investor who wants to own just one mutual fund. If you own just one specialty fund, you lose the advantage of diversification.

- ✔ **Fees:** A debate has raged over the past ten years about which is better: no-load or load mutual funds. All the studies in the universe indicate that paying a sales commission doesn't ensure a greater return. However, investing in a fund with high fees and high returns is better than investing in a fund with low fees and poor performance. Many times, you really do get what you pay for.

- ✔ **Purchase constraints:** Although some funds require a minimum initial investment of $5,000, many good funds don't. Also, if you enroll in a fund's automatic investment program, the minimum initial investment amount is usually waived. As well, many fund minimums are waived or substantially reduced for RRSP and RRIF investments. Unless there's a compelling reason for you to yield to a substantial minimum investment amount, tell the pushy sales representative to take a good long hike. With a smile of course!

For more resources about understanding and selecting mutual funds, see the Fund Library (www.fundlibrary.com). The Fund Library's Learning Centre has many helpful online articles (see Figure 10-2).

Figure 10-2:
Fund Library helps you learn about mutual funds by providing many free online primers and tutorials describing them.

Evaluating mutual fund performance

No hard-and-fast rules help you evaluate a mutual fund. The following easy-to-use guidelines, however, let you review the performance of your mutual fund investment candidates. After your assessment, each fund will require more analysis. Only funds that meet all the criteria should be selected for further research. These funds are likely to reduce your chances of losing money without lowering your returns.

- ✔ **Tax liabilities and returns:** All mutual fund performance is shown on a pre-tax basis. This is reasonable, since different investors are in different tax brackets. If you are investing through taxable accounts (which are different from non-taxable accounts, which might include your RRSP or other tax-exempt investments), you should compare only the after-tax returns of the funds you are analyzing. This comparison allows you to compare apples to apples instead of apples to oranges.

- ✔ **The impact of short-term performance:** Ignore short-term performance. Short-term returns are heavily influenced by fluctuations in the market and are valueless.

- ✔ **Inconsistent returns:** Avoid funds that have inconsistent returns when compared to unmanaged indexes. In other words, when you compare your fund to the appropriate benchmark, take into consideration the consistency of the two funds. If your fund is more volatile than the benchmark, it may have more risk than you expected.

- ✔ **Fund ranking when compared to like funds:** The fund's performance is ranked within the top 20 percent to 50 percent of its type. Make certain that your analysis compares growth funds to growth funds and value funds to value funds, and so on.

- ✔ **Fund ranking when compared to unmanaged indexes:** The fund's performance and risk level is better than an unmanaged index (indexes are influenced by the stock market, and not solely by fund managers) for time periods of one, three, and five years. Compare the fund's performance (before mutual fund costs). A broad-based Canadian stock fund should be compared to the TSE 300 (www.tse.com). A conservative Canadian equity fund that invests only in blue-chip stocks should be compared to the TSE 35 (the TSE's 35 largest-cap companies), and so on.

- ✔ **The fund's price-to-earnings (P/E) ratios are 15 to 25:** P/E ratios above 25 are high risk.

- ✔ **The fund's standard deviation:** The fund's standard deviation for three years is 15 or lower. Standard deviation information for Canadian mutual funds can be found with Morningstar Canada's Bellcharts service (www.morningstar.ca/Products/ProdBCPlusDataDownload.asp).

✔ **The fund's risk value:** Morningstar Canada's BellCharts rankings range from low-risk to high-risk values (or betas — a measurement of the volatility of a security with the market in general). A beta of 1 is low risk. Morningstar Canada (www.morningstar.ca) and its U.S. sister company (www.morningstar.com) rank mutual funds using their own *Morningstar Risk Values.* The respective Web sites explain how risk rankings are determined and what values you should look for.

The preceding list is a good starting point for your evaluation. As you become a more sophisticated investor, you'll likely modify, delete, and add criteria. This customization ensures that your mutual fund selections meet your individual risk-tolerance level and financial objectives.

The Ratings War

Mutual fund companies don't show you the standard deviation and the betas of their mutual funds. You don't have to make your investment decision without these bits of vital information, however. Many Web sites offer information on the ranking of mutual funds. Rankings are useful because they help you digest important performance and risk statistics into one measure. Here are a few examples of Web sites that offer free ranking of mutual funds:

✔ **Morningstar Canada** (www.morningstar.ca)

✔ **Morningstar U.S.** (www.morningstar.com)

✔ **GLOBEfund** (www.globefund.com)

✔ **CANOE Money** (www.canoe.ca); check out Figure 10-3

✔ **Barron's** (www.barrons.com)

The most comprehensive online rating resource is Morningstar Canada's BellCharts service (www.morningstar.ca/Products/ProdBCPlusDataDownload.asp). BellCharts excels at rating many forms of Canadian funds, including segregated funds.

In the best of times, the same fund can be a highly ranked CANOE winner and a number-one mutual fund by BellCharts. But sometimes a mutual fund's score can indicate a top performer by one rating service and a loser by another rating service. Why the difference?

Some mutual funds scores are *risk adjusted* and some are *absolute.* Risk-adjusted scores punish mutual funds for inconsistent returns and reward others for stability. For example, the risk-adjusted mutual funds rating can do the following:

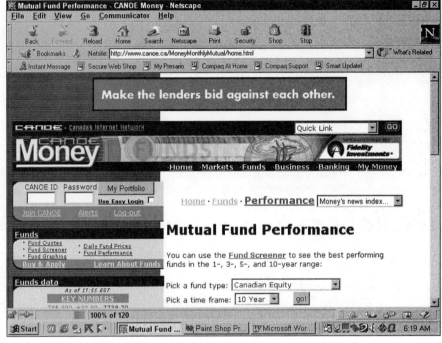

Figure 10-3:
In addition
to news,
CANOE
Money lets
you access
mutual fund
performance
statistics
and
rankings.

✔ **Penalize a fund for radically changing from its previous performance.**
For example, a fund can be penalized for *exceeding* its previous performance. In other words, the fund can receive a lower rating because of
unexpected increases in returns. This rating penalty can be just as bad as
an unexpected decrease in returns.

✔ **Reward mediocre fund performers.** A fund can receive a higher rating
because of its stability.

Conservative investors prefer to use risk-adjusted scores. Other investors
prefer to use the absolute numbers. However, the best approach is to have a
clear understanding of the differences in the ranking systems.

The analysis of mutual funds includes more research than selecting a fund
by its rating. Remember that the more informed you are, the better your
decision-making will be.

Finding Facts and Figures Online

This list of online information services can help you find the right mutual fund:

- **CANOE** (`www.canoe.ca`) provides rankings of the "best" and "worst" mutual funds. You can access current and archived articles about mutual funds.

- **Fund Library** (`www.fundlibrary.com`) lets you access detailed profiles on a wide array of Canadian mutual funds. It has a good investor learning centre on its site. Also, it provides a list of Web sites for most mutual fund companies operating in Canada. You can participate in its discussion forum, and hear what the experts have to say in its archived articles section.

- **GLOBEfund** (`www.globefund.com`), shown in Figure 10-4, offers tutorials for beginning mutual fund investors; it includes a glossary, a "Getting Started" section, and a "Wise Investor" section. It gives fund strategies, analyses of the Canadian mutual fund market, and links to Canadian mutual fund home pages. You can get concise profiles on a wide array of Canadian mutual funds, or even of mutual fund companies themselves. GLOBEfund lets you generate charts that compare the performance of a fund against a variety of criteria. GLOBEfund also allows you to prepare tailored reports on the value of your mutual fund holdings with its "Fundlist" tracker. You can sort the report to show which funds did best in the long term or to show change in value by percentage. You can see what individual investors are saying in its discussion forum.

- **Index Funds Online** (`www.indexfundsonline.com`) is a comprehensive resource for investigating Canadian and U.S. index funds. It has analysis, commentary, and links to articles and Web sites on index funds. The site explains types of indexes and lists funds tracking them.

- **The Investment Funds Institute of Canada** (`www.ific.ca`) lets you access a list of Web sites for most Canadian mutual fund companies.

- **Morningstar Canada** (`www.morningstar.ca`) is a key Web site for Canadian mutual fund investors interested in fund ratings. Morningstar Canada also offers in-depth mutual funds–related research, as well as some of the most active mutual fund discussion forums on the Net. Its BellCharts service lets you rate Canadian mutual funds based on criteria such as size, beta, and performance.

- **Mutual Funds Switchboard** (`web.onramp.ca/cadd/723mut.htm`) is an in-depth index that lists many Canadian mutual fund information sites.

- **The Street.com** (`www.thestreet.com`) provides fund profiles and scorecards of various mutual and index funds. You can search U.S. funds by asset size, category, fund symbol, or fund name.

Figure 10-4:
GLOBEfund
provides
you with
detailed and
professional-
looking
profiles of
most
Canadian
mutual
funds.

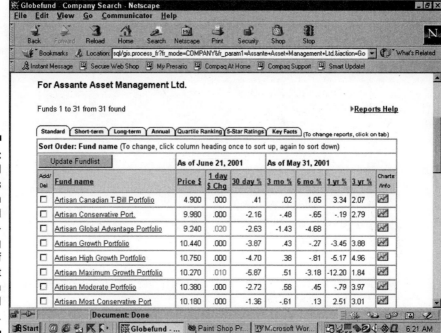

Chapter 11

Online Advice and Discussion about Investing

· ·

In This Chapter

▶ Locating online resources

▶ Finding online discussion forums

▶ Using bulletin boards, instant messaging, newsgroups, and mailing lists

· ·

*T*he Internet empowers you to do many things, but two of the most important are: to get very useful information and to communicate with others online. Along with corporate Web sites and sites that specialize in certain types of investments, you can also access traditional media sources that have a strong online presence and that have good investment resources. Very often they provide free and useful investment advice, just as they do in their regular print publications. In this chapter, we introduce you to some traditional media sources that can help you with your investment decisions.

One of the most popular features of the Internet is the ease of communication it provides. Discussion forums abound — including Web-based chat or bulletin boards, Usenet newsgroups, and mailing lists. Many investment supersites host active and popular discussion forums, usually as Web-based bulletin boards. Sometimes, these boards can be highly informative and entertaining. For example, they can help identify competitor companies, and often explain stock moves in a most animated way! But all too often, they can also be rife with conflict, deception, and plain old bad information. In this chapter, we introduce you to bulletin boards and to other online discussion forums that can help you make investment decisions. We also present some caveats about venturing into this exciting but sometimes unusual part of the Internet.

Traditional Media on the Net

You've seen — or perhaps even subscribed to — these publications: *Canadian Business, Report on Business,* the *National Post,* Gordon Pape's "Mutual Funds Update Newsletter," and *Profit.* Information, news, and advice are now online. Many media channels such as newspapers, magazines, and television networks have Web sites that can help you make informed investment decisions.

Newspapers on the Web

The online edition of the *Globe and Mail* (www.globeandmail.com) features its *Report on Business (ROB)* section. You get there by clicking the Business icon found on the home page. The ROB section provides a summary of the day's investing and business activity. This online version, containing bits and pieces from the print version, is free. The online edition does not contain the entire contents of the *Globe and Mail.* It does include a seven-day archive of selected parts of the newspaper, including the *Report on Business.* It also has features such as online calculators and links to ROBTV (www.robtv.com) and *ROB Magazine.*

The *National Post* (www.nationalpost.com) also has an online partial edition (shown in Figure 11-1), which includes the *Financial Post* section. You can access investment commentary about stocks, bonds, mutual funds, and sophisticated investments such as options, segregated funds, and more. This online version is free.

To get Canadian archived news, check out JournalismNet, at www.journalism net.com, shown in Figure 11-2. From there you can access past news and articles from Canadian newspapers and magazines. It's a good resource when you want to research a company, an investment issue, or an industry.

The *Wall Street Journal,* shown in Figure 11-3, is the definitive, international-scope investment publication — and it's available online at www.wsj.com. Because the full newspaper appears online, you have to pay an annual subscription fee ($59 U.S.). Yes, the price is pretty steep, but think about it this way: If you're retired up in the Laurentians, you know how hard it is to get an American paper. For the very serious investor, the *WSJ* is an online news resource to consider. It's always interesting to see how a positive or negative *WSJ* or *New York Times* (www.nytimes.com) article on a particular company affects the company's stock price on the same day.

Figure 11-1:
The
*National
Post*'s Web
site lets you
read part of
its print
version
online —
and it's free!

Figure 11-2:
JournalismNet
is a
repository of
Canadian
archived
news
articles.

Figure 11-3:
The Wall Street Journal has a full online edition, available for a fee.

Online investment magazines and tabloids

The largest business magazines also have an online presence:

- ✔ **Canadian Business** (www.canadianbusiness.com), shown in Figure 11-4, has articles about investing and business in general.

- ✔ **Report on Business Magazine** (www.robmagazine.com) has a monthly feature section that profiles a company or industry.

- ✔ **Barron's** (www.barrons.com) is still stuck in the smokestack industry, which is fine if you only want to invest in steel, energy, and mining companies. On second thought, that may not be such a bad idea, given the crash in new-economy stocks!

- ✔ **Fast Company** (www.fastcompany.com), shown in Figure 11-5, is required reading if you want to stay on top of investing in the high-tech sector.

- ✔ **Business Week** (www.businessweek.com) is strong on international business news.

- ✔ **Business 2.0** (www.business2.com) merged with eCompany Magazine, and has even better content than before.

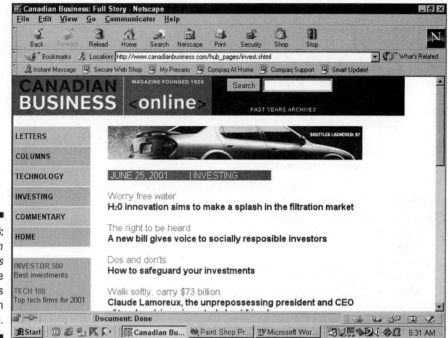

Figure 11-4:
Canadian Business lets you see parts of its print edition online.

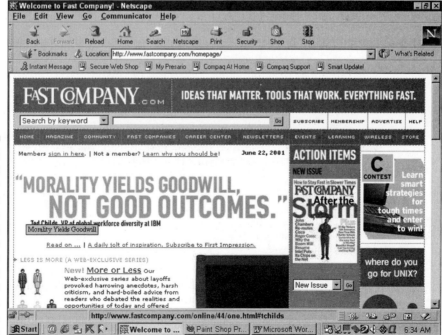

Figure 11-5:
Fast Company has an informative Web site that is geared to the business side of the high-tech industry.

- ✔ *Forbes* (www.forbes.com) focuses on American industry. It has a bias toward profiling blue-chip, old-economy companies.

- ✔ *Fortune* (www.fortune.com) is now a leader at profiling companies in the high-tech sector.

- ✔ *Investor's Business Daily* (www.investors.com) is a comprehensive source of investment news and statistics, and includes profiles of many companies. This publication provides readers with a good indication of overall market sentiment.

- ✔ *Red Herring* (www.redherring.com) is a *Business 2.0* clone, and has strengthened the quality of its content.

- ✔ *Worth* (www.worth.com) is good at profiling niche companies and emerging industries.

Most of the above Web sites publish feature and other articles for free. The balance of the articles is accessible only by paid subscription.

TV shows on the Web

Televised business newsmagazines have jumped onto the Web! Many of the CBC's *Newsworld Business News* stories can be found online at cbc.ca/business. From there, you can access archived news stories, check out program schedules (for shows such as *Venture* and *Money Weekly*), participate in message boards, and see what happened in the markets that day.

ROBTV (www.robtv.com), shown in Figure 11-6, is the online TV offspring of the *Globe and Mail*'s *Report on Business* section. You can click an icon to see a video clip of a story that aired on TV. You can also see the TV program lineup for features such as *Daywatch, Market Call,* and *Bottom Line.* Major business stories are also summarized on this Web site.

Some of the more popular U.S. business and investment TV programs have Web sites as well. These Web sites include MSNBC (www.msnbc.com), CNBC (www.cnbc.com) (shown in Figure 11-7), and CNNFN (www.cnnfn.com).

Always take what you hear on these TV shows — both the online and offline versions — with a grain of salt. Many guests appearing on these shows — and even the analysts — have their own (usually money-driven) agendas, and will create all kinds of hype to see those agendas satisfied!

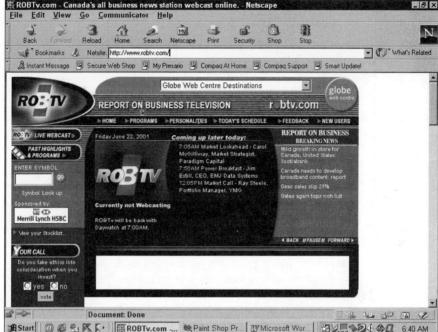

Figure 11-6:
ROBTV lets you view daily video clips from much of its program lineup.

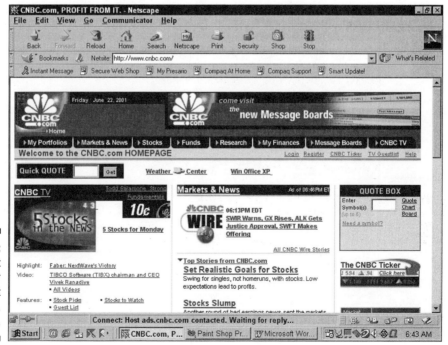

Figure 11-7:
Check out *CNBC* for insight into U.S. business.

Online newsletter advice

There are many investment newsletters on the Web. Anyone can be an online publisher. This fact alone should raise a few red flags for you. So when you're looking at free online investment newsletters, or are thinking of subscribing to one, stick with the names you know.

Gordon Pape is one of the best-known Canadian authorities on mutual funds and the financial markets. His Web site, at www.gordonpape.com, provides access to his newsletters and books — and to his advice. As well as providing ratings of mutual funds, Pape's site has useful links to mutual fund company pages and other financial destinations.

StockHouse (www.stockhouse.ca), shown in Figure 11-8, has scores of links to independent Canadian newsletters; links are organized by source, as well as by industry coverage.

Mutual Funds Online (www.mfmag.com) is an American site that provides comprehensive mutual fund and other advice. It's a useful resource if you're a global mutual fund investor.

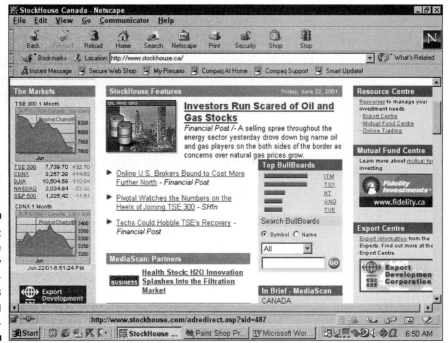

Figure 11-8: StockHouse has daily expert commentaries on promising companies.

Remember our advice at the beginning of this section? Of course you do, but it bears repeating: Make sure you have researched the credibility of any online publication before acting on its recommendation. Some sources you will have heard about; others will be obscure. The key here is research. Make sure the resource is good and free of bias.

Direct E-mail Advice

Direct advice usually refers to e-mail–driven advice given by individuals to individuals. It's essentially personal advice by computer. Online advice does not refer to Internet newsletters provided by banks, trust companies, or well-known authorities for the benefit of individuals. Although still scarce, online advisory services are expected to grow as investment advisers turn to the Internet to ply their trade.

We don't recommend that you act on online advice given by individuals — unless they are professionals and proven authorities in the investment field. Simply stated, the online medium is too risky, and e-mail investment advice is unnecessary. It's risky because your savings are at stake and there may be unseen, anonymous scam artists on the Internet, especially where money is so obviously involved. It's unnecessary because the same advice can be acquired in person or by other more conventional means.

The best course of action is to stick with the experts — proven and professional financial planners and experienced advisers who are trained to give investment advice. Getting such advice requires personal contact — the adviser has to know your financial circumstances and actually see your paperwork!

Discussion Forums

Discussion forums come in many shapes and sizes. They include Web-based bulletin boards, Usenet newsgroups, and mailing lists. All of these forums are electronic venues where groups of people can exchange information and ideas on investment topics. The topics usually concern publicly traded companies or investing issues, but you can even find forums on something as unexpected as treasury bills! These forums are convenient and are usually featured within popular investment Web sites. Web site forums attract the largest number of participants, and this often leads to many opinions and much discussion.

Web-based bulletin boards

Web-based *bulletin boards* (also called *message boards*) make it easy for participants to communicate with each other. Web sites that host bulletin boards frequently offer free features such as personal Web pages and e-mail addresses. All you have to do is register and choose a screen name, such as "Techspert" or "Stockhound." Yahoo! Finance (`finance.yahoo.com`) boasts one of the largest collections of message boards. Here are some other large Web-based boards:

- ✔ **GLOBEfund** (`www.globefund.com`) has a discussion forum specializing in mutual funds.

- ✔ **InfoMine** (`www.infomine.com`) is an e-commerce site that specializes in the Canadian mining industry. You'll find an informative, albeit specialized, discussion board for investing, general discussion, and special sectors.

- ✔ **Investing: Canada** (`investingcanada.about.com/finance/investing canada`) has a threaded discussion forum about individual companies, the economy, RRSPs, taxes, and other investment-related topics. Through its About.com parent site (`www.about.com`), you can access thousands of Web pages related to Canadian investments and investing.

- ✔ **The Motley Fool** (`www.fool.com`) has a comprehensive and popular discussion forum for a wide spectrum of industry sectors and investment options. Motley Fool was the first investment Web site to set up message boards for individual stocks.

- ✔ **Raging Bull** (`ragingbull.lycos.com`) is one of the most popular and active investment bulletin boards on the Internet. Board participants have been known to go on cruises together to celebrate a good stock pick! Although it's an American site, it has excellent board coverage of Canadian stocks — especially technology stocks. In fact, some new Canadian stocks can only be discussed here! It shows you the top bulletin boards in terms of number of daily posts and which ones are experiencing the most activity. A big plus is its "ignore" feature, which lets you block users who post offensive or annoying messages. It also does profiles on board members and rates them too! Click "Top 40 Membermarks" to see who is watching out for your posts!

- ✔ **Silicon Investor — Canadian Stocks** (`www.siliconinvestor.com/stocktalk`) lets you talk about any Canadian (click Canadian Stocks) or U.S. stocks. A list of companies is shown on its StockTalk page, along with the number of posts and the date and time posted. You can also call up an index of companies sorted by industry. Clicking a company name takes you to the forum. This site focuses on companies in the high-tech sector. It has very fast download times and is easy to use.

- **StockHouse** (`www.stockhouse.ca`) is a Canadian investment Web site that lets you access its "BullBoards" discussion boards about Canadian, U.S., Australian, and Hong Kong companies. Like Raging Bull, it has top-post, most-active-board, and ignore-poster features. An index of the most popular posts of the day is also displayed.

- **Sympatico Personal Finance** (`forums.sympatico.ca`) has a discussion forum in its Personal Finance area. It is geared more toward the discussion of general investment issues than to specific companies. You can talk about issues ranging from upcoming initial public offerings to offshore banking.

Internet chat

Internet chat rooms, like bulletin boards, provide another way for groups of investors to communicate with each other on the Internet. Chat sessions are hosted on many Web investor supersites and on almost all major portals (such as Yahoo! Chat or Yahoo! Clubs on the Yahoo! portal). They happen in real time, so you will likely get a reply within minutes, as compared to a message board, where a reply may take days, and can even involve attaching voice files to your messages. Although chat rooms are essentially real-time message boards, membership can be controlled and restricted more readily than in a regular public message board. The more "private" and "organized" nature of chat rooms helps keep the weirdos out!

As with Web-based bulletin/message boards, chat forums need a fair number of participants to be successful. If the investment chat forum is too small, it won't attract knowledgeable contributors. If it's too big, it can spin out of control because of lack of focus or the presence of *bashers* — posters who make inaccurate and disparaging remarks about a company. Ideally, you should look for a reasonably well-attended chat forum hosted by a reputable Web site.

Instant messaging

Private instant messaging (such as the AOL Instant Messenger service) is a natural extension of the bulletin board and chat phenomena, and is being adopted more and more as an Internet communication and information application for online investors. It's yet one more way for investors to stay in touch with one another, but in even smaller groups. It is almost completely private.

A final word about message boards: Bulletin/message boards are disliked by many, but needed by most. Once dominated by seasoned investors, they are now overrun by people posting insults and displaying rudeness. Also, *short* *sellers* (investors who will gain when the stock price falls) will sometimes try to frighten investors into selling an otherwise good stock by posting misinformation, or information that is taken out of context.

However, the boards can also be a good place to quickly find out why the price of a stock rose or fell so rapidly. A quick scan of the message boards can be an effective way to find a company press release, news article, or other relevant and reliable information about a company. Also, if you want to size up a company's competition, you can likely find that as well on a message board — courtesy of a post by a short seller!

Love them or hate them, bulletin boards are here to stay. Once you learn how to scan through them to separate the good information from the bad, though, you will find them to be informative — and even entertaining!

Usenet newsgroups

Newsgroups let you network with others to get or share information on a broad variety of topics, including investing.

Newsgroups reside by subject areas on an electronic organizational system called Usenet, and they are much like Web-based discussion or message boards where messages are posted. Newsgroups are easy to access since newsreader software is incorporated into most browsers, including Netscape Communicator and Microsoft Internet Explorer. You can participate in them (by replying to a question or by posting your own question) or you can just "lurk" (by viewing everyone else's questions and replies). You can even start a discussion.

Accessing newsgroups

How you get to one of the 100,000 newsgroups residing on the Internet depends on the type of Internet access you have. Several steps are the same, though. First, get newsreader software. Netscape Communicator and Microsoft Internet Explorer have built-in newsreader software. Or, you can get specialized newsreader programs such as Trumpet WinSock or WinVN at a computer store. Second, access a list of newsgroups through your software. AOL has an especially easy interface where you access Usenet by clicking the Internet Connection channel and then select the News Groups icon. Third, choose the newsgroup you want to join or subscribe to. Fourth, read the information posted. Finally, post your own message!

A list of newsgroups can be found at Deja News (`www.dejanews.com`), or through the associated Google Groups (`groups.google.com`) site. Once there, you can search for newsgroups by name or topic, or you can view a comprehensive list of newsgroups.

Types of newsgroups

To organize the mass of information available, there is a convention for categorizing newsgroups. There are several major global categories, topics, and subtopics. Nine major newsgroup categories are listed below.

Newsgroup categories

alt.	Open-ended discussion of any issue
biz.	Business and commercial topics
comp.	Computer-related issues
misc.	Other matters
news.	News and Internet information
rec.	Recreational and leisure activities
sci.	Scientific topics
soc.	Social issues
talk.	Topics open to discussion and debate

These are further divided into more topics. For example, the category "biz" may have a topic called "investments," or "biz.investments." Since investment is a broad topic, a subtopic may exist called "derivatives," or "biz.investments. derivatives." You can subscribe to all of the groups within "biz.investments" (there may be hundreds) or you can fine-tune things by subscribing to only "biz.investments.derivatives" (a lot fewer).

The best way to learn the do's and don'ts in Usenet is to join some newsgroups and observe how to post an article, how to follow up on a post, and what writing style to use.

Mailing lists

Mailing lists — another type of discussion forum — deal with specific topics. Unlike Web-based bulletin boards and Usenet newsgroups, however, mailing lists deposit all of their postings into your e-mail inbox. They are less popular conduits of communication. In a sense, they are not bona fide forums. They are like newsletters. But, like Web-based bulletin boards and Usenet newsgroups, they are organized by topic of interest and are meant for multi-party communication. Again, mailing list information comes to you; you don't go to it. A separate copy of the mailing list is e-mailed to each recipient on the list.

Mailing lists typically have fewer participants than newsgroups. That makes them less relevant for investing. But if you're looking for something very specific — such as trading in derivatives — give them a try. They tend to be more focused, less raucous, and less deluged by lousy information.

The way you get on a mailing list (to subscribe) depends on how the list is maintained — manually or automatically. You can also join a mailing list either through e-mail or via Web site subscription.

If a list is maintained manually, send an e-mail message such as "Please include me on your futures trading list." No fixed form is required since a person and not a computer reads the message. Be sure to include your real name and e-mail address to make the process faster and easier. Give the mailing list a few weeks to respond.

If a list is automatic, send an e-mail message to its administrative address with no subject heading and the following line as the body of the message: "SUBSCRIBE *listname your-name.*" Replace *listname* with the name of the mailing list, and *your-name* with your actual name. You need not include your e-mail address since it's automatically included as your message's return address.

You can find a mailing list through special indexes. For example, consult www.topica.com or paml.net for a list that suits your needs.

Part III
Tools of the Online Investing Trade

The 5th Wave
By Rich Tennant

"I couldn't get this stock-screening software to work on my PC, so I replaced the motherboard, upgraded the BIOS, and wrote a program that links it to my personal database. It told me I wasn't technically inclined and should set up a meeting with a financial adviser."

In this part . . .

You see how the Internet puts investment analysis tools at your disposal — tools that were previously available only to analysts. Find out how to screen for stocks and mutual funds that meet your personal investment criteria. See how you can calculate bond values and determine yield curves. Use the Internet to discover more about key ratios that can help you discover valuable investments. Also find out about the different ways to buy mutual funds and bonds — with or without an online broker.

Chapter 12

Internet Stock Screening

● ●

In This Chapter

▶ Becoming familiar with online stock screens

▶ Building your first stock screen

▶ Locating online and PC-based stock screens

▶ Using prebuilt stock screens

▶ Getting online stock recommendations from the experts

● ●

S tock screening boils down to finding the answer to one fundamental question: "Which stock (of all stocks) should I buy right now?" Of course, finding the answer to this question requires asking many more specific questions about stocks — questions that are difficult to answer without the help of computerized databases.

This chapter shows how you can use the Internet and PC-based stock screening tools to whittle down the universe of stocks to a manageable few candidates. You can then analyze your short list of stocks for a few gems that may bring you above-average returns. This chapter also tells you where to find daily or weekly results of prebuilt stock screens.

Finding the Best Stock Electronically

Screening is a process that permits investors to locate and distill information within a larger set of information. The Internet provides many screening tools to help you prospect stock issues. The goal of stock screens is to point out which stocks are worth your research and analysis time.

Some people believe that using a stock screen is like panning for gold. You use your computer to screen ("pan") for investment "nuggets" from a long list of possibilities. The individual investor sets the objectives of any single screen. Different people get different results because no two people have exactly the same selection criteria or investment philosophy.

Overall, the benefit of stock screens is that they let you generate your own ideas — ideas that generate profits based on your investor savvy. Stock screening programs allow you to go beyond finding good stock investments and assist you in finding the very best stocks.

To identify investment candidates, the stock screen uses your preset criteria, such as *growth* (stocks that are expanding faster than the market or their peers); *value* (stocks that have strong financial statements but are selling at prices below their peers); or *income* (stocks that provide higher than average dividends).

Depending on the criteria you select, you may have to run several iterations of the stock screen. For example, your first screen may result in several hundred possibilities. Because you can't investigate and analyze so many candidates, you have to run a second screen of these results. This fine-tuning should lead to a manageable list of investment candidates that you can research and analyze — perhaps between 10 and 20. It is likely that you can quickly pare this number down by using common sense and your investment experience.

Choosing the criteria for your first stock screen

Typically, you build a stock screen by accessing an online stock screening tool and filling out an online form. We offer examples of the variables used in these forms later in this chapter, in the section "Important Ratios for Screening Stocks." The first stock screen that you develop may include quantifiable variables that you believe are the most important — for example:

- **Earnings growth:** The percentage of change between current earnings and earnings for the last quarter or last year.

- **Recent earnings surprises:** The difference between predicted and actual earnings.

- **Price-to-earnings (P/E) ratio:** The current price of the stock divided by the earnings per share — that is, net income divided by the total number of common shares outstanding. Value stocks have P/E ratios below 10 or 12, and growth stocks have P/Es above 20. Technology stocks can have P/E ratios above 30 and still be considered good value if their current and expected growth rates are high.

- **Dividends:** The annual cash dividend paid by the company.

- **Market capitalization:** The number of outstanding shares multiplied by the current stock price of those shares. Market capitalization is sometimes abbreviated to *cap.* This value is a measurement of the company's size. Firms with high market capitalization are called "large-cap" and companies with low market capitalization are called "small-cap."

Fine-tuning your stock screen

After you select your initial screening criteria, you click Submit, Sort, or a similar command. A list of stock candidates appears. Often this list includes several hundred stocks. This number is still too large to research, so you should narrow this list by selecting more variables.

You may have some special knowledge about the industry you work in. You may have used certain products over the years and can use your knowledge to your advantage. However, keep in mind that a good product doesn't necessarily mean a good company. You may want to filter out companies that you just don't understand. You may also want to filter out companies about which you lack information. Without at least some basic information, you can't perform a complete analysis.

Using your stock screen results

After you complete your second stock screen and sort the data, you should have a list of about 10 to 20 companies. Start a file for each firm and begin to gather data for your analysis. At this point, you may discover that some companies aren't worth additional research — a finding that further reduces your short list. For example, the company may have filed for bankruptcy, or it may be targeted for federal investigation. Maybe the company recently paid a large fine for shady dealings, or the executive management was recently indicted for fraud, misconduct, or some other crime.

Check out the stock screen at Daily Stocks (www.dailystocks.com). The Daily Stocks screen handles only U.S. stocks, but the Web site itself has comprehensive analyses and news about Canadian stocks as well. After you reach the Daily Stocks home page, click either Advance Stock Screen or Basic Stock Screen. The basic stock screens are prebuilt. The advanced stock screens allow you to enter the industry and criteria that you feel are important. You can then query the database for fundamental and historical stock information by using your own investment criteria.

Important ratios for screening stocks

Every industry has its own language, and the financial industry is no exception. In the following sections, we define the key terms that the finance industry uses for stock screening variables. Figure 12-1, on the next page, shows Hoover's StockScreener (www.stockscreener.com), which uses up to 20 variables and sorts the results alphabetically. Hoover's StockScreener screens more than 7,800 publicly traded companies, including major Canadian companies and most Nasdaq small-cap stocks. Each stock screen's results are hyperlinked to a Hoover's *company capsule* (a snapshot of the company), as well as to the company's home page, stock quotes and charts, regulatory filings, and investment news.

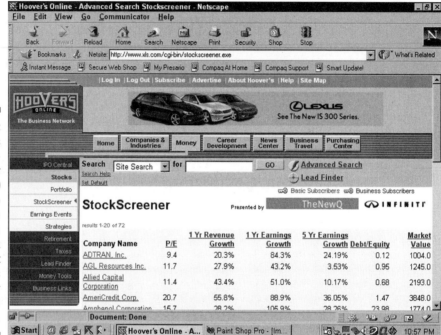

Figure 12-1: Hoover's Stock-Screener uses 20 variables to assist you in finding a stock investment that meets your financial objectives.

Here are some important concepts that the finance industry uses for stock screening variables. They are worth knowing as you build and fine-tune your own stock screens.

Beta

Beta is the measurement of market risk. The beta is the relationship between investment returns and market returns. For example, risk-free Canada Savings Bonds have a beta of 0. If the beta is negative, the company is inversely correlated to the market — that is, if the market goes up, the company's stock tends to go down. If a stock's volatility is equal to the market, the beta is 1. In this case, if the stock market increases 10 percent, the stock price increases 10 percent. Betas greater than 1.0 indicate that the company is more volatile than the market. For example, if the stock is 50 percent more volatile than the market, the beta is 1.5.

Book value

Book value is the original cost, less depreciation of the company's assets, less the outstanding liabilities. (*Depreciation* or *amortization* is the means by which an asset's value is expensed — or spread — over its useful life for accounting and tax purposes.)

Cash flow to share price

The ratio of *cash flow to share price* is the company's net income plus depreciation or amortization (expenses not paid in cash) divided by the number of shares outstanding. For companies that are building their infrastructure (such as cable companies or new cellular companies) and, therefore, don't yet have earnings, this ratio may be a better measure of their value than earnings per share (EPS).

Current ratio

Current ratio is current assets divided by current liabilities. A current ratio of 1.00 or greater means that the company can pay all current obligations without using future earnings. The *quick ratio* is current assets minus inventory, divided by current liabilities. It measures the readiness of a company to meet its current obligations in a matter of days.

Debt-to-equity ratio

To determine the *debt-to-equity ratio,* divide the company's total amount of long-term debt by the total amount of equity. (*Equity* is defined as the residual claim by shareholders of company assets after creditors and preferred shareholders have been paid.) This ratio measures the percentage of debt the company is carrying. Many firms average a debt level of 50 percent. Debt-to-equity ratios greater than 50 percent may indicate trouble. That is, if sales decline, the firm may not be able to pay the interest payments due on its debt.

Dividends

Dividends are paid quarterly out of retained earnings. However, some high-growth companies reinvest earnings and don't pay dividends.

Dividend yield

Dividend yield is the amount of the dividend divided by the most current stock price. You can use dividends as a valuation indicator by comparing them to the company's own historical dividend yield. If a stock is selling at a historically low yield, it may be overvalued. Companies that don't pay a dividend — many Canadian technology stocks don't declare dividends — have a dividend yield of zero.

Earnings per share (EPS)

Earnings is one of the stock's most important features. After all, the price you pay for a stock is based on the future earnings of the company. The consistency and growth of a company's past earnings indicate the likelihood of stock price appreciation and future dividends. *Earnings per share* is often referred to as EPS.

Market capitalization

Market capitalization is calculated by multiplying the number of outstanding shares times the current stock price of those shares. Market capitalization is sometimes called *market value*.

P/E ratio

You calculate the *price-to-earnings ratio* by dividing the price of the stock by the current earnings per share. A low P/E ratio indicates that the company may be undervalued. A high P/E ratio indicates that the company may be overvalued.

Price-to-book value

Price-to-book value is the current price of the stock divided by the book value. If the current stock price is below the price-to-book value, the stock may be a real bargain. On the other hand, impending unprofitability or unjustified levels of intangible assets (such as goodwill) may be the reason.

Return on equity (ROE)

Return on equity (ROE) is usually equity earnings as a proportion of net worth. You divide the most recent year's net income by shareholders' equity (*shareholders' equity* is assets minus liabilities) to calculate the ROE.

Shares outstanding

The term *shares outstanding* refers to the total number of shares for a company's stock. To determine the firm's outstanding shares, you need the most recent data. The shares outstanding can be calculated by taking issued shares on the balance sheet and subtracting treasury stock. *Treasury stock* is stock issued but not outstanding by virtue of being held (after it is repurchased) by the firm.

Using Online Stock Screens

Web-based stock screens can require between 2 and 30 variables. Their computerized stock databases can include anywhere from 1,100 stocks to more than 9,000 stocks. As well, some computerized stock databases are updated daily, weekly, or monthly. The best stock screen is the one that includes your personal investment criteria. A few examples follow:

> ✔ **Adviceforinvestors.com** (www.adviceforinvestors.com) has stock screens for Canadian companies. The monthly subscription fee is $10, under the economy subscription option. There are many screening criteria to select from, and this site also lets you access technical indicators to see where the stock price may be headed in the future.

✔ **Globeinvestor.com** (`www.globeinvestor.com`) also has Canadian-oriented stock screens (see Figure 12-2). The service is free, and lets you view current and most recent quarter information about companies that met your criteria and were listed for you. From the list, you can click on handy icons to access a given company's financial statements, profile, and more.

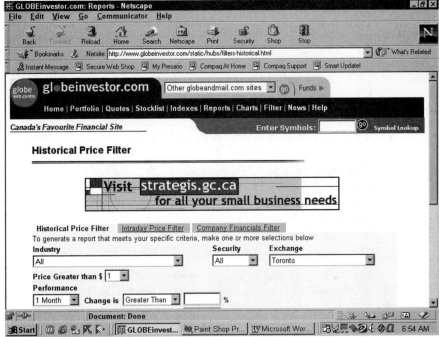

Figure 12-2:
Globe-investor.com
lets you
screen
information
about
Canadian
companies.

✔ **Multex Investor's NetScreen** (`www.multexinvestor.com`) allows you to screen for stocks by using any of 20 variables. To access the stock screen, go to the home page and click Screening. This stock screen features comparisons of variables, user-defined variables, comparison of variables to a constant, use of a variable more than once, and use of operators (greater than, less than, equals, and so on). The database is updated weekly. Your screening results are limited to no more than 200 companies at a time. Some of the larger inter-listed Canadian companies (such as Nortel, JDS Uniphase, and ATI Technologies) are covered.

✔ **Microsoft MoneyCentral Investor** (`moneycentral.msn.com/investor`) is free and has lots of features. You can select from more than 500 criteria to quickly create a list of companies that meet your standards, or, if you'd rather, you can use a pre-existing search and modify it to suit your needs. If you find a company in the results list that looks interesting, it's easy to export the symbol to your portfolio so you can keep an eye on it.

Once you have crafted just the right search, you can save it and run it again later. You can vary the number of matches you'll see in the results list from 1 to 100, or change the sort order by just clicking a column heading. You can also use Investment Matcher, a way to find companies with a similar market cap, average daily volume, price-to-sales ratio, and other specific criteria.

✓ **Nasdaq (**www.nasdaq.com**)** has its own stock screening tool, but it's limited to companies listed on Nasdaq-AMEX and the NYSE. It uses most of the variables mentioned in this chapter, and the database is updated daily. The screening tool is free.

✓ **ResearchMag (**www.researchmag.com**)** requires you to register (for free) before you begin. The stock screen has 12 basic variables that screen more than 9,000 stocks. The basic service is free of charge, but you need to subscribe to use the advanced stock screen. Subscription information can be found on the Web site.

Using Stock Screening Software

PC-based stock screens use their own stock screening software and data-bases. The advantage of these programs over Web-based stock screens is that they use hundreds of variables to screen stocks. PC-based screens are also a lot faster! We describe a few examples in this section.

Equis International — MetaStock (www.metastock.com**)** is a technical analysis software product that includes a stock search engine, real-time charting, and an analysis tool. The program is compatible with Microsoft Office 97 or Microsoft Office 2000, which means that you can download data to an Excel spreadsheet or embed charts in Word. You set the rules to identify trends and highlight important ratios. Click on a Canadian or U.S. stock price, and the program links your Internet browser to a free Web site that provides the current stock prices. When you purchase the software, you receive a CD-ROM with a historical database of more than 2,100 different U.S. securities, Canadian stocks, mutual funds, futures, and indexes. The price of MetaStock 6.5 for Windows is $349 U.S.

Figure 12-3 shows the home page of MetaStock software. The makers of MetaStock use their software program to make stock recommendations. For example, they show the top five stocks that had the biggest gains over the past week, measured on a percentage basis. For example, a $20 stock that increases in price to $25 has a 25-percent gain.

Telescan's ProSearch Module (www.telescan.com**)** allows you to target your best investment opportunities with its stock screening program. Select from 207 variables to isolate stocks that have the highest performance based on

Figure 12-3:
MetaStock
can help
you by
screening
stocks and
providing
real-time
price
quotes.

your investment goals. The program includes the Analyzer Module, which performs in-depth technical and fundamental analysis using data from Telescan's 20-year historical database. The program, which sells for a hefty $395 U.S., also includes Quotelink, a data downloader, and Optimizer programs.

Telescan provides many screen results of the Telescan Prospector online. The Web page shows the results of various Telescan stock searches. The company computes more than 25 million search combinations every week to find the searches that have worked the best or worst over the past 12 months. The latest searches are available every Monday. The firm displays the best 25 stocks for categories including Nasdaq stocks, NYSE stocks, and AMEX stocks, as well as micro-cap stocks, and small-, medium-, and large-cap stocks. This service is for the serious investor.

Using Those Terrific Prebuilt Stock Screens

The Internet provides many prebuilt stock screens that use preselected criteria. Some of these screens may make your work easier because they already include the investment criteria that you feel are most important. We describe a few examples in this list.

✔ **MarketPlayer** (`www.marketplayer.com`) requires you to register, but it's free. After you do so, click Screening. MarketPlayer provides instructions, sample screens, and an advanced stock screening engine. Instructions for using the engine are easy to understand, but you should allow some extra time for getting used to the program. MarketPlayer, shown in Figure 12-4, features simple and industry stock screens that you may find useful. With over 100 screening ratios, MarketPlayer offers a unique screening environment for the serious investor. (If you're an experienced online investor, the prebuilt sample screens may provide some ideas about how you can improve your own screens.)

Figure 12-4:
Market-
Player has
advanced
screening
features for
the serious
investor.

✔ **The Motley Fool** (`www.fool.com`) offers a weekly discussion of its stock screens of U.S. companies. Stocks are listed alphabetically as well as by descending percentages.

✔ **Quicken.com — Popular Stock Searches** (`www.quicken.com/investments`) uses a large database that's owned by an independent financial information company, called Disclosure. Figure 12-5 shows the Quicken.com prebuilt stock screen for Popular Searches (at the Search entry page, just click Popular Searches).

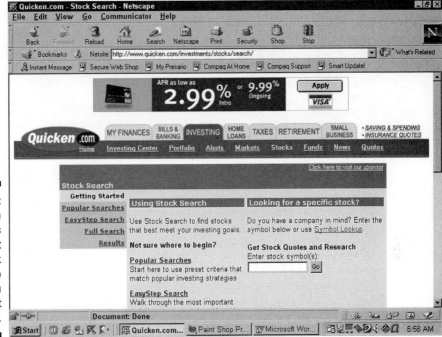

Figure 12-5:
Quicken
provides
prebuilt
stock
screens to
help you
select
stocks.

Quicken's Stock Evaluator compares your search results and explains the benefits and limitations of using each variable as a stock-selection criterion. The prebuilt stock screens are divided into three categories:

- **Popular Search:** Uses preset criteria that match the most popular investing strategies.

- **EasyStep Search:** Walks you through six steps that use important variables one step at a time. Each step provides definitions about the variable and shows why the variable is important in your stock search.

- **Full Search:** Uses 33 variables on one page and many advanced search options.

✔ **Zacks** (www.zacks.com) is one of the very few Web sites on the Internet that has a screening tool for Canadian stocks. It allows you to screen stocks on the Toronto Stock Exchange, where most Canadian public companies are listed.

Determining Your Own Investment Criteria for Stock Screens

This section outlines several ways to set up stock screens that may be beneficial for your research. We offer a few examples of ways that you can build stock screens to discover specific categories of stocks. We've chosen the categories of growth stocks, income stocks, and value stocks for these examples.

Screening for growth stocks

Growth stocks are expanding at rates faster than their counterparts. They have different degrees of risk and are a way of betting on the future. Your stock screen for growth stocks may consider the following criteria:

- **Basic growth:** Any stock that has earnings growth of 15 percent or more in one year.

- **Long-term growth:** Any stocks that grew 15 percent or more in one year over the past five years. (Companies must have historical EPS records of over five years.)

- **Earnings for growth:** Stocks that have a price-to-earnings ratio that is equal to or less than the growth rate of the stock plus its dividend yield.

- **Aggressive growth companies with low P/E ratios:** Stocks with annual earnings growth of more than 24 percent and P/E ratios of less than 15. (P/E ratios of less than 15 are preferable, but rare in the current market.)

Screening for income stocks

Income stocks tend to be stodgy, boring, slow-growth companies that are nevertheless steady income producers. You may want to include dividend yield in your stock screen for income stocks. For example, you may screen for any stocks with a dividend yield that's at least equal to the TSE 300 and never falls below 4 percent. (This criterion rules out growth stocks that don't pay dividends.)

Screening for value stocks

Value stocks are companies that have strong financial statements and good earnings but are traded at stock prices that are less than their industry peers. Some criteria that you may want to include in your stock screen for value stocks include the following:

✔ **Book value:** Stocks for which the book value of the company is less than 80 percent of the average TSE 300 stock.

✔ **Debt-to-equity ratio:** Stocks for companies with a debt-to-equity ratio of 50 percent or less.

✔ **Price-to-earnings ratio:** Stocks for which the average of the company's five-year earnings is not less than 70 percent of the average P/E ratio of the TSE 300 or S&P 500. Don't include stocks with a P/E ratio greater than 12, unless perhaps it's a technology stock. In that case, consider using a slightly higher multiple to allow for potentially higher growth rates. (A low P/E ratio may indicate that the stock is selling at a bargain price.)

✔ **Underpriced stocks:** There are three criteria for underpriced stocks:

- Small-cap stocks with *quick ratios* (current assets minus inventory divided by current liabilities) greater than 1.0 and return on assets (ROA) greater than 0.

- A price-to-earnings ratio (P/E ratio) that is half of that industry's average

- A price-to-book-value ratio of 80 percent or less and a price-to-sales ratio of 33 percent or less

Screening for Investment Bargains

Investors are always searching for a *competitive edge* that will allow them to *beat the market.* (Beating the market is usually defined as selecting stocks that outperform — that is, provide greater returns than — the TSE 300 for Canadian stocks or the S&P 500 for U.S. stocks.) The following are several stock screen variables that you may want to factor in to your stock selection strategy. However, observe your risk-tolerance level. After all, you want to sleep at night.

Stocks selling below book value

Some stock screens allow you to sort for stocks that have a current selling price that is below book value. *Book value* is defined as the depreciated value of a company's assets (original cost less accumulated depreciation or amortization) less the outstanding liabilities.

Purchasing stocks selling at below book value may be a bargain hunter's dream but will require additional research on your part. A company's total assets are often the accounting values of assets purchased over time; in other words, the historical price of an asset less depreciation or amortization. For example, the firm may have fully depreciated a 20-year-old building. The sales value of the building may be in the millions, but the value listed on the balance sheet may be zero. (This difference causes the book value to be understated.)

Or the building may have environmental problems (because of improper disposal of industrial wastes, for example) that will cost the owners millions to clean up. In this case, the book value is overstated.

The prudent investor determines why a company is selling below book value before he or she purchases the stock. Check out the company's annual, quarterly, and other miscellaneous reports filed with SEDAR (www.sedar.com), FreeEDGAR (www.freeedgar.com), or the Securities and Exchange Commission (www.sec.gov).

Try different approaches to your research. For example, you may be able to discover some interesting facts about the company if it was a failed merger or acquisition candidate. If a large corporation or an investment bank didn't want to buy the company, you may want to follow its lead.

Stocks selling below liquidation value

Your bargain hunting may guide you to screening for stocks that are selling below their liquidation value. *Liquidation value* of a company is defined as the dollar sum that could be realized if assets were sold independently or piece-meal, instead of selling the company as a whole. For example, say that no market demand exists for the company's hula-hoops or buggy-whips, and the company discontinues that product line. The machinery used to manufacture this product still bears value. The appraised value of the manufacturing equipment is determined as a separate collection. The values of the firm's ongoing or discontinued operations are not factored into this price. A company's assets are listed in company annual reports. The Thomson Investors Network site, at www.thomsoninvest.net, is a good online source for these reports, which are free. From the Thomson Investors Network home page, click on the Stocks icon at the top of the page, and then click on the EDGAR Search feature to access the reports.

Stocks selling at below liquidation value may be valuable, but you should consider the priority of claims if the company is forced into bankruptcy. Claims against company assets are paid in the following order: (1) secured creditors, (2) expenses incurred for administration and bankruptcy costs, (3) expenses incurred after filing bankruptcy, (4) salaries and commissions (not to exceed a set amount) that were earned within three months of filing bankruptcy, (5) federal, provincial, and local taxes, (6) unsecured creditors, (7) preferred stock, and finally, (8) you, the common shareholder.

Stocks with low P/E ratios

The *price-to-earnings (P/E) ratio* is the current price of a stock divided by the earning for one share of stock and is the value that the investment community places on $1 of the company's earnings. For example, if the current price of the stock is $60 and the earning per share (for the past 12 months) is $3, the P/E ratio is 20 ($60/$3). *Note:* In Bay Street–speak, the earnings per share (EPS) for the past 12 months when used in the preceding formula is often called the *trailing P/E ratio*. You are likely to see the trailing P/E ratio listed as a variable in the online stock screens.

P/E ratios vary by industry, so unless you find out the industry average, you can't determine whether a stock has a low P/E ratio. Luckily, Hoover's (www.hoovers.com) Company Capsules and Zacks Company Reports (www.zacks.com) provide this information for free. Zacks Company Reports include those of many Canadian companies. When analyzing a P/E ratio, you want to look at the trend of the company's P/E ratio over the past five to seven years. Companies that the investment community expects to grow will have higher P/E ratios than others in the same industry.

Bargain hunters may want to set the variables in their stock screens for low P/E ratios because a company with a P/E ratio of 20 is a more expensive stock than one with a P/E ratio of 10. However, companies with low P/E ratios may be cheap for good reason. For example, one way to analyze the P/E ratio is to compare it to the company's growth rate. The company's P/E ratio and growth rate should be equal. (*Remember:* The stock price is the present value of all the future earnings.) Therefore, if the P/E ratio is low, the company may be plagued by slow growth.

What a low P/E ratio is or what it indicates may be difficult to determine. For example, the company may have a low P/E ratio because investors are bailing out, which can drive the stock price down and make the stock appear inexpensive. Say that that $60 stock we mentioned a little earlier drops to $30 per share. The P/E ratio will be reduced to 10 ($30/$3). The stock is now half-price, but it may not be a good purchase if the company is headed toward bankruptcy or has another major problem.

Companies reporting deficits

You may want to set up your stock screen to determine which companies in a certain cyclical industry are reporting *deficits* (losses). Cyclical stocks are dependent on external environmental factors, such as the national economy, housing sales, and consumer confidence. You can check out these good online sources of industry information: LexisNexis (www.lexis-nexis.com) and Statistics Canada (www.statcan.ca). Cyclical stocks have peaks (high points) and valleys (low points) in their revenues, profits, and stock prices. These peaks and valleys can mean that some cyclical companies with strong foundations may be experiencing flat earnings or deficits due to their business cycles.

Be certain that you understand the company's business operations. High fliers can crash and burn. For example, you may want to avoid companies that have no earnings and stock prices based on planned new products, corporate restructuring, or strategic partnering.

The trick with cyclical stocks is to purchase the stock when it's in a valley in the cycle and sell when it's near the peak. A good indicator that the upward part of the cycle may be about to begin is when the P/E ratio is high and the EPS (earnings per share) is low. Other external environmental factors may indicate that the stock is approaching its peak. For example, a sudden drop in housing starts might indicate that your shares in a furniture company are near their peak and it's time to sell.

Prospective turnaround candidates

Using stock screen variables to locate companies that are laggards in sales, earnings, and profits is one way to locate turnaround candidates. The value of investing in turnarounds is that the stock may increase two to three times what it originally was as the company becomes successful. (A rare few companies will increase by 10 times. The 40 times increase for Chrysler may be the biggest increase on record.)

Young companies often have ups and downs, but mature companies that have problems frequently don't get a second chance to improve their fundamentals. These fallen angels often have problems with inconsistent product quality, respond slowly to changing market conditions, and have high operating costs, low employee involvement, poor customer service, and inadequate methods of allocating resources. Often, management is negative, risk-averse, and bureaucratic. All these factors prevent the company from becoming competitive. The result is that analysts and investors are waiting for a turnaround that never appears.

The preceding situation highlights how timing is everything when investing in troubled companies. The company has to survive long enough to get well. For troubled companies, a larger, more mature company that owns real estate and has cash on hand is superior to a small company with limited resources and rented office space. After all, the company needs to be solvent in order to make a comeback.

Don't be fooled by quick profits when the company starts slashing budgets and implementing a recovery plan. These short-term gains will likely disappear as customers become wary of doing business with the troubled company. The comeback road is bumpy. Many companies get off to false starts and then stumble. Some pick themselves up again. Others never do.

Chapter 13

Valuing Bonds Online

● ●

In This Chapter

▶ Making sense of why bond values change

▶ Determining the value of any type of bond

▶ Discovering the easiest way to determine your bond returns

▶ Buying and selling bonds

▶ Using a hot strategy for reducing bond risk

● ●

*I*n this chapter, we show you how to analyze a variety of fixed-income investments. We explore the benefits of savings bonds, explain new regulations, and discuss the limitations of this type of investment. For online investors who wish to know how to pay the right price for a bond, or when to bail out of one, this chapter shows how to value all types of bonds and determine bond yields (returns). Doing so may sound complicated, but with a little practice you'll be calculating your returns in no time. This chapter also provides a hot strategy that can protect you from interest-rate risk.

Treasury Securities and You

The federal government sells Canadian treasury securities to the public in order to pay off maturing debt and raise the cash needed to operate the Canadian government. The Bank of Canada auctions them every other week. There are three general types of treasury securities, in both Canada and the United States. A U.S. treasury bill, which is a popular form of treasury security, has a minimum purchase requirement of $10,000 U.S. Canadian treasury bills require minimums from $5,000 (for terms of 6 to 12 months) up to $25,000 (for 30- to 60-day terms). A U.S.-denominated Canadian treasury bill (guaranteed by the Canadian government) has a minimum requirement of $100,000 U.S. The chief difference between the U.S. and Canadian treasury securities, as seen in the following list, is the life of the obligation.

- ✔ **Treasury bills (T-bills)** mature in three months, six months, or one year. Treasury bills are purchased at a discount, so interest is actually paid. For example, you'll write a cheque for $10,000 and the government refunds the discount (which equals the interest rate determined at auction). In other words, your return is the difference between the purchase price and the maturity value.

- ✔ **Treasury notes (Canada notes)** are considered intermediate-term securities and mature in 2 to 10 years. Canada notes are denominated in U.S. dollars and provide interest payments to note holders.

- ✔ **Treasury bonds (Canada bonds)** are long-term securities that have maturities ranging from 10 years to 30 years. They are sold by auction to securities dealers and banks.

Online sources for more information

Government information is often written in a way that makes purchasing treasuries seem more difficult and complex than it really is. But don't get discouraged. For more information about understanding and purchasing Canadian and U.S. treasury securities, refer to the following online resources:

- ✔ **Bank of Canada:** This comprehensive site, located at `www.bankof canada.ca`, provides auction dates and news about Canadian treasury securities.

- ✔ **BondCan:** This site is located at `www.bondcan.com`, and provides detailed overviews about the bond market from a Canadian perspective. It also provides links to other Web resources dealing with Canadian bonds.

- ✔ **CIBC Economics Online:** CIBC's online economics site at `www.cibc.com/ english/business_services/economics/index.html` lets you access research and overviews about Canadian government bonds, interest rates, and the provincial, national, and global economies. It also publishes leading economic indicators, the latest economic forecasts, and industry analyses. See Figure 13-1.

- ✔ **GovPX:** This site, located at `www.govpx.com`, provides quotations of U.S. government securities. The site also provides active lists of treasury bonds, notes, and bills with each financial instrument's coupon rate and maturity date. Lists include buyers' bid prices, sellers' asking prices, changes from the prior trading day, and yields. It also has useful links to related sites.

- ✔ **Quote.com Street Pricing:** This site, located at `www.quote.com`, provides quotes for U.S. and Canadian treasury securities and government agency securities. Specific information includes interest rates and spreads, quotes on active treasuries, and quotes on government agency securities. Cost is $9.95 U.S. per month for the basic service.

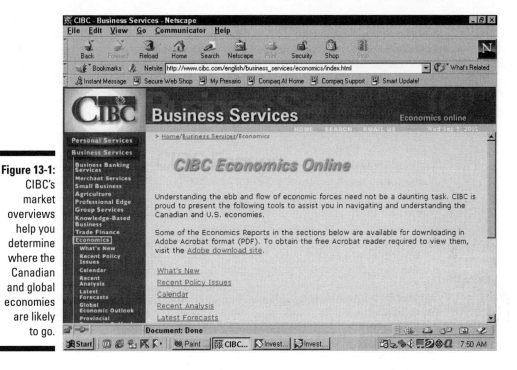

Figure 13-1:
CIBC's market overviews help you determine where the Canadian and global economies are likely to go.

> ✔ **Zero coupon bonds and strips:** You can get an explanation of these more sophisticated treasury securities from the Federal Reserve Bank of New York at `www.ny.frb.org/pihome/fedpoint/fed41.html`.

The Math of Bonds

The bond market is dominated by institutional investors (insurance companies, pension funds, mutual funds, and so on) that account for 80 to 85 percent of all trading. However, the impact of individual investors can also be felt through the purchases of mutual funds that specialize in bonds.

The following section shows the valuation process of bonds and the relationship of interest-rate changes to the value of bonds. We provide several easy-to-use approaches that take the mystery out of determining your bond yield.

Calculating bond values

One such approach is calculating the value of a bond.

A bond issued by a corporation is called a *debt instrument*. The bond states how the debtholder (investor) is repaid. Generally, these terms are normal debt arrangements. The borrower makes interest payments and then pays the principal at a predetermined date. Several things make bonds complicated, such as provisions to convert the bonds to common stocks at a predetermined stock value or terms that allow the bond issuer to retire the bond before maturity.

The value of a bond is based on the investor's overall assessment of the bond's worth at a given point in time. The receipt of future interest payments, the repayment of principal, and the credit rating or riskiness of the bond usually drive these assessments. You aren't obligated to hold a bond until maturity, and bonds are traded freely in the marketplace.

Calculating the value of a bond involves determining the present value of the interest payments and the eventual recovery of the principal. *Present value* means discounting the future cash flow to calculate how much you're willing to pay today for those future receipts.

At times, calculating the yield on bonds can seem more complicated than it really is. For example, if you purchase a one-year treasury bill for $9,500 and redeem it in 12 months at full face value ($10,000), your gain is $500 (subject to Canadian income tax). To determine your yield, use the following formula. (We assume your holding period is one year):

Face value – Price / Price = Annual return

$10,000 – $9,500 / $9,500 = 0.526 or 5.26%

See the section "The easy way to value your bond returns" later in this chapter, where we show you how to calculate the yield for a bond that has a maturity term greater than one year. Yield is a key performance indicator for bonds.

Creating yield curves

A *yield curve* is a diagram that illustrates the relationship of bond yields to maturities on a specific day. Yield curves can be used to decide which type of bond is best for your financial objectives. Bond yields and maturities are posted daily at the *Globe and Mail*'s Web site (www.globeandmail.com) and at the *Wall Street Journal* Interactive Web site (www.wsj.com). Go to their respective business sections to find the link.

On a piece of graph paper on the horizontal axis, plot the maturities of treasury securities from left to right starting with the shortest maturity of 30 days to the longest maturity of 30 years. Then on the vertical axis, plot the yield of each treasury security. Next, connect the dots to make a yield curve. See the curve descriptions in the following list to find out what your results indicate:

✔ If the short-term rates are higher than the long-term rates, then the yield curve becomes *inverted,* or has a downward swing to it, which tells you that this situation tends to be *bearish* for the market. In times like these, monetary policy is likely to be tight; the Bank of Canada or Federal Reserve will push up short-term rates.

✔ If the short-term rates are lower than the long-term rates, then the yield curve is *positive,* or has an upward swing to it, which usually indicates that investors are willing to tie up their money in long-term commitments to reap higher rewards.

✔ If the short-term rates and the long-term rates are the same (or nearly the same), then the yield curve appears to be flat.

The yield curve approach also works for other types of bonds, such as government agency, municipal, or corporate bonds. Remember that you need to include in the curve only bonds with the same level of risk, such as all AA-rated corporate bonds.

The easy way to value your bond returns

Bonds are often quoted at prices that differ from their stated (or *par*) values, a situation that can be troublesome for investors who want to determine the yield of the bond. Still, many ways exist to calculate the yield value of a bond. In our opinion, the *approximate yield to maturity (YTM)* method provides the easiest way to determine a bond's current yield.

To calculate the approximate yield to maturity, you need the following information:

✔ Annual interest payment (I)

✔ Principal payment (P)

✔ Price of the bond (B)

✔ Number of years to maturity (M)

Using these values, you calculate the approximate yield to maturity (YTM) by using the following formula:

$$YTM = \{I + [(P - B) \div M]\} \div [(0.6 \times B) + (0.4 \times P)]$$

For example, what is the yield to maturity on a 12-year, 7-percent annual coupon, $1,000 par value bond that sells at a discount for $942.21? Here are the calculations:

$$YTM = \{70 + [(\$1{,}000 - \$942.21) \div 12]\} \div [(0.6 \times \$942.21) + (0.4 \times \$1{,}000)]$$

$$YTM = [70 + (57.79 \div 12)] \div (565.33 + 400)$$

$$YTM = (70 + 4.82) \div 965.33$$

$$YTM = 74.82 \div 965.33$$

$$YTM = 0.0775$$

$$YTM = 7.75\%$$

If your required rate of return is 8 percent, you should *not* purchase the bond because the approximate yield to maturity (7.75 percent) doesn't meet your financial requirements. Conversely, if the bond has a return that is equal to or *greater* than 8 percent, the bond meets your objectives and is a "buy" candidate.

Note: If the value of the bond is discounted (that is, sells below its par value — in this case, below $1,000), the yield to maturity (YTM) is greater than the 7-percent coupon rate.

A hot bond strategy

More Canadians have invested in bonds than in any other security. Some of the advantages of bonds are that they offer regular interest payments that are higher than money-market accounts; they can be tax-exempt; and they offer a way to stay ahead of inflation.

Some of the limitations of investing in bonds are interest-rate risk (if interest rates go up, the value of your bond goes down) and credit rating risk (if your bond gets downgraded, its value goes down). Holding foreign bonds exposes you to exchange-rate risk (if the Canadian dollar goes up relative to the foreign bond, you get less money back at maturity). Also, unless you own a treasury security, your principal investment isn't guaranteed by the government the way bank deposits are protected by the Canada Deposit Insurance Corporation (CDIC).

Several investment advisers say that one way to reduce your exposure to interest-rate risk is to create a *bond ladder*. Each rung of the bond ladder consists of a different bond maturity. For example, the first rung of the bond ladder may consist of bonds that mature in 1 year; the second rung may consist of bonds that mature in 2 years; and so on, for 10 years. In effect, you are staggering the maturities over time.

The yield of the 10-year bond ladder is less than 20-year bonds, but the ladder provides diversification. As each rung matures, you can reinvest the funds in the same or better ways to conserve your principal. The benefits of this approach are some protection from declining interest rates and low maintenance on your part.

If this bond ladder scheme seems too complex, you can always invest in a bond mutual fund. But keep in mind that bond mutual funds rarely "beat the market" and have more risk than individual bonds. Some aggressively managed bond funds include risky investing strategies that can be a real gamble. On the other hand, one of the advantages of a bond mutual fund is that you often get to own a share of bonds that are $50,000, $100,000, or $250,000 each — something that you may not be able to achieve as an individual investor.

More Online Bond News, Rates of Return, and Advice

For more information about bond markets, commentary, rates, and news, see the following online resources:

- ✔ **E*Trade Canada (**www.etrade.ca**)** provides a Daily Bond Market Commentary that includes financial data about bonds, and discusses political, economic, and other events that can affect the price of bonds. It's a great source for background information about bonds.

- ✔ **SmartMoney.com (**www.smartmoney.com**)**, shown in Figure 13-2, provides key interest rates, bond market updates, a bond calculator, and a glossary. Educational articles include bond strategies, short-term bond investing, bond allocation, and a bond primer. Yup, this site is the "James Bond" of bondsites.

Figure 13-2:
SmartMoney.com is a good place to learn more about bonds.

Where to Buy Bonds

Tens of thousands of Canadians own bonds of various stripes. In fact, about $1 billion of Canada Savings Bonds are sold each year. Three sources exist for purchasing CSBs and other bonds:

- **Banks, credit unions, and other financial institutions:** Many Canadian financial institutions are qualified as savings-bond agents. These agents accept the payments and the purchase orders for Canada Savings and other bonds, and forward the orders to the Bank of Canada (or, in the case of U.S. savings bonds, to a Federal Reserve bank).

- **Employer-sponsored payroll savings plans:** More than 5,000 Canadian employers participate in employer-sponsored payroll savings plans, and some chartered banks offer Canada Savings Bonds through installment plans.

- **Federal Reserve banks:** If you want to buy U.S. savings bonds, you can write to a regional Federal Reserve bank and ask for an application. The "Fed" allows you (even though you are a Canadian) to purchase savings bonds by mail. A U.S. Savings Bond page can be found at the Web site for the Federal Reserve Bank of New York (www.ny.frb.org/pihome/svg_bnds). This site provides the addresses of the 12 regional Federal Reserve banks. (Of course, you can also buy U.S. savings bonds through most Canadian financial institutions.) You can also purchase treasury securities through the Fed's Internet purchase program, *Buy Direct!,* or by calling 1-800-943-6864. Tender forms and payments may also be submitted electronically through your financial institution or government securities broker or dealer.

You can get more information about savings bonds from the following Internet sources:

- **BondCan** (www.bondcan.com)**:** This site provides a market overview of Canadian bonds. Learn how economic and political developments influence Canadian bond prices.

- **Market Analysis of Savings Bonds** (www.bondinformer.com)**:** An expert on U.S. bonds gives a market analysis of short- and long-term interest rates for savings bonds.

How to buy 'em

You can get more information about buying and selling Canadian treasury bills and Canada Savings Bonds by going to the Bank of Canada's Web site (www.bank-banque-canada.ca/english/intro-e.htm). You can even see if there is an unclaimed bank account or unredeemed bond in your name!

Canadians who invest in U.S. treasuries and savings bonds can obtain all the order forms, instructions, auction dates, auction results, and other related information at the Bureau of the Public Debt Web site (www.publicdebt.treas.gov). You can download and print forms, send e-mail requests for forms, or ask that forms be mailed to you. The ability to purchase U.S. treasury securities without a broker is a great money-saving feature for investors. Check out the special rules for Canadians who wish to buy U.S. securities.

You can also buy and sell fixed income securities at E-Bond (www.ebond.ca), a Canadian online bond discount broker. At this site, you can access live rates, investor news, and your account — 24 hours a day. You can trade online or by phone. This broker deals with all areas of the bond markets, including federal government bonds, provincial and federal zero coupons, along with a selection of high-grade corporate debt.

Rolling over, cashing in, or selling your treasury securities

Canadian and U.S. treasury bills mature at various intervals of time. When your treasury bill matures, you have two choices. First, you can roll over your investment and reinvest in the face value of another T-bill (with the same or a different maturity). Second, you can cash in and have the proceeds deposited to your holding account. For example, say that your $15,000 T-bill with a maturity term of 13 weeks matures. You can elect to reinvest in another $15,000 T-bill for 13, 26, or 52 weeks. If you choose not to reinvest your $15,000 at maturity, your holding account is credited with $15,000, or a cheque for $15,000 is sent to your home.

A third T-bill disposition option exists. You can sell your treasury securities before they mature, through a broker. But this will cost you extra money in commissions.

If you need to sell your U.S. treasury security, the U.S. federal government will help you. You can sell directly through Treasury Direct — without a broker. The government gets quotes from different dealers and offers you the best price. The fee is $34 U.S. for each security sold. You can even have the proceeds from the sale of the treasury security deposited directly into your chequing account, less the transaction fee. See www.publicdebt.treas.gov/sec/secbsr.htm for additional information.

Chapter 14

Valuing, Screening, Buying, and Selling Mutual Funds

. . . .

In This Chapter

▶ Using online screening tools to find mutual fund values

▶ Investigating top screen sites

▶ Using an electronic broker

▶ Knowing when to sell

. . . .

*T*his chapter gives you all the basic online tools for identifying mutual fund candidates. We describe five types of online screening tools that can help you choose the mutual fund that best meets your needs. These mutual fund screens vary from simple to more advanced. We believe you'll find that the best online mutual fund screen is the one that includes the criteria that are most important to you.

What Am I Screening?

Before you can screen mutual funds, you have to know where to find the large online mutual fund databases. More information about these databases is provided in chapters 6 and 10. It may be worthwhile to briefly list the major ones again, and to introduce some new ones as well:

✔ **The Fund Library** (www.fundlibrary.com) lets you access detailed profiles on a wide array of Canadian mutual funds.

✔ **GLOBEfund** (www.globefund.com) has a large database of mutual fund profiles. GLOBEfund also has online tools to help you place a value on your mutual fund holdings.

✔ **Morningstar Canada** (www.morningstar.ca) has a comprehensive listing of Canadian mutual funds. Click on Fund Profile to access an overview of just about any Canadian mutual fund out there.

✔ **Standard & Poor's (**`www.funds-sp.com/win/en`**)** world fund database, shown in Figure 14-1, provides fund information and monitoring for over 45,000 funds around the globe on a daily, weekly, and monthly basis. It also supplies summaries on the funds it monitors.

Figure 14-1: Standard & Poor's has information about mutual funds that are offered globally.

How to Screen Mutual Funds Online

The Internet provides a variety of mutual fund screening tools that sort thousands of U.S. and Canadian mutual funds by criteria that you select. For example, you may want one type of fund for your children's education — something long-term because you don't need the money for 10 to 20 years — and a different fund for your retirement to help you get a steady stream of income and to reduce your current tax liabilities. With online screening tools, you can evaluate several funds that meet your financial needs.

Most investment screening Web sites are free. But there's always an exception. Morningstar Canada's (`www.morningstar.ca`) BellCharts feature is, in our opinion, the most powerful mutual fund screening tool for Canadian funds. But it will cost you a fee. Its subscription rates are accessible on its Web site.

Screening a list of mutual funds residing in a database is an inexpensive way to isolate mutual funds that meet your special criteria. Be wary that some databases list funds incorrectly or have outdated information; however, they are useful for pruning a long list of candidates to a manageable short list.

Some mutual fund screening programs — for example, Quicken's Mutual Fund Finder (`www.quicken.com/investments/mutualfunds/finder/`) and MSN Investor (`moneycentral.msn.com/investor`) — are for beginners. Others, such as ResearchMag (`www.researchmag.com`), require practice. Some mutual fund screens allow you to download the data to your spreadsheet so that you can do additional analysis.

Each screening site uses different criteria to sort mutual funds. You have to decide which criteria you care about and then use the site that offers the criteria you want. Any way you look at it, the selection of the right mutual fund is still up to you.

Here's an overview of the features of five mutual fund screens that are best for beginning online investors:

✔ **Quicken.ca (`www.quicken.ca`),** shown in Figure 14-2, provides its Canadian mutual fund screen free of charge. At the Quicken.ca home page, click on Top Funds, and then click Fund Screener to access a mutual fund screen that you can tailor. The screen includes segregated funds. Its variables include minimum return, load, minimum investment, RRSP eligibility, and asset size.

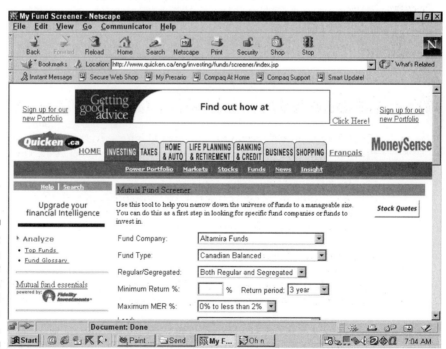

Figure 14-2: Quicken.ca has an array of Canadian mutual fund performance screens.

✔ **Microsoft MoneyCentral Investor** (`moneycentral.msn.com/investor`) is free and has lots of features. You can select from a predefined fund search or perform a custom search using criteria that you define. The MoneyCentral Fund Finder lets you search a database of over 8,000 funds. The custom search criteria include the fund family name, investment focus, the fund's historical performance, overall rating, the minimum initial investment, risk ranking, and load status.

✔ **Morningstar Canada** (`www.morningstar.ca`) has a screening tool called Fund Selector, which lets you screen Canadian mutual funds by fund sponsor, fund category, load type, RRSP eligibility, fund assets, management expense ratio, Morningstar rating, and rate of return. At Morningstar Canada's home page, click the Fund Selector icon.

✔ **Morningstar U.S.** (`www.morningstar.com`) offers a free, independent service that evaluates mostly U.S. mutual funds. At Morningstar's home page, click the Mutual Fund Screen icon to access this screening tool.

✔ **Quote.com Mutual Fund Screening** (`www.quote.com`) is cost-free with your free registration. This prebuilt mutual fund screen covers only U.S. mutual funds. Click Funds to get there.

The following three mutual funds screens are great for more experienced investors:

✔ **ResearchMag** (`www.researchmag.com`) is a free service that is definitely for the experienced investor. However, after you get familiar with its 40 research variables, the service is easy to use. ResearchMag requires your free registration. To access the screen from ReseachMag's home page, click Mutual Fund Screens. To save time and to avoid making the same mistakes over and over, be sure to keep a list of what works and what doesn't. The program searches more than 3,500 equity mutual funds. You can copy screen results to a spreadsheet.

✔ **Smart Money Interactive** (`www.smartmoney.com`) has a do-it-yourself mutual fund finder that searches a database of over 6,000 U.S. mutual funds. You can screen for dozens of factors. For more help, the screen provides current averages for factors like EPS, ROE, and so on. To analyze your selections, click Analyze First 15 Funds. This function sorts your best candidates so that you can compare your results.

✔ **Thomson Investors Network** (`www.thomsoninvest.net`), shown in Figure 14-3, has free mutual fund (and stock) screens. On the home page, click Funds. Next, click Fund Screening and select the characteristics of the mutual fund you are seeking. Click Submit to enter your choices. This site lets you screen both Canadian and U.S. funds. One drawback is that you can't copy search results to a spreadsheet program.

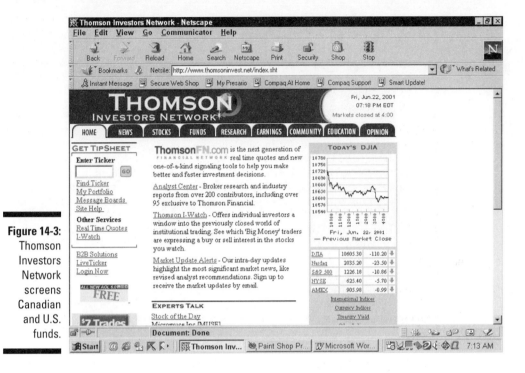

Figure 14-3:
Thomson
Investors
Network
screens
Canadian
and U.S.
funds.

Buying Mutual Funds Online: No Broker Needed

When you have decided which mutual fund best suits your portfolio, you can purchase it without a broker. All you have to do is contact the company directly. Table 14-1 lists a few online mutual fund companies. The table shows the name of the mutual fund company and its Internet address.

Table 14-1	Examples of Online Mutual Fund Sources
Company	*Internet Address*
AGF	www.agf.com
AIC Funds	www.aicfunds.com
Altamira	www.altamira.com
Fidelity Funds	www.fidelity.com
Greenline Mutual Funds	www.tdcanadatrust.com
Mackenzie Funds	www.mackenziefinancial.com
Talvest	www.talvest.com

Buying Mutual Funds Online: Using an Electronic Broker

You can purchase mutual funds through registered representatives of banks, trust companies, stockbrokers, discount brokers, and financial planners. To purchase mutual funds via the Internet, go to an online broker's Web site. (We list a few examples later in this section.)

Register by completing the online application form. You have to provide information about your income, net worth, social insurance number, and the type of account you desire. Sometimes you can open an account based on the quality (creditworthiness) of your information. However, to have a fully functioning account, brokerages are required to have your signature on file. After they have your signature on file, you can buy or sell as much as you want.

After you open your account, you can log on to the Internet, go to your brokerage Web site, and enter orders by completing the online form. You can access your account at any time, check all your investments, and monitor your investments by using online news or quote services.

You have the following options for selecting an electronic broker:

- **A deep-discount broker:** The least-expensive type of broker ($7 to $15 per trade); no recommendations; contacting a human if an error occurs is often difficult.

- **A discount broker:** Less expensive than full-service brokerages; no recommendations; minimal human contact.

- **A full-service broker:** Full commissions, recommendations, advice, and personal service.

Here are a few examples of online deep-discount brokers:

- **E*Trade Canada (**www.etrade.ca**)** charges no fee as long as funds are held for at least 90 days. However, the fund companies may charge fees themselves.

- **Ameritrade (**www.ameritrade.com**)** is a New York–based firm that charges a flat rate of $8 U.S. per trade. This firm trades stocks, funds, and options. An initial investment of $2,000 U.S. is required to open an account. If you're wondering where this firm came from, the organization is a consolidation of Ceres, Aufhauser, and eBroker.

- **CSFB Direct (**www.csfbdirect.com**)** offers no fee and for-fee trades for thousands of mutual funds. The company also trades stocks, bonds, and options.

The Right Time to Sell Your Mutual Funds

If your fund becomes one of the worst performers, consider selling. You need to look at more than just the fund's rating, though. Here are a few guidelines for determining when to sell a fund:

- ✔ Look at the performance of comparable mutual funds. If a similar fund's overall performance is down 10 percent but your fund is down 16 percent and its performance consistently trails its peers, it may be a loser.

- ✔ If your fund has drifted from its original investment objectives, then it's not meeting your asset allocation goals. You'll lose all the benefits of diversification if you have two mutual funds investing in the same asset class.

- ✔ Keep track of changes in your fund's management. If the fund hires a new money manager, that person may have a different investment strategy.

- ✔ You may want to sell if your mutual fund's management expense ratio (MER) has crept up, or if you inherited the fund. High MERs reduce your returns and make the fund less profitable than similar funds with lower expenses.

- ✔ In a volatile market, you may discover that you are a more conservative investor than you imagined. If you can't sleep at night, sell your fund.

- ✔ You are going to pay taxes on your capital gains. If one of your mutual funds is posting negative returns, you may want to consider selling it to offset your tax liabilities.

- ✔ If the fund increases by three or four times its original size in a short time period and its performance starts to decline, you may want to sell. As the fund keeps growing and growing, the professional money manager can't invest in the securities he or she knows and loves best, so the fund may start to acquire poor- or average-performing assets.

- ✔ Consider your needs. If you purchased the fund for a specific purpose and your life circumstances change, you should sell the fund and purchase one that meets your needs — even if the fund is doing well.

Funds that underperform in the short term can still be sound investments. For example, some Canadian funds did not outperform the TSE in the past three years, but their average total returns over the past three years exceeded 20 percent.

The Investing Online For Canadians For Dummies, 2nd Edition Internet Directory

The 5th Wave — By Rich Tennant

"I'm not saying I believe in anything. All I know is since it's been there, our online investment picks have been posting 50% higher returns."

In this part . . .

Throughout the pages of *Investing Online For Canadians For Dummies,* 2nd Edition, we describe dozens of Internet resources that can assist you in your wealth-building efforts. In this part of the book, we provide you with a listing of the sites you are most likely to use for analyzing investment candidates, selecting the right financial assets for your objectives, monitoring your portfolio, and buying and selling your investments online.

The Investing Online For Canadians For Dummies, 2nd Edition Internet Directory

In This Directory

▶ Discovering some of the most highly rated Internet investment sites available and navigating your path to profitability

▶ Gaining easy access to great online services, from online trading and stock quote services to electronic brokerages and investment education

▶ Constructing a successful portfolio with online information about all types of investments

The Internet has a wide variety of resources for Canadian online investors, and this directory provides a sampling of some of the latest and greatest online investing sites available at this time. We don't claim that this guide is exhaustive. The constant growth and change that characterize the Internet make it almost impossible to create a directory to live up to such a claim.

The Internet is a continually evolving resource. Some Web sites listed in this directory (and elsewhere in this book) may have been revised or gone away because of mergers with larger sites. Other investment Web sites just vanish without reason. If a site has moved, you may find a link to the new location. If not, try a search engine (like AltaVista or Google) to locate the resource you need.

Since the Canadian stock market represents only 2 percent of the world equity market, and because many Canadian investors also own U.S. securities, this directory will focus on both Canadian and U.S. Internet resources.

D-4

About Those Micons

To give you as much information as possible, this directory uses *micons*, small graphics that point out some of the special features and attributes of a Web site:

$ This site charges an access fee. We use this micon if most of the site's content — or the most important content — is available only to paying subscribers.

    You need a special piece of software — a *plug-in,* such as Shockwave or Real Audio — to get the most out of this site.

    This site features shopping opportunities.

    This site has software that you can download.

    This site is one of many on the Internet that require your free registration.

    The site has interactive discussion forums where you can communicate with other online investors.

    Sites identified by this micon offer special chat rooms where you can interact with other visitors or investment experts. Participation in chat rooms often requires registering at the site.

Analyst Evaluations

Finding out what the experts are saying about your investment selection is often useful. Here are a few of our favourite sources for analysts' evaluations.

Zacks Investment Research

http://my.zacks.com

$ ◫

Analyst commentary for the individual investor: To get a quote on a specific U.S. or large Canadian public company's shares, just enter its stock ticker symbol and click Go. You can purchase company research reports from Zacks and access free analyst commentary on companies, sectors, and the economy as a whole.

Other Stuff to Check Out

www.standardandpoors.com
www.bloomberg.com
www.bridge.com
www.briefing.com

Basics of Investing

If you're looking for good investor starting places, try the Web sites we list in this section.

Canstock

www.canstock.com

$ ◫

Canadian-focused starting point: Canstock provides investment primers, lets you access free quotes, allows you to set up a personalized portfolio of up to 10 stocks, and lets you personalize market information. Canstock also provides fee-based financial content and analytical tools for investors. Enhanced services include real-time stock quotes, analytical tools, breaking business news, detailed company information, comprehensive mutual fund data and profiles, and more.

InvestorGuide

www.investorguide.com

Start here: InvestorGuide features newsletters, articles, stock analyses, and links to thousands of investment sites. Plus, the site features loads of educational materials that can help you figure out what you want to do with your money, and why. Much of this educational information is goal-oriented, so it contains information about saving for university or community college, in addition to investments in general.

Other Stuff to Check Out

www.canadianbusiness.com
www.teachmefinance.com
www.invest-faq.com
http://university.smartmoney.com
www.fool.com/school.htm
www.quicken.com/investments

Bonds

Bonds (sometimes called fixed-income investments) can be short-term or long term, high-risk (like junk bonds) or low-risk (like treasury bonds). If you own mutual fund shares that include bonds, you may already be a bond investor. Check out the following sites for bond-related information.

D-6 Broker Fraud and Complaints

Bondcan

www.bondcan.com

"Eh"-rated debt: This is one of the best online resources for individuals investing in Canadian bonds. It lists news about the Bank of Canada, dispatches from all the provincial banks, and government statistics. The site also features a message board, a glossary, links to articles, historical yields, and more.

E-Bond

www.ebond.ca

Trading bonds: E-Bond is a Canadian online bond brokerage/investment firm. It provides most Canadian fixed-income security buyers/sellers with rates for required terms. At E-Bond's site, you can access live rates, investor news, and your E-Bond account (if you have one) — 24 hours a day. You can trade online or by phone. It deals with all areas of the Canadian and foreign bond markets, including federal government bonds, provincial and federal zero coupons or strips, along with a selection of high-grade corporate debt.

Other Stuff to Check Out

www.stls.frb.org/fred/data/irates.html
www.investinginbonds.com
www.moodys.com

Broker Fraud and Complaints

If you suspect that your broker is not as honest as you once thought, you can voice your complaint to the right people using the Internet. Many of these organizations follow up on your complaint and keep you informed of its status.

Better Business Bureau

www.bbb.org

Your complaint will be heard: The Better Business Bureau has an online complaint form, as well as a list of companies with a history of irregularities. It has links to your local Canadian Better Business Bureau.

National Fraud Information Center

www.fraud.org

Help others by reporting fraud: The U.S. National Fraud Information Center forwards your complaint to the appropriate organizations and includes it in the center's Internet fraud statistics (which may not get your money back, but may be helpful to other online investors).

Ontario Securities Commission

www.osc.gov.on.ca

Check up on your broker: The Ontario Securities Commission (SEC) has an online complaint process. The OSC is woefully understaffed, so don't keep your fingers crossed for too long if you're waiting for results. However, it's better to have OSC's complaint process than to have no process at all.

Other Stuff to Check Out

www.cipf.ca
www.osfi-bsif.gc.ca
www.bcsc.bc.ca

Canada Savings Bonds

You can purchase Canada Savings Bonds at banks or credit unions. Also, many employers offer payroll deduction plans that allow you to purchase savings bonds.

Bank of Canada

www.bankofcanada.ca

The government promotes its bonds: The Bank of Canada provides information about past and upcoming series of savings bonds, as well as about interest rates and savings bond maturity periods.

Market Analysis of Savings Bonds

www.bondinformer.com

Easy for anyone to understand: One expert provides a market analysis of short- and long-term interest rates for savings bonds. Although this is a U.S. site, much of this analysis can be applied to the Canadian bond market.

Company Profiles and Press

If you're thinking about investing in a company, you can do much of your research about the company online. For example, you can read the company's quantitative and qualitative profile, or develop your own company profile based on your online research and analysis. You can also access recent company news to get a better idea regarding what has been said by, or about, a company.

Adviceforinvestors.com

www.adviceforinvestors.com

$

All-in-one Canadian solution: More of a professional resource than StockHouse Canada, this site enables you to buy full research reports. These reports provide executive names, sales figures, insider trading data, and ratio analyses. This site also has free information about most Canadian companies, including charts, news, and industry comparisons. You can also find market commentaries and some information on U.S. public companies.

Hoover's Online

www.hoovers.com

$

Good freebies — great, if you pay the fee: Hoover's Online has free and fee-based information on 8,500 companies. Although most covered companies are of U.S. origin, some of the larger Canadian companies are also profiled. At Hoover's, you can search company ticker symbols, locations, and sales. Company profiles include the firm's address, phone numbers, executive names, recent sales figures, and company status. Hoover's is generally considered to be the U.S. equivalent of Carlson Online.

Other Stuff to Check Out

www.canadanewswire.ca
www.technometrica.com
www.prnewswire.com
www.businesswire.com
www.freeedgar.com

www.edgar-online.com
www.sedar.com
www.irin.com
www.10kwizard.com

Direct Public Offerings

In a direct public offering (DPO), a company bypasses an underwriter and offers its shares directly to the public. This procedure has both good points and drawbacks. The Internet provides information and materials about many DPOs. A DPO may not be available to Canadian residents if it is being offered by a U.S. company, so talk to the issuing company's investor relations department to see where you stand.

The Direct Stock Market

www.dsm.com

Companies for sale, info for free: The Direct Stock Market provides information about companies that are issuing direct public offerings. It provides a central online repository for the distribution of these companies' prospectuses and documents. You can also find an exchange for over-the-counter and bulletin board shares, and regular Webcasts disseminating investment information.

Earnings Estimates

When determining the value of a stock, you often need to estimate the direction of a company's earnings. Compare your

earnings hunches with the experts' at the following Web sites.

First Call

www.firstcall.com

$

A reliable source: The First Call database follows most U.S., and large- to mid-cap Canadian public companies. It also tracks more than 100 industry groups, several commodities and economic indicators, plus the Dow Jones Industrial Average, the S&P 500, and the TSE 300. Most of the useful stuff here costs you, but it's good if you're a serious investor.

Yahoo! Finance

http://finance.yahoo.com

A free and comprehensive source: The Yahoo! Finance section of the huge Yahoo! portal provides summaries of analyst estimates. Click the Research icon to get earnings estimates and ratings on most U.S. and large Canadian companies.

Zacks Investment Research

http://my.zacks.com

 $

A long-standing favourite: Zacks provides estimated earnings reports that are based on broker opinions. The site includes a listing of current earnings surprises, recommendations, and the company's annual balance sheet and income statement. Although Zacks is based in the U.S., it covers most of the larger Canadian public companies. Zacks also reports on what hundreds of expert analysts around the U.S., Canada, and elsewhere are saying about stocks you can invest in. Some of these reports are free; others require you to pay a fee. All reports are top quality.

Economic Information

Before you invest, checking out the big picture is always a wise idea. Find out how our economy is doing, both nationally and provincially. For example, if the Canadian economy weakens, analyze how this will affect your domestic investment selections.

Statistics Canada

www.statcan.ca

 $

Just the facts: Statistics Canada is a combination free and for-fee Web site. Basic demographic and statistical information is usually free. But when the statistics you want become more specific, you'll likely have to pay a fee to get that information. Statistics Canada provides basic and detailed information about industry, statistics, and general business. It produces reports on areas that may impact the Canadian stock market — labour, production, shipments, inventory balance of trade, retail, and wholesale. It also provides reports on inflation, which can move stock markets seconds after release!

Census Bureau

www.census.gov

 $

How many, exactly: The Census Bureau is the U.S. counterpart to Statistics Canada, and it provides similar industry, statistical, and general business information. *Current Industrial Reports* gives production and inventory statistics.

Industry Information

Compare the performance of your investment candidate to the industry standard. How is the company performing? Is the company an industry leader or fighting for market share? Find out by researching the company's industry at the following Internet sites.

LexisNexis

www.lexis-nexis.com

$

One of the most comprehensive and reliable information databases in the world: LexisNexis has a wide variety of business and legal databases, and recently added a new database of 10- to 20-page market summaries of particular industry sectors or demographic markets. As well, the LexisNexis database includes the *Market Share Reporter* (from 1991 to the present) and *Computer Industry Forecasts*. LexisNexis has a service geared especially for Canadians who seek Canadian information.

Strategis

www.strategis.ic.gc.ca

Everything you need to know about Canadian industry, and still more: Industry Canada has developed one of Canada's most useful and comprehensive Web sites. You can search by industry to find information about industry trends and perform comparative analyses to U.S. industries. The overviews of certain industries are very well researched, and are accessible for free at this site. You can access a company directory, and worldwide links to relevant sites are also available.

Other Stuff to Check Out

www.technometrica.com
www.trainingforum.com
www.quicklaw.com

Initial Public Offerings (IPOs)

Usually, in an initial public offering (IPO), a company offers shares to the public for the first time. Purchasing shares in an IPO may be one way to get in on the ground floor of a new investment opportunity. Investing in an IPO is also an excellent way to lose your shirt. In Canada, it's still difficult to get in on an IPO, so most of the sites listed next are of U.S. origin. As a Canadian, you may or may not be able to participate in a U.S. IPO. Check your eligibility for U.S. IPOs with your broker.

Everything about IPOs

www.moneypages.com/syndicate/stocks/ipo.html

An IPO primer: This Web page contains an informative article about the advantages and limitations of initial public offerings. Start here.

IPO Central

www.ipocentral.com

News of a turbulent field: IPO Central provides the most recent IPO filings, weekly pricing, commentary, and informative articles. Its IPO profile pages are concise, and provide a great financial snapshot of any company about to go public. This Web resource is part of the Hoover's empire, so it's reliable.

IPO.com

www.ipo.com

A great site for the knowledgeable IPO investor: IPO.com is a portal to online resources for IPO investors. Here, you can find the latest pricing information and news in an attractive, frequently updated format that you can easily refer to.

Other Stuff to Check Out

http://biz.yahoo.com/reports/ipo.html
www.ipodata.com
www.ipomonitor.com
www.ipo.com
www.ostman.com
www.iposyndicate.com
www.ipomonitor.com
www.edgar-online.com/ipoexpress/

Interest Rates

The Internet can help you find the best savings rate in Canada.

Bank of Canada

www.bankofcanada.ca

Canadian rates and bonds: This site provides auction dates and news about Canadian treasury securities. You can also get information about the prime lending rate at any given day.

BondCan

www.bondcan.com

Bond market overviews: This site provides detailed overviews about the Canadian bond market, and provides links to other Web resources dealing with Canadian bonds and interest rates.

CANNEX

www.cannex.com

Rate quotes: This Canadian Web site compares interest rates on an array of fixed-income investment options — including term deposits and GICs — offered by Canadian banks, trust companies, credit unions, and other financial institutions. It also covers fixed-income investments offered in the U.S. and Australia.

Industry Canada's Financial Service Charges Calculator

www.strategis.ic.gc.ca/SSG/
   ca00669e.html

All-purpose interest rate shopper: This site shows interest rates offered by financial institutions throughout Canada. It includes trust companies and credit unions. It has a questionnaire to help you assess your banking habits and offers suggestions to save costs.

Investor Databases

When researching an investment candidate, investors often use specialized databases to find that elusive piece of data. Here are a few online databases.

FinWeb

www.finweb.com

Free advice from an academic expert: FinWeb has links to the finance and economics departments of many universities, commercial sources, and financial institutions. This U.S.-focused financial supersite includes high-quality recommendations, and all links are screened for content.

FreeEDGAR

www.freeedgar.com

 $

Annual reports and other regulatory filings: The FreeEDGAR service is like SEDAR, but offers much more. For example, it provides registered users with an e-mail alert every time a certain firm files a document, and links you to that document.

SEDAR

www.sedar.com

Regulated filings galore: Publicly traded companies are required to file company information and disclosures with provincial securities regulators. These reports are entered into a government-sponsored database called SEDAR — The System for Electronic Data Analysis and Retrieval. Downloadable data — such as financial statements or annual reports — can be accessed in their original formats by individual investors.

Other Stuff to Check Out

www.gsa.gov
www.thomasregister.com

Investor Supersites

Investor compilation sites are excellent sources for beginning investors. These investor starting points are also good sources for finding new investor Web sites.

Canadian Financial Network (CFN)

www.canadianfinance.com

One-stop research: CFN is a repository of over 6,000 Canadian and foreign online financial resources. According to CFN's home page, the resources referred to are outlined in enough detail to allow you to stop searching from Web site to Web site and start targeting the information you want. CFN is geared to Canadian investors and can be a useful resource for researching various types of financial management issues. This site has links to information resources that cover stocks, bonds, mutual funds, brokerages, futures, and more.

InvestorGuide

www.investorguide.com

A good place to start: InvestorGuide is a well-organized directory with links to thousands of investor-related sites. InvestorGuide includes site reviews, summaries, and an extensive section on initial pubic offerings (IPOs).

StockHouse

www.stockhouse.com

One-stop investment supermarket: StockHouse has a daily Canadian market commentary, charting tools, newsletters, and interviews with industry experts. It has very active discussion boards for Canadian and foreign stocks.

The Syndicate

www.moneypages.com/syndicate

Ask questions, get answers: The Syndicate includes informative articles on investor

topics, more than 2,000 links to related investor sites, and information on brokers, bonds, and more.

Wall Street Research Net

www.wsrn.com

Share and share alike: Wall Street Research Net focuses on U.S. stock market research. The site includes a very large set of links to company information, the economy, market news, investor reports, quotes, mutual fund indexes, and more. While some of the content is free, you need to pay a subscription fee for the full online version.

Mailing Lists

Mailing lists are special e-mail programs that direct all incoming mail to a list of subscribers. Get new insights and advice from savvy investors by joining a topic-specific mailing list.

CataList

www.lsoft.com/lists/listref.html

A list of lists: CataList lists more than 21,000 mailing lists and is searchable by site, country, and number of list subscribers. Note that the listed lists aren't all about financial matters — they're about many different subjects.

Holt Stock Report

http://metro.turnpike.net/holt

Of particular interest to day traders and options people: The Holt Stock Report provides indexes, averages, information about foreign markets, new stock highs and lows, currency exchange rates, gold prices, interest rates, lists of the most active issues on the NYSE, Nasdaq, and

AMEX, stocks with today's volume up more than 50 percent, and stocks that have reached new highs and lows. You can access a Web site too.

Municipal and Treasury Information

Local levels of Canadian government often issue municipal bonds (sometimes called *munis*). Treasury securities (sometimes called *treasuries*) are issued by the Canadian and U.S. federal governments. Both types of investments can help you diversify your portfolio, providing some tax protection and predictability in the process.

CIBC World Markets
www.cibcwg.com/bigar/bigarrpt.shtml

Canadian municipals: This site provides information on many types of Canadian bonds, including provincials, municipals, federal agency, corporate, and federal instruments. It has a comprehensive Broad Investment Grade Analysis of Return Index that tracks historical rates of return on all broad bond categories, including municipals.

Investor Learning Centre of Canada
www.investorlearning.ca

Informed Canadian resources: Provides references and links to additional resources dealing with the Canadian treasury and overall bond market.

Kirlin: About Investments
www.kirlin.com

All about treasuries: This site provides a good overview of the U.S. treasury security market.

Other Stuff to Check Out
www.economeister.com
www.govpx.com

Mutual Fund Screens

How is a particular mutual fund likely to perform? You can get some sense of this from online screening tools. They allow you to look before you leap, investment-wise.

The Fund Library
www.fundlibrary.com

The best of the best funds: The Fund Library lets you screen a wide array of Canadian mutual funds. You can screen by fund type, or look for the best — or worst — historical performers.

GLOBEfund
www.globefund.com

A big mutual fund database: GLOBEfund has a large database of Canadian mutual fund profiles. You can screen the GLOBEfund list of mutual funds by performance and other variables.

Mutual Funds: Companies and Funds

In this section, we list mutual fund companies that manage many funds. Purchasing a mutual fund directly from a fund company has some benefits. One advantage is that some companies allow you to swap your investment in one of their funds for another of their mutual funds, at no charge.

Altamira
www.altamira.com

A Canadian giant: Altamira is one of the largest mutual fund houses in the world. Altamira's Web site has news about new fund offerings, mutual fund primers, online investment and retirement planning advice, and more.

TD Mutual Funds
www.tdcanadatrust.com/mutual funds

A good beginner's site: If you're a beginning investor, you'll appreciate this site's useful advice. This Web site includes online prospectuses and a list of the firm's financial services. This family of funds has a wide variety of no-load offerings.

T. Rowe Price
www.troweprice.com

Price quotes and more: T. Rowe Price provides daily mutual fund prices, brief updates of fund performance, and more. You have the option of downloading a prospectus or having one sent to you by mail.

Vanguard
www.vanguard.com

On the cutting edge: Vanguard has about 90 funds that do not charge sales fees. Vanguard is one of the largest mutual fund companies in the U.S. The site includes fund descriptions, downloadable prospectuses, an education centre for investors, and more. You can also sign up to receive your statements by e-mail.

Mutual Funds: Information Services, Performance, and Screening

Uncertain about which mutual fund is best for you? Wondering about which fund was last year's star? Looking for a certain type of fund to invest in? The Internet provides lots of mutual fund information resources.

Morningstar Canada
www.morningstar.ca

 $

All about Canadian funds: Morningstar Canada's BellCharts feature provides rankings of all Canadian mutual and segregated funds. You can rate Canadian funds on the basis of several criteria such as size, beta, and return. You can even tailor the criteria to suit your needs. BellCharts is available on an annual, quarterly, and monthly paid subscription basis.

CANOE Money
www.canoe.ca/Money

Ratings of mutual funds: CANOE is the online home of Sun Media. This site provides rankings of the "best" and "worst" mutual funds. You can access current and archived articles about mutual funds.

CBS MarketWatch — Mutual Funds

http://cbs.marketwatch.com

Eye on funds: CBS MarketWatch provides articles, news, market data, fund research, links to fund sites, mutual fund tutorials for new investors, portfolios, and a stock chat room. Click the Mutual Funds box to see the fund information.

EDGAR for Mutual Funds

www.edgar-online.com

Quick and dirty (and free) searching: EDGAR for Mutual Funds is a Web site that provides prospectuses for more than 7,000 mutual funds. If you know the name of the fund you are interested in, you can investigate the fund's activities at this site.

The Fund Library

www.fundlibrary.com

Loads of information: This Canadian site lets you access detailed profiles on a wide array of Canadian mutual funds. It has a good investor Learning Centre on its site. Also, it provides a list of Web sites for most mutual fund companies operating in Canada. You can participate in its discussion forum and also hear what the experts have to say in its archived articles section.

GLOBEfund

www.globefund.com

Information galore: GLOBEfund is the online face of the *Globe and Mail*. It supplies advice to investment newcomers, reviews of investing books, interviews with financial experts, and a glossary. It provides descriptions of fund strategies, analyses of the Canadian mutual fund market, and links to Canadian mutual fund home pages. You can get concise profiles on a wide array of Canadian mutual funds, or even of mutual fund companies themselves. GLOBEfund lets you generate charts that compare the performance of a fund against a variety of criteria. GLOBEfund also allows you to prepare tailored reports on the value of your mutual fund holdings with its Fundlist tracker. You can sort the report to show long-term performance or percentage change in value. You can see what others are saying in its discussion forum.

Index Funds Online

www.indexfundsonline.com

 $

About index funds: Index Funds Online is a comprehensive resource for investigating U.S. (and a handful of Canadian) index funds. It has analysis, commentary, and links to articles and Web sites on index funds. The site explains types of indexes and lists funds tracking them.

The Investment Funds Institute of Canada (IFIC)

www.ific.ca

Mutual fund yellow pages: IFIC lets you access a list of Web sites for most Canadian mutual fund companies. It has articles and statistics about the Canadian mutual fund industry.

Morningstar Canada

www.morningstar.ca

 $

Authoritative information about Canadian funds: Morningstar Canada is a comprehensive Web site for investors looking for information on Canadian mutual funds. Morningstar Canada offers ratings, in-depth mutual funds–related commentary, as well as powerful mutual fund screening tools.

MSN MoneyCentral Investor

http://investor.msn.com

Investment wizardry: Now free, MSN MoneyCentral Investor includes the Fund Research Wizard, which can help you identify mutual funds that meet your needs. The Wizard provides several options. First, you can select one of almost a dozen prebuilt screens. Second, you can build a mutual fund screen that includes all the variables you feel are important. Each type of mutual fund screen is easy to use, and you can copy the results to your spreadsheet.

Mutual Funds Interactive

www.fundsinteractive.com/profiles.html

An excellent centre of information: Mutual Funds Interactive has recommendations, analysis tools, and links to other useful sites. Plus, you can find profiles of many top money managers.

Quicken.ca

www.quicken.ca

The online presence of a personal finance software leader: Quicken provides its Canadian mutual fund screen free of charge. At the Quicken.ca home page, click Find Top Funds, and then click Fund Screener to access a mutual fund screen that you can tailor. The screen includes segregated funds. It has variables that include minimum return, load, RRSP eligibility, and asset size.

SEDAR for Mutual Funds

www.sedar.com

Easy (and free) searching: SEDAR provides prospectuses for most Canadian mutual funds. This site is user-friendly and allows you to download documents so that you can read them later.

News

The Internet offers online news from many large news organizations. Often these organizations will send brief versions of the daily business and investor news or breaking news directly to your e-mailbox free of charge.

Bloomberg Personal Finance

www.bloomberg.com

$

Loaded with timely news, data, and analyses of financial markets and businesses: Find data on securities, statistics, indexes, and research for free. Additional levels of service are available for a fee, including portfolio tracking, online stock quotes, company news, mutual fund information, and at-home delivery of the monthly magazine.

CBS MarketWatch

http://cbs.marketwatch.com

$

Comprehensive: CBS MarketWatch combines the resources of CBS News and Data Broadcasting Corporation: This Web site has many free and fee-based services.

CNNfn
www.cnnfn.com

News, articles on investment topics, and professional advice on money management: Major global stock indexes, stock quotes, currency rates, commodities, and interest information are also available. CNNfn offers links to official company Web sites, a glossary of business terms, general references, and government resources. At your request, free daily news briefings are sent to your e-mailbox.

Reuters moneynet.com
www.moneynet.com/home/moneynet/ homepage/homepage.asp

Sponsored by Reuters to provide you with financial data: Moneynet.com is a convenient Web site from which to get quotes, financial and company news, charts, research, and market snapshots. If you're looking for free online portfolio management, this site has Portfolio Tracker, one of the better portfolio management programs on the Web.

ROBTV
www.robtv.com

Another newspaper creation: This site is the online offspring of the *Globe and Mail*'s *Report on Business*. You can click an icon to see a video clip of a story that aired on TV. You can also see the TV program lineup for features such as DayWatch, This Morning, and Bottom Line. Major business stories are also summarized on this Web site.

Other Stuff to Check Out

www.gsa.gov
www.newsalert.com
www.nightlybusiness.org
www.cnbc.com
www.ft.com
http://finance.yahoo.com

www.moneycentral.com
www.wsjradio.com
www.kiplinger.com
www.on24.com
www.earningswhisper.com
www.cyberinvest.com
www.thomsoninvest.com
www.money.com
www.bbc.co.uk/business
www.chinaonline.com
www.uk-invest.com
www.businessdaily.com

Newsgroups

Newsgroups contain discussions about a range of subject areas. The content of these discussions ranges from the ridiculous to the sublime. By using the search engines we list in this section, you may find a newsgroup that's a good source for opinions on various investments.

Google Groups
http://groups.google.com

Usenet without the hassle: You can use this site to search more than 50,000 Usenet newsgroups (including those directly, indirectly, and not at all related to investments) for the information you are seeking. Searches can be by group, subject, or dates.

Usenet Info Center Launch Pad
http://sunsite.unc.edu/usenet-i

Beginners' information: If you're new to Usenet, the resources here can help you get up to speed.

Newsletters

If you subscribe to an online newsletter, you may receive issues several times a day, daily, weekly, biweekly, monthly, or quarterly. Investor newsletters may be free or for-fee, and they may have hard facts and breaking news or chatty items about the market's latest events. They may also be completely full of hot air. Here are some of the better ones.

Gordon Pape

www.gordonpape.com

$

An authority: This well-known Canadian author's Web site provides fee-based access to his newsletters and books. In addition to providing ratings of mutual funds, Pape's site has useful links to mutual fund company pages and other financial destinations.

Holt Stock Report

http://metro.turnpike.net/holt

All-encompassing news and comment: The Holt Stock Report can be delivered to your e-mailbox daily. This newsletter provides all the market statistics you need for your investment decision-making.

InvestorGuide Weekly

www.investorguide.com/weekly.htm

Internet for fun and profit: InvestorGuide Weekly is designed to keep you informed of new Web-related developments in the areas of investing and personal finance. It includes links to articles on how to use the Internet for investing, new and improved Web sites, investing in Internet companies, and electronic commerce.

Newspapers

Get the news in quick summaries and then read the full story at your leisure, all online. Many online newspapers let you customize your paper so you get just the news that interests you.

The *Globe and Mail*

www.globeandmail.com

Newsworthy stuff: This site provides a summary of the day's investing and business activity. This online partial version, containing bits and pieces from the print version, is free. The online edition of the *Globe and Mail* contains a seven-day archive of selected parts of the newspaper, including *Report on Business*. It also has some additional features such as online calculators and links to related sites.

National Post

www.nationalpost.com

From the Canadian business news leader: *National Post* also has a partial online edition, which includes the very popular *Financial Post* section. You can access investment commentary about stocks, bonds, mutual funds, and sophisticated investments such as options, segregated funds, and more. This site is free.

NewsDirectory.com

www.newsdirectory.com

Newspaper and magazine central: NewsDirectory.com's search tool lets you access online newspapers and magazines by title and region. It contains links to hundreds of Web sites for published material from local and specialty papers, magazines, and major news services.

InfoBeat

www.infobeat.com

Tailored news: InfoBeat enables you to select user profiles that highlight finance, news, weather, sports, entertainment, or snow. To subscribe, just go to the Web site and enroll. You can also get updates sent to you by e-mail.

Newspaper Association of America

www.newspaperlinks.com

All online papers: The Newspaper Association of America offers comprehensive indexes to the online versions of major newspapers, searchable and browsable.

Online Brokerages

Electronic brokerages often charge the lowest commissions available. Each commercial enterprise charges a different fee and has its own unique features. Online brokerages are generally as accurate as their full-service counterparts.

Charles Schwab Canada

www.schwabcanada.com

A long-time discount house goes online: Schwab's Internet trading site offers downloadable trading software, online trading, account information, quotes, and more.

E*Trade Canada

www.etrade.ca

Fast and competent pioneer: E*Trade charges a flat rate for online trades. It's one of the original online brokerages.

Sun Life Securities

www.sunsecurities.com

Insurance companies too: Sun Life has a user-friendly online trading Web site.

TD Canada Trust

www.tdcanadatrust.com

Banks are in the online brokerage game too: TD Canada Trust offers a range of online brokerage services through its TD Waterhouse arm.

TD Waterhouse

www.tdwaterhouse.ca

Do-it-yourself, online: TD Waterhouse features equity and option trading, retirement accounts, and trading on margin.

Other Stuff to Check Out

www.actiondirect.com
www.sdbi.com
www.cibc.com
www.invesnet.com
www.hsbcinvestdirect.com
www.quick-reilly.com
www.datek.com

Online Calculators and Charts

If you have a hard time with the math of personal finance, the Internet can help you. The Net provides many online financial calculators that can do all the math you require. It can also pull up stock price/volume charts that show the numbers over time, and even compare the results to those of other companies or indexes.

Altamira Resource Center Net Worth Calculator

www.altamira.com/icat/toolbox/netcalc.html

What you're worth, dollar-wise: The Altamira Resource Center suggests that one of the primary financial goals in life is to increase net worth. Therefore, this site provides an online calculator that's designed to help you determine your current net worth.

FinanCenter

www.financenter.com

Calculators by the bagful: The FinanCenter provides many online calculators that can help you with your personal finances and investment decision-making. Just click an icon (budget, investments, retirement, and so on) and select the appropriate calculator.

Other Stuff to Check Out

www.clearstation.com
www.wavechart.com
www.equis.com
www.tradingcharts.com

Portfolio Management: Online Tools

Many online portfolio management programs exist that can monitor your investments, track their performance, and send you end-of-the-day messages to notify you of major changes. This section lists just a few examples.

Thomson Investors Network

www.thomsoninvest.net

Tracking, by e-mail and on the Web: Thomson Investors Network provides free and fee-based services. Subscribers and registered guests can use the Web site's portfolio tracking services (which include end-of-the-day quotes sent to your e-mailbox).

Yahoo!

http://edit.my.yahoo.com/config

Do you Yahoo?: Yahoo! has a personalized portfolio program. To create portfolios, just enter a portfolio name and then add the ticker symbols of your investments, separated by commas.

Other Stuff to Check Out

www.moneynet.com
www.financenter.com
www.smartmoney.com/si/tools/oneasset
http://my.excite.com
www.quicken.ca

Push Technology

In the past, you had to laboriously search the Internet for that one vital piece of missing investment information. Now you can use push technology to bring that needed information directly to your desktop computer.

BackWeb

www.backweb.com

Intelligent screen savers: BackWeb flashes the news you select across your screen when you're not using your computer. BackWeb has a total of 50 channels to select from, and is free and downloadable.

Marimba

www.marimba.com

Use Java technology: Marimba can distribute software updates and corporate information directly to your computer. When Marimba detects new or updated information that you're interested in, it retrieves the data and saves it on your hard disk. You can view it at your leisure. The program is free and downloadable.

Quote Servers

The Internet provides many quote servers that provide real-time and delayed stock, mutual fund, bond, option, and treasury security prices. These servers are the bread and butter of any investment Web site. Here are a few examples of online quote services and their features.

Historical Stock Data for S&P 500 Stocks

http://kumo.swcp.com/stocks/

For hard-core analysts: Here, you can download files containing historical information for the stocks that make up the S&P 500 stock index (as well as those that were part of it in the past). The files can be used with analysis software.

Interquote

www.interquote.com

Real-time quotes: Interquote provides real-time, continuously updated quotes with the help of a special Windows program.

PC Quote

www.pcquote.com

Quotes, now: PC Quote offers many free services and five levels of fee-based service. Free services include ticker symbol look-up, current stock prices, portfolio tracker, company profiles, and Zacks Investment Research broker recommendations.

Quote.Com

www.quote.com

Not just current quotes: Quote.com provides a basic as well as a value-added service. This Web site provides both Canadian and U.S. quotes. This is noteworthy because there are not very many U.S.-based Web sites that can give you quotes for stocks listed on all Canadian exchanges. Quote.com provides a layered level of packages, ranging from free to as much as $130 per month. The free service lets you get delayed quotes and hour-to-hour charts. The free service also lets you build your own tailored financial page. You can track nine types of information, including your portfolio, news about a company, and ratings on new U.S. issues. Their fee-based service is essentially a "you get what you pay for" service. This includes real-time data, options information, and the ability to day trade with ease.

Other Stuff to Check Out

> www.canada-stockwatch.com
> http://quote.pathfinder.com/money/quote/qc
> http://finance.yahoo.com
> www.ragingbull.com
> www.stockhouse.ca
> www.411stocks.com
> www.spcomstock.com
> www.bullsession.com
> www.freerealtime.com
> www.money.net
> http://quotes.quicken.com
> www.cnnfn.com
> www.stocksmart.com
> www.thomsoninvest.net

Retirement Planning

Can you retire early? Check out the guidance that the Internet offers, and maybe you can say goodbye to your day job earlier than you think.

Deloitte & Touche Canada
www.deloitte.ca

Tax law, translated: Deloitte & Touche provides help interpreting the tax lingo of the Canada Customs and Revenue Agency. This site has archived summaries of new tax laws and provides Registered Retirement Savings Plan (RRSP) tips. Following each tax-law change, this site offers suggested action steps that you may want to consider.

RetireWeb
www.retireweb.com

Retirement 101: Developed by an actuary, this site attempts to answer your questions about retirement issues — on both the number crunching and qualitative side of things. RetireWeb grasps the concept that you not only have to plan for your future retirement, but you also have to manage retirement issues if you're already retired. The site is geared to Canadians at all stages of adult life.

Retirement Planning: Calculators

Need to do a few calculations for your retirement planning? These Web sites can do the math for you.

AGF
www.agf.com

Planning calculators and worksheets: AGF's online retirement planning calculators can assist you in determining the savings needed to retire with "X" dollars, and more. You can experiment with different savings amounts so that you can see the effect these amounts will have on your retirement lifestyle.

Fidelity Investments

http://personal.fidelity.com/toolbox

Retirement calculators, among others: Click the toolbox icon and go to a page with lots of links to online calculators. One of these calculators is for retirement planning. Use the calculator to determine the value of your nest egg at retirement, estimated savings surplus or shortfall, and estimated additional annual savings needed.

Other Stuff to Check Out

www.tdcanadatrust.com
www.altamira.com
www.clarica.com

Stock Screens: Online

Stock screens can help you whittle down your list of investment candidates. Your creative searches can reveal stocks that have just the characteristics you're looking for.

Multex Investor's NetScreen

www.multexinvestor.com

 $

Do your own sifting: Multex Investor's NetScreen feature allows you to screen for stocks using any combination of categories and variables. The database is updated weekly.

MSN Investor

http://investor.msn.com

Loads of data: MSN Investor has a stock screen called Investment Finder that searches 8,000 companies to find securities that meet your specific criteria. The program uses dozens of variable combinations. You'll have better luck with this site (surprise, surprise) when you use the latest version of Microsoft Internet Explorer.

ResearchMag

www.researchmag.com

Applied research: The stock screen has 12 basic variables that screen more than 9,000 stocks. To use the advanced stock screen, you must be a subscriber. The subscription cost is based on the number of reports you use per year.

Other Stuff to Check Out

www.fortuneinvestor.com
www.marketplayer.com
www.dogsofthedow.com
www.insidertrader.com
www.zacksadvisor.com
www.equitytrader.com
www.great-picks.com
www.netcurrentasset.com

Stock Screens: Prebuilt

Online prebuilt stock screens can assist you in finding the stocks that are worthy of your additional analysis. (Remember, the best prebuilt screen is the one that screens for the things that *you* believe are important.)

D-24 Tax Preparation and Online Assistance

Market Player

www.marketplayer.com

Power tools: Market Player provides a relatively advanced stock-screening engine. Instructions about how to use the engine are easy to understand, but you should allow some time for figuring out the program. Market Player has many prebuilt screens that you may find useful. You can also play stock-picking games here.

The Motley Fool

www.fool.com

The original stock chat site: Motley Fool offers a weekly discussion of its stock screens. Motley Fool provides screen results that pick out companies that missed or beat analysts' consensus estimates by 9 percent or more. Stocks are listed alphabetically as well as by descending percentages.

Tax Preparation and Online Assistance

If you're struggling with your taxes, the Internet can help you to get the right tax forms and rules, get tax planning advice, and complete and file your tax return.

Canada Customs and Revenue Agency

www.ccra-adrc.gc.ca

Help with tax administration: This site's Web pages are filled with administrative information: guides, publications, technical papers, brochures, and forms related to just about every Canadian tax issue

around. If you run a business from home, you can access the most current payroll deduction formulas. You can also access Web pages that deal with trusts, your general rights and obligations as a taxpayer, and more. Also, if you're missing a certain tax form and don't want to hear the CCRA's busy signal — or worse, wait in line at one of their offices to get the form — then pay their site a visit. You can download tax forms online with ease.

INTERtax

www.foxall.com

$

Another way to file taxes: INTERtax, from Foxall Income Tax Services, allows you to e-mail your basic tax information through online forms. Foxall compiles and processes your personal tax information and e-mails duly completed forms to you. No software is required. All you do after that is print out copies and send them to the CCRA. The cost of their service is about $20 for a basic tax return.

KPMG

www.kpmg.ca

Straight from the experts: An accounting firm's Web site is probably a good resource for online tax advice. At KPMG, you can access archived articles that can help you save taxes and resolve some tax issues. KPMG's site has information about RRSPs, general tax tips, home business advice, and more.

Other Stuff to Check Out

www.eycan.com
www.deloitte.ca
www.pwcglobal.com/ca
www.intuit.com/canada/quicktax
www.cantax.com

Part IV
Trading and Tracking Online

The 5th Wave   By Rich Tennant

Wanda had the feeling that her husband's new portfolio management program was about to become interactive.

In this part . . .

You figure out how to trade stocks with an online broker. Study what to look for in an online brokerage. Find out what most Canadian online brokers are charging and what services they provide. Know the caveats of day trading. Let the Internet show you how you can avoid online fraud.

Chapter 15

Brokers and Online Trading

• •

In This Chapter

▶ Checking out online brokerages

▶ Finding the type of brokerage that meets your needs

▶ Opening your electronic brokerage account

▶ Increasing your profits by choosing the right trading techniques

▶ Understanding day trading

• •

Several factors have come together to drive an explosion in self-managed investing. The Internet has enabled individual investors to get the kind of information that was once the domain of investment professionals. Baby boomers are paying off their mortgages and are now investing heavily for retirement, while younger generations are more aware than ever about the importance of investing. Last but not least, the recent volatility in equity markets has driven home the importance of being an active investor and knowing when to move investment capital into cash, bonds, or other defensive issues.

In this chapter, we show you how to save money on trades, gain unlimited control over your investments, and enter trades from your computer 24 hours a day, 7 days a week. You just need to get the hang of a few online trading basics and recognize the risks that any investor faces.

This chapter describes three types of brokers: full-service, discount, and deep-discount. Each type of broker offers a different range of services. Internet deep-discount brokers are generally the least expensive, but they offer bare-bones services. Not all brokers are alike. Occasionally, an inexpensive broker costs you more money. For example, if you require real-time stock quotes and subscribe to an online service, you'll pay about $30 per month. If you select a broker that has a commission rate that's higher than some others but includes free online securities quotes, you may save money. This chapter also describes some of the added features of brokerages. This information can help you decide which brokerage is right for you.

Online trading accounts require you to complete an application form and to open and maintain a minimum cash account balance. While your electronic brokerage is processing your account (which takes two to three weeks), you can turn to this chapter to find out where you can practise trading online and how to increase your profits by using the right trading strategies. This chapter concludes with a section that explains the dangers of day trading for beginning investors. Discover what gear day traders need, how much cash they require, what they look for, and how they trade.

Finding a Brokerage Firm

For each trade, you pay commissions ranging from a few dollars to hundreds of dollars per order. Commissions can take a large bite out of your profits. For example, assume that you invest $2,000 and pay a $200 commission to a full-service broker. Your securities must increase to $2,200 for you to break even. One way to avoid high commissions is to use a discount broker or a deep-discount broker.

A full-service broker researches many companies and securities, helps you organize your goals, and gives you advice on specific securities that match your financial goals. These firms often use a *commission schedule* to calculate the fees that they charge their customers. For example, if you purchase 10 shares of a stock that costs $47 per share, the commission may be $47 (a commission rate of 10 percent). If you purchase two shares of a stock that costs $75 per share, the commission may be $35 (a commission rate of about 23 percent).

All brokers administer your securities. They maintain a paper trail and computer backup of your transactions, and calculate your gains (or losses). (But most do not provide you with performance reports that would measure things like percentage gains or losses.) As well, they track how many shares you own, when the stock splits, and when dividends are paid.

As a general rule, full-service brokers provide recommendations and inform you of initial public offerings (IPOs), insider trading, and legal concerns about your investments. For example, if you own stock in a firm that is a takeover target, a full-service broker notifies you and provides you with any relevant information regarding offers to buy your stock. When you want to buy or sell securities, the full-service broker decides what type of order to place and oversees its implementation.

In the past, discount brokers offered no advice and conducted no research. Today, many discount brokers, such as TD Waterhouse, E*Trade Canada, Charles Schwab Canada, and Quick & Reilly offer "full-service" advice, IPO information, and research to customers who want that type of service. Consumers have the option of seeking advice for special transactions or placing orders directly. The discount broker receives your touch-tone telephone order and relays it to the firm's floor broker, who in turn contacts the individual who executes your order. The discount broker then confirms that your order has been completed.

Deep-discount brokers are electronic brokerages in every sense of the word; contact with a human broker is rare and may cost you more money. Deep-discount brokerages often start as subdivisions of discount or full-service brokerages. They may offer lower prices by automatically accepting touch-tone telephone orders and Internet-based stock orders. A recent innovation to online trading is the addition of full-service online brokerages. These companies often provide discount pricing, 24-hour phone service, branch offices throughout the nation, and high-quality online research. For example, TD Waterhouse (`www.tdwaterhouse.ca`) excels at doing these sorts of things. Some of its services will be described later in this chapter.

Caveats about Using U.S. Online Brokers

A few years ago, if Canadians wished to open a trading account with a U.S. discount broker, doing so was not much of a problem. All they did was fill out a form, send over some cash, and start trading. But recent changes to Canadian securities regulations mean that Canadians who use U.S. discount brokers are breaking the law.

Because this law is difficult to enforce, many Canadians are tempted to ignore it to take advantage of lower trading commissions. We recommend that you not break the law. One key practical reason is that if you do proceed with a U.S. broker and later enter into a dispute, you have no legal remedy beyond what the firm is willing to do to assist you.

On the other hand, although clients of Canadian brokers can complain to the OSC (Ontario Securities Commission) or the Investment Dealers Association of Canada, to be fair, there is only so much that these types of Canadian organizations can do to help you. Like many government agencies, they are understaffed and not equipped to enforce law violations.

Finally, it is important to note that U.S. brokers cannot serve Canadian clients without first registering with a provincial securities commission, and without setting up a physical office in Canada. If you plan to sign up with a U.S. broker that accepts Canadian clients, first ask whether it is duly registered and whether it has a local office.

Checking Out Prospective Brokers

The Canadian Investor Protection Fund (CIPF) is overseen by the Canadian investment industry and provides coverage for Canadians making investments through its members. It insures brokerage accounts similar to the way the Canada Deposit Insurance Corporation (CDIC) insures bank accounts. The CIPF covers customers' losses of securities and cash balances, including mutual funds, for amounts up to $500,000. However, the amount of cash losses that you can claim as part of this limit may not exceed $60,000. Coverage applies only if a particular financial institution becomes insolvent. You aren't covered if the market corrects! (More on the CIPF in Chapter 17.)

You're wise to look into the background of a Canadian brokerage firm before investing, by checking with your provincial securities regulator. Using a search tool, type in "Ontario Securities Commission," "British Columbia Securities Commission," and so on. Most of these Web sites have phone directories. Someone there can tell you whether the broker you're considering is registered.

Getting Online Trading Services for Less

As we mention at the beginning of this chapter, no two brokerages are alike. Furthermore, individual brokerages may change their services and fees to keep pace with their competitors. To find the online broker that best meets your needs, you must investigate the prices, services, and features that various brokers offer.

Make certain that your brokerage doesn't charge you for services that are free elsewhere. For example, say that an online brokerage charges a flat fee of $25 for your trade. If the brokerage adds a postage and handling fee of $5 for your transaction, the actual cost is $30. That's 20 percent higher than you expected. Here are some other hidden fees:

- ✔ Higher fees for accepting odd-lot orders (less than 100 shares)
- ✔ Higher fees for certain types of orders (see "Increasing Profits with Simple Order Specification Techniques" later in this chapter)
- ✔ Fees for sending out certificates (some firms charge $50 per certificate)
- ✔ Fees to close your account
- ✔ Fees to withdraw funds from your trading account

Trading online at a discount

You can't measure broker service with a formula. You have to look at both financial and non-financial criteria.

Cost is one factor. Look at how much each broker charges in commission for different levels of trades. Assess the quality of online trade execution by talking to others who use a service you are considering. Are real-time quotes available? Is research material available? What is the overall ease of use of the service? Examine the availability of mutual funds. Does the broker provide online screening tools?

Product selection is another important factor. You want to be able to trade things like guaranteed investment certificates, gold and silver certificates, municipal bonds, futures, Canadian and foreign equities, and so on.

Response time has to be quick. Phone each firm to see how long it takes for the broker to respond. E-mail each broker under consideration with a few questions. Ask for an application to be sent by mail. Again, evaluate the response time.

All Internet brokers can handle any type of basic transaction with a minimum of human contact. Recently, deep-discount brokers have flourished on the Internet. This evolution has lowered the cost of doing business and fuelled a fierce price war. Now many reputable online brokerages can complete your trade for $25 or less. Table 15-1 lists several examples of deep-discount brokerages. The commission structure is in Canadian funds, unless otherwise indicated.

Table 15-1	You Can Trade Online at a Discount	
Brokerage Name	*Web Address*	*Commission Structure*
Ameritrade	www.ameritrade.com	$8 U.S. flat rate + $5 U.S. extra for limit orders
Bank of Montreal Investorline	www.bmoinvestorline.com	$25*
Charles Schwab Canada	www.schwabcanada.com	$33*
CIBC Investor's Edge	www.cibc.com	$28*
E*Trade Canada	www.etrade.ca	$27*

(continued)

Table 15-1 *(continued)*

Brokerage Name	Web Address	Commission Structure
Merrill Lynch HSBC	www.mlhsbc.ca	$29*
National Bank InvesNET	www.invesnet.com	$25*
Quick & Reilly	www.quickandreilly.com	$15 U.S. flat rate
Royal Bank Action Direct	www.actiondirect.com	$29*
Scotia Discount Brokerage	www.sdbi.com	$20*
Sun Life Securities	www.sunsecurities.com	$29*
SureTrade.com	www.suretrade.com	$8 U.S. flat rate
TD Waterhouse	www.tdwaterhouse.ca	$29*

Note **(*):** Based on a market order to buy 500 shares of a Canadian stock quoted at $17. However, commission rates vary widely depending on the quantity of shares, the price of shares, and the exchange (Canadian or foreign) the share is traded on. Most are flat fees but up to a maximum amount, after which fees may rise (similar to U.S. brokers shown above). These figures are for comparative purposes only.

The U.S. brokerage commission structures listed in Table 15-1 use notations such as the following: 0 on at least 1,000 @ $5 U.S.; $15 U.S. on market orders less than 1,000 @ $5 U.S.; $20 U.S. on limit orders for Nasdaq, less than 5,000; $20 U.S. + $0.01 for limit orders over 5,000 shares. Here's what this notation means:

- ✔ The commission fee is $0 U.S. on a minimum order of 1,000 shares that are priced at $5 U.S. or more. (Total cost $0.)

- ✔ The commission fee is $15 U.S. on *market orders* (instructions for the broker to immediately buy or sell a security for the best available price) of 1,000 shares that are priced at $5 U.S. or more. (Total cost $15 U.S.)

- ✔ The commission fee is $20 U.S. on *limit orders* (trading orders that specify a certain price at which the broker is to execute the order) for the Nasdaq (an automated nationwide communications network operated by the National Association of Securities Dealers that connects brokers and dealers in the over-the-counter market) of less than 5,000 shares. (Total cost $20 U.S.)

✔ The commission fee is $20 U.S. plus $0.01 (a penny) for limit orders of 5,000 shares or more. For example, if you want a limit order for 6,000 shares, the fee is $20 U.S. for 5,000 shares plus $10 U.S. for the quantity over 5,000 ($0.01 U.S. × 1,000), for a total cost of $30 U.S.

Finding online brokers with no or low initial account minimums

One of the things that many investors may find prohibitive about online trading is the initial minimum deposit required for opening a cash account. This means that the broker already has your money when you request a trade. Just like everything else on the Internet, though, this requirement is changing. Today, most of the brokerages listed in Table 15-1 do not ask for initial account minimum deposits. Check with the broker before signing up.

Checking Out Special Features

Commission structures range widely from firm to firm because some Internet brokers include special or added features. When deciding which broker is best for you, factor in some or all of the features that we list in this section. First, consider whether each broker offers the following in your cash account:

✔ Low minimum amount required to open an account

✔ Low monthly fees with minimum equity balance

✔ No additional charges for postage and handling

✔ A summary of cash balances

✔ A summary of order status

✔ A summary of your portfolio's value

✔ Confirmation of trades (via e-mail, phone, or Canada Post)

✔ A historical review of your trading activities

✔ No charges for RRSP account maintenance

✔ Consolidation of your money market, investments, chequing, and savings accounts

Second, consider whether each broker offers the following account features:

✔ Unlimited cheque-writing privileges

✔ Dividend collection and reinvestment

- Debit cards for ATM access
- Interest earned on cash balances
- Wire transfers accepted
- No RRSP account inactivity fees or surcharges

Third, find out which of the following types of investments the broker enables you to trade:

- Stocks (foreign or domestic)
- Options
- Canada Savings Bonds; provincial savings bonds
- Government of Canada and U.S. government treasury bills
- Bankers' acceptances
- Commercial paper
- Mortgage-backed securities
- Bonds (corporate or agency)
- Bonds (municipal)
- Treasury notes
- Zero coupon bonds
- Guaranteed investment certificates
- Precious metals
- Mutual funds
- Investment trusts

Finally, determine whether the brokerage offers the following analytical and research features:

- Real-time online quotes
- Reports on insider trading
- Economic forecasts
- Company profiles and breaking news
- Earnings forecasts
- End-of-the-day prices automatically sent to you

One feature that's of interest to frequent traders is real-time quotes. Some brokerage firms offer real-time quotes for free, other firms offer a limited number for free when you open an account or make a trade, and several firms charge $25 a month for nonprofessional, real-time quotes.

Another great feature, this one offered by E*Trade Canada (www.etrade.ca), is the E*Trade "60 Second Advantage." This program lets you trade TSE-listed stocks in 60 seconds or less — or the trade is free (subject to limitations). Under the 60 Second Advantage program, if E*Trade Canada doesn't execute your order in 60 seconds or less, they will waive the trading commission.

Some conditions apply to this offer. The order must be a market order for a TSE-listed equity security. Certain types of orders, such as mutual fund and option orders, are excluded. Your order must be placed between 9:45 a.m. and 3:45 p.m. EST (Eastern Standard Time) on regular TSE trading days. For the commission to be waived, execution time for your order must exceed 60 seconds (measured from the time the order is submitted to the E*Trade Canada Web server to the time of the confirmation of the initial fill of the order). This program is suitable for the fast-paced world of day traders, discussed later in this chapter.

How to Open Your Online Brokerage Account

Internet brokerage firms are basically cash-and-carry enterprises. They all require investors to open an account before trading — a process that takes from two to three weeks to complete. Minimum account balances are becoming a rarity these days, but a few online brokerages still require that the book value of cash and securities that you own at any given time exceeds a minimum amount. Since most Canadian brokerages do not require minimum account balances, you can open an account with only a nominal deposit. However, there are only so many shares of Nortel that you can buy economically with $300 in your account!

When you place an order, your Internet broker withdraws money from your cash account to cover your trade. If you sell stock or receive a dividend, the Internet broker adds money to your cash account. If you develop a good history, your Internet broker may allow you to place trades without funds in your cash account if you settle within three days. All Internet brokers require that you complete an application form (which you can download online by following the downloading instructions given at the Web site) that includes your name, address, social insurance number, work history, and a personal cheque, certified cheque, or money order for the minimum amount (if any) needed to open an account. Some brokers accept wire transfers or securities of equal value. Canadian and U.S. law requires all brokerages to have your signature on file. Figure 15-1, on the next page, shows the online application form for E*Trade Canada (www.etrade.ca).

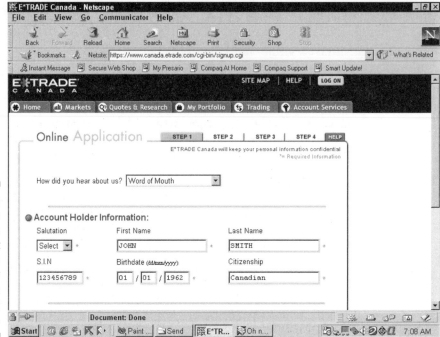

Figure 15-1:
E*Trade
Canada
makes it
easy to
apply for
an online
trading
account.

To speed up the process, you can complete application forms online or fax them to the Internet broker. You must then follow up by sending the completed, written, and signed forms via Canada Post within a preset (usually two-week) time frame, or the account is cancelled. The Internet broker then verifies all the information on the form and opens your account. Investors receive a personal identification number (PIN) by mail. After you receive your PIN, you're ready to begin trading.

Some of the major Canadian online brokers include the following:

- **Bank of Montreal Investorline** (www.bmoinvestorline.com)
- **Charles Schwab Canada** (www.schwabcanada.com)
- **CIBC Investor's Edge** (www.cibc.com)
- **E*Trade Canada** (www.etrade.ca)
- **Merrill Lynch HSBC** (www.mlhsbc.ca)
- **National Bank InvesNET** (www.invesnet.com)
- **Royal Bank Action Direct** (www.actiondirect.com)
- **Scotia Discount Brokerage** (www.sdbi.com)
- **Sun Life Securities** (www.sunsecurities.com)
- **TD Waterhouse** (www.tdwaterhouse.ca)

Increasing Profits with Simple Order Specification Techniques

In the past, brokers recommended the order specifications for your stock transactions and confirmed that your transaction was completed. Order specifications define how your request is completed. One type of order specification is called a *day order*. Day orders are good only on the day you place the order. Specifying security execution orders was one of the expert services that brokers used to justify their fees.

Another type of order is the *Good Till Cancelled* (GTC) order. The investor decides when the order expires but is uncertain about the order being executed. If no one in the market takes the order within the specified time (anywhere from several hours to several decades), the order is cancelled. In other words, the order lasts until the customer cancels the order. For example, an investor wants to buy a certain company's shares, but not until the shares are a few dollars cheaper. The investor specifies a GTC order and determines when the order will expire. If the company's shares reach the predetermined limit (today, tomorrow, next year, or next decade), the order is filled.

Figure 15-2 shows the home page for TD Waterhouse (`www.tdwaterhouse.ca`), a popular full-function brokerage service. Trading online puts you in charge.

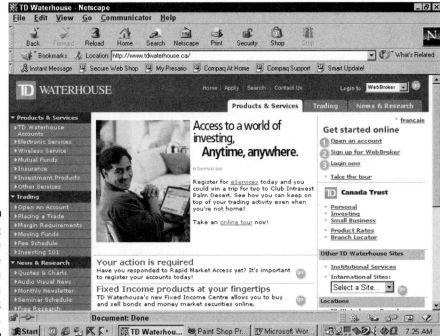

Figure 15-2: TD Waterhouse lets you start trading at the click of a mouse.

As you look over your online order form, you'll notice different ways of specifying how the order should be executed. In the past, a full-service broker decided which approach was best. With online trading, you select the method you feel is best. Many online brokerages (for example, Charles Schwab & Co., Inc., at `www.schwab.com`, and CSFBdirect, at `www.csfbdirect.com`) have handy demos that can assist you in practising trading online.

E*Trade Canada's E*Combat (`www.etrade.ca/combat`) is an investment simulation game where you can invest in stocks in a virtual environment and become better prepared for the real thing. Prizes are awarded to the best performers! The four most popular ways to specify your stock order are as follows:

- **Limit orders:** Any order in which the buyer or seller specifies the top price he or she is willing to pay. For sell orders, the *limit* specified is the minimum price at which the investor is willing to sell. For buy orders, the limit is the maximum price that the investor is willing to pay.

- **Market orders:** Any order (buy or sell) to be executed immediately at the *best effort* price available. In other words, the investor wants to buy or sell a stated number of shares at the best price at the time the order is placed.

- **Stop:** After a security reaches the price set by the investor, the order becomes active. When the order is activated, that investor is guaranteed that the order will be executed. However, the investor isn't guaranteed the execution price.

- **Stop-limit orders:** After a security reaches the investor's predetermined price, the order is activated. The order can be executed only at the set price or better, so the order may not be completed.

You may want to use a *limit order* when purchasing or selling *odd lots* (less than 100 shares of any one stock). This type of order can increase your profits. Odd lots rarely get the best price because they must be bundled with other orders.

The Dangers of Day Trading

Lower trading commissions, improved information technology, and changes in government regulations make day trading possible. After the crash of October 1987, Nasdaq mandated the development and implementation of the Small Order Execution System (SOES). SOES is designed to protect small investors and is a forced execution system for orders up to 1,000 shares. The Nasdaq computer automatically executes the SOES order without any hesitation, which allows day traders (sometimes called SOES bandits) to immediately enter and exit transactions when they see changes in a stock.

Day trading involves buying and selling stocks for your own account. Traders buy and then sell stocks within minutes, profiting by market changes in an effort to profit $0.125, $0.25, or $0.50 per share. It's not unusual for a day trader to make over 175 trades per day. Day traders primarily use the Nasdaq because it's twice as volatile as the NYSE and three times as volatile as the TSE (meaning that traders have two to three times as many opportunities to make short-term profits).

This section on day trading is for educational purposes. Day trading is not recommended for beginner investors. Keep the following in mind as you read this section: (1) studies indicate that day trading has proven to be riskier and less successful than long-term trading; (2) day trading is for experienced investors who can afford to lose all of their investment; (3) day trading at your home or office often requires an initial investment of $5,000 or more for communications equipment, financial information services, and special software. During the last bear market, many day traders lost their proverbial shirts! That's because most day traders still trade hoping for a rise in share price, and do not try to short-sell a stock.

Day trading appears to be a simple process. For example, say that you purchase 1,000 shares of Dell at $46 per share for a total cost of $46,000 from a market maker. A *market maker* represents an institution (such as TD Waterhouse, Merrill Lynch HSBC, and so on) that wants to *make a market* in a particular Nasdaq stock. You then sell the same shares for $46,250. The stock would then be worth $46.25 per share. The difference is $250 less a commission of $50 ($25 to buy and $25 to sell) for a gain of $200. In this example, the profit is $200.

What is day trading?

One of the first steps in understanding day trading is to define the players. What day traders really focus on are the activities of market makers. The market maker is a specialist on an exchange or dealer in the over-the-counter market who buys and sells stocks, creating an inventory for temporary holding. Market makers provide liquidity by buying and selling at any time. But they aren't under any obligation to buy or sell at a price other than the published bid and ask prices.

The downside of being a market maker is that you are obligated to purchase stocks when no one wants them. The upside of being a market maker is that you get to pocket the profits of a spread. A *spread* is the difference between a bid and ask price. For example, a stock with a bid and ask price of 15/15¼ has a spread of ¼. The bid price is $15 and the sell price is $15.25. If the market maker sells 1,000 shares at $15.25, the market maker profits by $250.

Spreads are often just a few cents for each stock. However, these pennies quickly become dollars because of high trading volume. Last year, Nasdaq market makers earned $2 billion from spreads. Day traders have sliced into some of these profits. Recent reports indicate that market maker spreads are down by 30 percent.

The existence of several kinds of spreads has caused some confusion. The following list defines some spreads.

- ✔ **Dealer spread:** The quote of the individual market maker. A market maker never earns the entire spread. The market maker needs to be competitive on either the bid or offer side of the market. The dealer is unlikely to be at the best price (the highest price if selling and the lowest price if buying) on both sides of the market at the same time.

- ✔ **Inside spread:** The highest bid and lowest offer being quoted among all of the market makers competing in a stock. Because the quote is a combined quote, it's narrower than an individual dealer quote.

- ✔ **Actual spreads paid:** The narrowest measure of a spread, because it's based on actual trade prices. The actual spreads paid is calculated by measuring actual trade prices against the inside quote at the time of the trade.

Spotting the signals for day trading

Day traders can spot many buy-and-sell signals. Stocks that are good day trading candidates have "a surprise in earnings" (earnings reports that are above or below analysts' expectations) or are the subjects of buyout rumours. Day trading software programs connected to electronic communication networks (ECNs) can help day traders target changes in inside quotes or track stock candidates. Some programs create real-time line graphs for trend analysis and comparison to other stocks or indexes (such as the Dow Jones Industrial Average). Charts are created for different time periods (intraday, daily, or yearly). Day traders use these charts to look for buy, sell, and exit signals.

Day trading is the ultimate in market timing. Not only does the day trader have to pick the "right time" to enter the market, but also the "right time" to exit — decisions that must be made 150 to 200 times in one day.

Having What It Takes to Be a Day Trader

Besides a stoic nature, day traders need large amounts of cash (which they can afford to lose) and lots of time. Experienced day traders suggest that it takes about $100,000 to get into the business of day trading. Such an amount serves as risk capital that the day trader must be able to afford to lose. Day trading is a full-time job that requires the day trader to be ready to act each weekday from 9:30 a.m. to 4:00 p.m. Day traders have to be good winners and good losers. Inexperienced traders can easily lose between $3,000 and $4,000 per day (or even more). Some traders leverage their capital by trading on margin, which means that the brokerage establishes credit for its customer/trader. For example, $100,000 of capital can support $200,000 of security purchases. This credit arrangement is called *leveraging* and provides an opportunity to gain — or lose — big money.

Many brokerage and investment advisers offer one- to five-day seminars on day trading that can cost anywhere from $900 to $2,500. Check out the Canadian Society of Technical Analysts (CSTA) Web site (www.csta.org), shown in Figure 15-3, to learn more about day trading and related seminars and events.

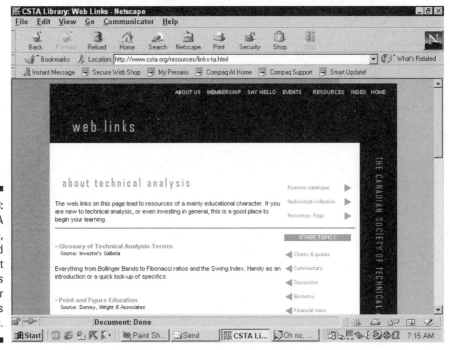

Figure 15-3:
At the CSTA Web site, you can find out about seminars and other happenings for traders.

Gearing Up for Day Trading

Currently, about 5,000 professional day traders are up and running in the U.S. and Canada. Most day traders work from when the market opens until it closes (from 9:30 a.m. to 4:00 p.m.). The new CDNX exchange, based in Vancouver, closes at 4:30 p.m. Traders can average 175 trades per day and rarely hold stocks overnight or longer. Day traders can trade from home, office, or specialized brokerage trading floors.

The day trading puzzle contains many pieces. Some individuals like remote trading at home or in an office. Some want to telephone their SOES brokers with their limit orders. New software enables day traders to do one-stop shopping by combining a decision-support system with real-time live quotes and an electronic clearing network. The type of hardware and software you select depends upon your personal day trading system. And as the industry introduces new products and services or as regulations change, you may need to revise and update your approach.

Getting ready (to day trade)

The following lists the hardware needed to get started in day trading. Installation of the Internet connection may take time, so plan ahead:

- **Computer workstations:** Day trading requires a computer with a Pentium processor or equivalent (minimum of 300 MHz/64MB of RAM). The modem should have a baud rate of at least 56 Kbps.

- **Direct Internet connection:** Day traders often need a permanent Internet address for high-level data exchanges and fast connectivity (in this business, seconds mean dollars). Cable and telephone companies provide this service for between $40 and $300 per month.

Making the investment decision

Nasdaq Level II real-time quotes show, for each stock listed, how many shares each market maker wants to buy or sell; the quotes also indicate changes as orders are processed and filled. This assists day traders in forecasting when a stock will move and in what direction. Nasdaq Level II real-time quotes show the *depth of the market.* Day traders need Nasdaq Level II real-time quotes to be effective.

Some organizations, like eSignal (www.esignal.com), offer many trading tools for the active and mobile trader, such as wireless real-time quotes and news. Most U.S. brokerages — and some Canadian brokerages — offer free quotes to customers too.

Day traders can use stock monitoring decision-support software with a computer, modem, and data connection. These computer programs are often connected to day trader brokerages (which are different from Web-based online brokerages and are found mostly in the U.S.) to provide access to ECNs. (Connectivity can cost up to $2,500 and is usually paid by the brokerage.) Day traders who aren't electronically connected must telephone their limit orders to their SOES brokers. The SOES broker then enters the order into an ECN.

In addition to the hardware day traders need, they may also use day trading decision-support software. Some day trading decision-support software includes real-time quotes to improve investment judgments. The following software helps day traders make investment decisions:

- **PC Quote** (`www.pcquote.on.ca`): This software provider has teamed up with Charles Schwab Canada to provide you with one of the fastest information feeds available — 1024k via T1 access. PC Quote 6.0 is a complete suite of trading tools, including quotes, charts, analytics, Nasdaq Level II Market Maker quotes, Market by Price on the TSE, and CDNX. You can download data into Excel. Check out their Web site for pricing packages.

- **Power E*Trade Canada** (`www.etrade.ca/power`): Power E*Trade starts you off with 25 free trades. This service is designed for day traders, who are provided with powerful tools, key information, and priority customer service. Enhanced services include streaming real-time quotes, a streamlined trading desk, free Nasdaq Level II Quotes, and preferred access to offerings in E*Trade's IPO Centre (see Figure 15-4).

- **Power Trader** (`www.powertrader.com`): Power Trader Software is a Vancouver-based company that specializes in products that manage and analyze securities information. The software allows for direct U.S. and Canadian market access for fast executions and confirmations and for real-time quotes in Canadian and U.S. markets. You also get point-and-click order submissions to the Island ECN. Multiple screens, charting, graphs, and analysis are available. Monthly service fee information can be obtained at their Web site (see Figure 15-5).

- **KillerKey** (`www.castleonline.com`): This U.S.-based software provider offers data packages with charts and news, and automated account information. Free Nasdaq Live Level I quotes. Nasdaq Live Level II quotes are $150 U.S. per month and waived upon the execution of 100 orders or more per month. Castle Online brokerage commission rates for SOES, Select Net, and Island ECN trades cost $20 U.S. for up to 10,000 shares. There is an additional $1 U.S. charge for partial executions, and $0.15 U.S. for ECNs other than Island. A minimum of $5,000 U.S. is required to open an account. KillerKey and Java Trader software is free and downloadable.

Figure 15-4:
Power
E*Trade has
lots of tools
and services
for Canadian
day traders.

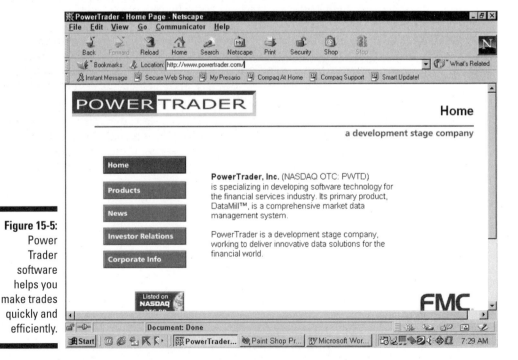

Figure 15-5:
Power
Trader
software
helps you
make trades
quickly and
efficiently.

✓ **Nasdaq Level II** (`www.elitetrader.com`): Nasdaq Level II includes time-of-sales, real-time news, real-time quotes with customizable layouts, intraday and historical charts, options analytics, and more. The firm provides a two-week trial for $25 U.S. plus exchange fees of $50 U.S. per month for all trades. (Check out the free online tutorial.)

In 1971, Nasdaq became a true electronic market allowing traders to buy and sell through a network of computers. Market makers could display their best bids and execute offers and orders instantaneously over Nasdaq Level II workstations.

This electronic trading system uses Nasdaq's Select Net, which is an anonymous electronic communication system between the trader and the market maker to buy or sell stock. The system allows the trader to specify the desired stock and have the order placed directly to watching market makers.

Beginning in 1997, day traders (customers) could display bids and offers through an alternative system called an _Electronic Communications Network (ECN)_. ECNs are supported and staffed by the brokers of day traders.

ECNs allow traders to display their orders to other customers. Trader orders can be matched and traded with other customer orders before they reach the Nasdaq Level II system. This gives individual traders a competitive edge and a higher probability of a successful trade. If a match isn't made through an ECN, the order enters the SOES system and it instantaneously appears on the Nasdaq Level II system. Good examples of ECNs are the following:

✓ **Attain** (`www.attain.com`): Now a SEC-approved electronic clearing network, the Attain ECN is a proprietary system used by subscribers (brokers/dealers) to post bids and offers for their clients (day traders) in a certain over-the-counter security. Attain ECN is an alternative to the traditional market-making price quote system on Nasdaq.

✓ **Island** (`www.isld.com`): An alternative trading system that matches buy orders with sell offers in Nasdaq stocks. If Island can't find a match, it allows orders to receive direct representation in the marketplace as Nasdaq Level II quotes. Prices vary, so check the Web site for details. Island is itself now a public company.

Chapter 16

Tracking and Monitoring Your Portfolio

• •

• •

*P*ortfolio management may sound like a lot of work, but knowing how much you own in cash, stocks, bonds, and other investments is important. Without portfolio management, how can you determine whether your returns are meeting your financial requirements? Are you missing opportunities by not buying or selling securities at the right time?

This chapter covers three Internet-based approaches to managing your portfolio. The first approach is using Web-based portfolio tracking tools that can be customized and that often provide e-mail alerts on price changes and end-of-the-day quotes. The second approach to portfolio management is using PC-based tools that are free, offer free trials, or cost only a few dollars. These programs use your Internet connection to automatically update portfolio quotes. (If you already have Microsoft Money 2001 Deluxe or Quicken 2001 Deluxe, we show you how to use the portfolio feature and update price quotes in just a few clicks.) The third portfolio management approach is using your online broker's free portfolio management program. Your broker knows all about your buying and selling habits. He can automatically update your portfolio, and you don't have to wait until the end of the month to determine the value of your investment decisions. We conclude this chapter by discussing the difficulties of measuring portfolio performance and risk.

Why Manage Your Investments?

You may select the best investments, but if you don't have a way to track your gains and losses, you can lose time and money. Good record keeping is invaluable for calculating your taxes, preparing for retirement, doing estate planning, and taking advantage of opportunities to increase your personal wealth.

Sources on the Internet can assist you in keeping careful records of every stock, mutual fund, bond, and money-market security you own. Setup time can be as little as ten minutes. You can update and monitor your portfolio once a week or once a month. Your investments can be in one portfolio (for example, your retirement fund) or many (say, your retirement fund, an emergency fund, and your children's education fund). You can also track investments that you wish you owned or that you're considering for investment.

The Internet offers programs that automatically update your portfolio with daily price changes and re-tally your portfolio's value. Many portfolio management programs can perform the following tasks:

- ✔ Help you determine how much you own in cash, stocks, and bonds
- ✔ Show you how these investments line up with your asset allocation targets
- ✔ Indicate what returns (capital gains or losses) you're receiving
- ✔ Compare returns to your financial requirements
- ✔ Integrate your investment account information with your banking, tax, and budgeting information needs
- ✔ Alert you that securities are at the prices at which you want to buy (or sell)

How often do you need to monitor your investments? Monitoring once every two or three days is a little aggressive, once a week is average, and once a month is enough for some investments. You should monitor equities more often than you would bonds. While it's important to monitor your investments, it's even more important to have a life!

Tracking the Right Information

If you own more than one investment, you probably want to compare the performance of your investments. The more investments you have, the harder this task is. Many novice investors find it difficult to determine whether they're making money, losing money, or just breaking even. To determine how your investments are performing, you need to look at the following data:

✔ **52-week high and low:** The highest and lowest selling price in the previous 365 days

✔ **Dividend:** The annual per-share amount of cash payments made to shareholders of the corporations

✔ **Dividend yield percentage:** The total amount of the dividend paid in the past 12 months divided by the closing price (the price at which the last trade of the day was made)

✔ **Growth rate:** How much the dividend increases from one fiscal year to the next

✔ **P/E ratio:** The ratio of the closing price to the past 12 months' earnings per share

✔ **Volume:** The number of shares traded in one day

✔ **High, low, close:** Highest selling price of the day, lowest selling price of the day, and closing selling price

✔ **Net change:** The difference between the day's closing price and the previous day's closing price

You can compare these amounts and ratios to the performance of your other investments, the firm's previous performance, the industry, and the market indexes (for example, the TSE 300).

If you own several securities, how do you keep track of all this data? Once again, the Internet provides an answer. The Internet has hundreds of Web- and PC-based portfolio management programs that are just waiting to assist you. Some of them are free, others are fee-based, and some are automatically set up for you by your online broker.

Your Portfolio Management Options

The Internet offers three types of portfolio management programs:

✔ **Web-based portfolio management programs:** Investor supersites, Internet portals, and large news organizations generally sponsor online portfolio management programs. These programs usually don't require any software downloading, and they constantly update your portfolio. Limitations of these programs are that they don't offer many features, such as customized graphs or charts, fundamental analysis, or tax-planning tools.

✔ **PC-based portfolio management programs:** These programs present portfolio tracking as a feature of a personal software program like Quicken 2001 Deluxe (www.quicken2001.com) or Microsoft Money 2001 Deluxe (www.microsoft.com/money). PC-based portfolio tracking can be done with a software program downloaded from the Internet. These programs can be very inexpensive or free. PC-based portfolio tracking programs usually have more choices and functions than Web-based portfolio management programs. Most programs have utilities to help you with tax planning and budgeting, since your investment activities can affect the taxes you pay and the budgets you make. Many handle both Canadian and U.S. stocks. Limitations of this approach are that you must download the proprietary software and you may have to *import* (transfer data from one source to another) stock quotes.

✔ **Portfolio management with your online broker:** Portfolio management with your online broker is automatic. Your online broker knows what you traded, so the brokerage can automatically update your portfolio. The advantages of using your broker's portfolio management system are that you don't have to manually add transactions and that your portfolio always reflects the current value of your investments.

In the following sections, we offer examples that detail the features and functions of these three types of portfolio management programs.

Using Web-Based Portfolio Management Programs

Many Web sites provide online portfolio tracking services. Some of these services are free and others are fee-based. The aim of Web-based portfolio management tools is to help you make better investment decisions and thus increase your capital gains. Each Web-based portfolio management program offers something different. In the following sections, we describe just a few examples.

Don't let the fascination of having your portfolio online tempt you into overtrading (buying or selling) your investments.

Investor compilation, or *supersites,* provide, among other things, free and fee-based portfolio tracking. Investor supersites often require your free registration and are supported by advertisers. Other compilation sites provide different levels of services, costing from nothing up to $8 or $10 per month. The benefits of tracking your portfolio at one of these sites is access to the vast repositories of investor information, data, and tools that they offer. That is, if you want to research or analyze something in connection with your portfolio, you don't have to go to several investor sites to get the job done, which can save you time and money if you need to make a quick investment decision. In the following sections, we profile several of these investor compilation sites.

CANOE Money

CANOE Money (www.canoe.ca/MyMoney), shown in Figure 16-1, provides a personal portfolio of your Canadian stock holdings. It updates your portfolio at the end of each day. The portfolio management program requires your free registration. CANOE's portfolio tracker handles as many portfolios as you want. CANOE also has a portfolio tracker for Canadian mutual funds. To access the portfolio management Web page from the CANOE Money home page, click My Portfolio.

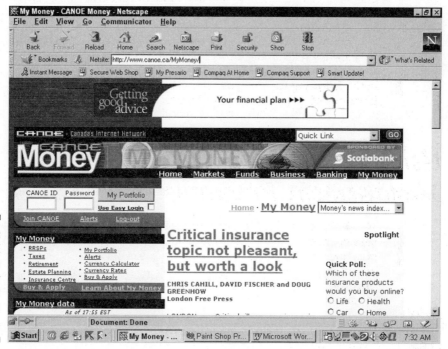

Figure 16-1:
CANOE Money can track your stock and mutual fund positions.

CANOE also provides e-mail alerts to notify you of changes in your portfolio. CANOE Money sends an e-mail to you containing your Portfolio Snapshot. The Snapshot has the latest figures for each of your portfolio holdings, plus updates on major stock indices and the Canadian dollar exchange rate. You choose when you receive your Snapshots: on a daily, weekly, or monthly basis.

From the Canoe Money homepage, you can also find links to information about RRSPs, taxes, retirement planning, insurance, and currency rates.

CBS MarketWatch

CBS MarketWatch (portfolio.marketwatch.com), a free program, allows you to create an unlimited number of portfolios and track up to 200 ticker symbols for options, mutual funds, and stocks on all the major exchanges in each portfolio. You can also customize price and value views to display the data. Prices are automatically updated every five minutes. Other features include news and quotes (the data you need are linked directly to your portfolio); custom views (tailor your portfolio to show data the way you want to see them); allocation analysis by security, symbol, and asset class; financials (including detailed balance sheets for all the securities in your portfolio); and charting.

Globe Portfolio

Globe Portfolio (www.globeportfolio.com), shown in Figure 16-2, is no longer just about mutual funds. Globe Portfolio now offers a new stock portfolio tracker (much like CANOE's) in addition to its comprehensive mutual fund tracking program. It tracks other investments as well. The service is free.

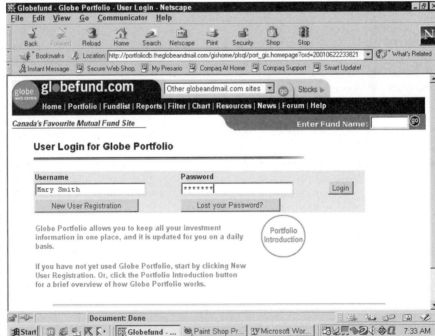

Figure 16-2:
Globe Portfolio calculates and compares the performance of your investments to market benchmarks.

If you want to track mutual funds, Globe Portfolio allows you to determine your daily gain or loss as compared to the previous day, beginning of the month, or beginning of the year. It calculates performance using a return on investment measurement called "internal rate of return," or IRR. IRR is useful when you want to compare the performance of your mutual funds to benchmark indexes like the TSE 300 or TSE 35. You can perform such a comparison on a fund-by-fund or total-portfolio basis. The portfolio tracking program takes into account investments and withdrawals made at various points in time. This ensures that your returns are not distorted.

For all types of securities, Globe Portfolio tells you how much money you made — or lost — on a given day. It tracks all your investments on one page, and lets you determine whether you are outperforming, for example, the TSE and Dow Jones indexes. Plus, the value of your U.S. holdings is automatically converted to Canadian loonies! Globe Portfolio provides new printer-friendly reports that are specially formatted to save paper and printer ink. Recent enhancements include automatically adding mutual fund distributions, stock dividends, and stock splits to your portfolio. Also, if you make regular contributions to your investment portfolio, you can set up a recurring transaction to instruct Globe Portfolio to automatically update your portfolio on the appropriate days.

National Post Online

Many large news organizations provide portfolio-tracking services that can make your portfolio tracking very convenient if you already use one or more of these news sources. The portfolio-tracking functions of online news organizations generally require the security's ticker symbol, quantity you purchased, purchase price, and date of purchase. In return, your portfolio tracker shows today's delayed market price, today's change, market value of your shares, the value of your investment, and your gain or loss.

The *National Post* Online edition (www.nationalpost.com), shown in Figure 16-3, is one such news service. The Your Portfolio feature allows you to create up to three custom portfolios for Canadian equities, and one portfolio for U.S. equities, each consisting of up to 100 stocks or mutual funds. Recent enhancements to this online tool include an application that converts the value of U.S. securities held in your portfolio to Canadian dollars, and a data field containing a running total of gains or losses. Portfolio holders can now sign up to receive e-mail notification of security prices and relevant news alerts. *National Post* Online has most of the bases covered, and it's free. If you feel uncomfortable about tracking your portfolio online, you can opt for a free password-protection option at this site.

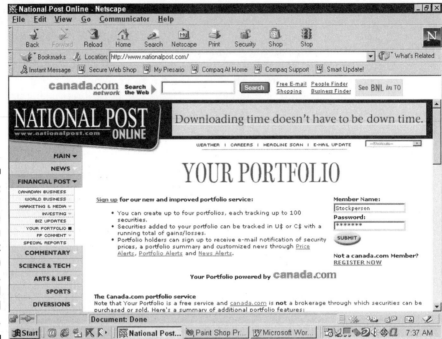

Figure 16-3:
*National
Post* Online
lets you
track a mix
of Canadian
and U.S.
stocks and
mutual
funds.

Quicken Power Portfolio

You can access Quicken.ca's Web-based Power Portfolio (www.quicken.ca) by clicking the Power Portfolio icon on Quicken.ca's home page. Registration is free of charge. Once you open an account, you can create a portfolio to track your investments, post messages to the Quicken.ca message boards, and subscribe to e-mail newsletters. This feature is nowhere near as powerful as the software version of Quicken, Quicken 2001 Deluxe, discussed later in this chapter. But it is free and is based on much of the same portfolio tracking technology.

Reuters Money Network

Moneynet (www.moneynet.com), a Reuters-sponsored investment supersite, features a free, easy-to-use Web-based portfolio management program called Portfolio Tracker. This program can create up to 30 customized portfolios for as many as 40 stocks, mutual funds, and options in each portfolio. The easy-to-read grid includes a security symbol, company name, price or NAV (net asset value) of a mutual fund, volume, high, low, and date/time stamp.

At the Reuters Moneynet home page, click Portfolio Tracker. To create a portfolio, click Add Securities, enter a portfolio name or multiple portfolio names, and then add investments and the number of shares (optional). After you build a portfolio, the program automatically monitors the market for you. Reuters Moneynet handles both Canadian stocks and mutual funds.

Stockpoint

Stockpoint Portfolio Management (`investor.stockpoint.com`), shown in Figure 16-4, provides a personal portfolio, stock news, and end-of-the-day e-mail portfolio updates. The portfolio management program requires your free registration. Stockpoint Portfolio Management allows you to download current share options in a Quicken software format and handles up to 50 U.S. and Canadian stocks, mutual funds, and stock indexes (so that you can compare the performance of your investment selections). To access the portfolio management Web page from the Stockpoint home page, click Portfolio.

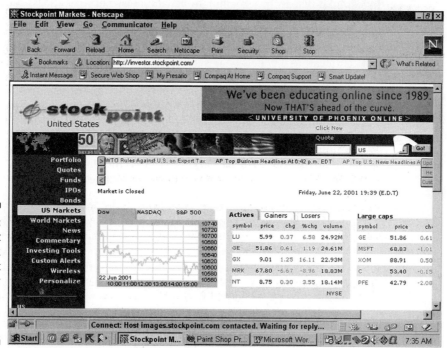

Figure 16-4: Stockpoint can track and export your Canadian and U.S. stocks.

This portfolio management program includes the last traded price, each day's price changes, the percentage of each day's price changes, and the current value of each holding. It calculates the capital gains and losses and the percentage of capital gains and losses from the initial purchase price that you entered when you set up the portfolio. The program provides information about volume and moving averages of several securities at once. You can click the Export button to download all the portfolio information to Quicken software for more analysis. Some limitations of Stockpoint's portfolio management program are that it doesn't provide any fundamental analysis or graphing and that you must add all stock splits manually.

Thomson Investors Network

Thomson Investors Network (www.thomsoninvest.net) has free and fee-based services. Registered guests have free use of the U.S. and Canadian portfolio-tracking services with end-of-the-day quotes sent to your e-mailbox and limited access to other site services. This site includes a wide variety of high-quality investment research, screening tools, and news services (S&P Comstock, First Call, Institutional Shareholder Services, and more).

Guests are allowed 25 portfolios containing 25 securities each. The My Portfolio feature displays values in fractions or decimals (for Canadian stocks), account history, and commissions. Micro-icons indicate charts, and alerts or breaking news about your investment are available. For example, click the News icon and the news page appears. Articles include company news, changes in credit ratings, and other pertinent information about your investment.

You can receive an evening FlashMail — an e-mailed snapshot of your portfolio at the end of the business day with news and other information affecting your portfolio — and can use LiveTicker as your real-time portfolio-monitoring tool.

You can create a customized view by following a few online instructions and adjusting for stock splits. Specifically, the portfolio management function includes the following:

- **The Today's Market view** shows the price for the last trade, change, high and low prices, volume, position, and value. Positions are either long or short. Long positions are the traditional buy-and-hold strategies. A short position is where the investor borrows stock from a broker and then sells it. When the stock price drops, the investor purchases the original number of shares and returns them to the broker. The difference from the sales price and the repurchase price is the investor's profit, less broker fees.

✔ **The fundamental view** shows last traded price (delayed 20 minutes), P/E ratio, EPS, dividend rate, market capitalization, 52-week highs and lows, price-to-book ratio, and value.

✔ **The graphical view** compares the best and worst performers in the portfolio. If this view shows that a stock is dragging your returns to a lower-than-acceptable level over a period of time, you may want to consider selling.

✔ **The closed position view** indicates your tax liabilities, and this is helpful when tax season rolls around.

Membership is $20 U.S. per month or $200 U.S. per year for unlimited access, which includes a *live ticker* that you can detach and use on your computer's desktop for real-time indexes and delayed stock quotes. Other membership services include FlashMail (reports sent directly to your e-mailbox), 25 mutual fund reports and 25 company reports per month, company and mutual fund screening tools, and intraday updates of market news and analyses. Thomson also includes municipal bond news, bulletin boards, chats with experts, and an education centre. Additional company reports cost $2.50, and additional mutual fund reports cost $1.50.

My Yahoo!

Portals are not to be outdone in the portfolio tracking business! Portals are colossal Web sites that are designed to be the Internet user's first window onto the Web — the first page that comes up when the user accesses the Web. Often, portals can be personalized so that the user can get news, sports, current portfolio data, or interest rate information before moving on to other sites. Yahoo (www.yahoo.com), Lycos (www.lycos.com), and Excite (www.excite.com) are examples of portals.

Figure 16-5 shows the My Yahoo! personalized portfolio program (my.yahoo.com). (Other portals have similar features.) To use the free portfolio, you need to set up an account with My Yahoo! Click the Log In link that appears on the Portfolio line and then click Create an Account. Click the Edit link that appears and enter a portfolio name. Add the ticker symbols of your Canadian or U.S. investments, separated by commas where indicated. You can also enter indexes like the S&P 500 or TSE 300 for comparison purposes. You can use the same ticker symbol to record separate purchases. Enter or edit the number of shares or purchase prices by clicking the Enter More Info button at the bottom of the page.

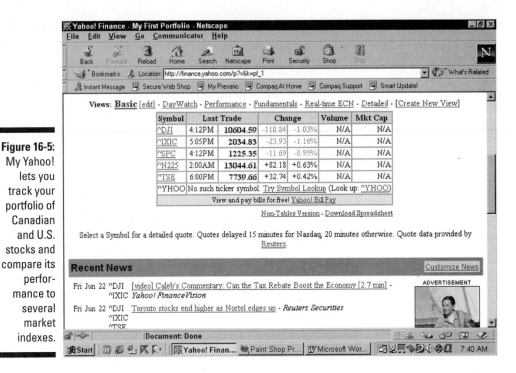

Figure 16-5:
My Yahoo!
lets you
track your
portfolio of
Canadian
and U.S.
stocks and
compare its
perfor-
mance to
several
market
indexes.

Quotes are delayed by 15 minutes for Nasdaq and 20 minutes for other exchanges. Portfolio management information includes company ticker symbol, price at the last trade, amount of price change at last trade, trading volume, number of shares held, the total value of the issue, dollar and percentage of change between the purchase price and the current value, amount paid per share, and dollar capital gain or loss and percentage of capital gain or loss.

The program provides charts, news, research, regulatory filings data, and related information. Recent headlines that link to news stories about your portfolio investments appear at the bottom of the page. You can get your information by signing in on any computer (remember to use the sign-out feature to make certain that others can't pry).

You can view your portfolio in a floating window, which lets you track your portfolio even when you leave My Yahoo! Just click the stacked pages icon in the top right-hand corner of the portfolio module. If you get tired of seeing your portfolio, click the X sign to close the floating window.

Zacks Investment Research

Zacks Investment Research (www.zacks.com) is a sophisticated investment research organization that provides free and fee-based services, including portfolio trackers. Portfolios set up at Zacks can include up to 20 Canadian or U.S. stocks in a single portfolio. (Also, you can purchase portfolios that go to separate e-mail addresses.) To begin your portfolio, just click Portfolio and give your e-mail address. On the next screen that appears, enter the ticker symbol and the number of shares you own or wish to own. (As a free service, Zacks provides portfolio alerts that are sent to your e-mailbox.) Portfolio alerts include daily closing prices, changes in prices, and trading volume. Portfolio information also includes Zacks Investment Research scores of your securities (using their own ranking system), analysts' earnings per share estimates, and buy/hold/sell recommendations, in addition to reported earnings per share surprises, news, EPS report dates, and declared dividends.

You can use daily alerts for monitoring stocks on your Watchlist. You can have e-mail alerts sent to you daily or weekly. When you begin your free subscription, Zacks includes a 30-day free trial of news and analysts' reports on the portfolio. The basic subscription gives you up to 35 ticker symbols per report for $19.95 U.S. per year. Extended subscriptions provide you with up to 100 ticker symbols per report for $29.95 U.S. per year. Plus subscriptions get you up to 200 ticker symbols per report for $59.95 U.S. per year.

Using PC-based Portfolio Management Software

If you want more analysis, including graphs of your investments' performance, tax data, and price and volume alerts, you may want to consider a PC-based portfolio manager (a software program that operates on your PC). For example, you can select Microsoft Money 2001 Deluxe or Quicken 2001 Deluxe (which you may already use for your online banking), shareware, or free Internet programs. In the following sections, we describe a few examples of PC-based portfolio management programs.

Personal finance programs

Personal finance software programs often offer much more value than what you pay for. These programs let you access online banking, organize your personal finances, understand what you have and what you owe, and organize your financial accounts for the beloved Canada Customs and Revenue Agency. Also, these programs track and analyze your portfolio's performance. In most personal-finance software programs, your portfolio's gains and losses are automatically used for your net worth calculations. With many of these programs, if you are connected to the Internet you can automatically update securities prices. Two popular personal finance software programs are Microsoft Money 2001 Deluxe and Quicken 2001 Deluxe.

Microsoft Money 2001 Deluxe

Microsoft Money 2001 Deluxe (www.microsoft.com/money) is a personal-finance software program that can help you stay organized by tracking activities in your savings and chequing accounts, and it can do your banking and bill-paying online. You can also manage your investments by downloading quotes and brokerage statements from the Internet. You can plan your retirement and more. This program costs $65 U.S. (or $99 Canadian) and includes a free six-month subscription to *MS Investor* (investor.msn.com).

Microsoft Money 2001 Deluxe's portfolio management function allows investors to view performance, holdings, quotes, fundamentals, positions, and the asset allocation of the portfolio. You can track employee stock options and create a Watchlist of investment candidates. Portfolio information is linked via your hard drive to MSN Investor (investor.msn.com). However, to access MSN Investor you must pay an additional $9.95 U.S. per month.

Here's how to automatically update the price of a security in your portfolio:

1. **Open the portfolio window that holds the security whose price you want to update.**

2. **Click the Update Price button. The Update Price dialogue box opens.**

   The program automatically updates all the securities that you checked in the drop-down box and selects the investments whose prices you want to update.

3. **Click the Up Call button. If this is the first time you have used the program, provide your Internet Service Provider's required user ID and password.**

   The program automatically updates securities prices.

Quicken 2001 Deluxe

Quicken 2001 Deluxe (www.quicken2001.com) is a personal-finance software program that can assist you with your home and small business finances, and help you prepare for retirement and educational costs. The Quicken 2001 Deluxe portfolio's table-style format is easy to read and can be organized into customized views. It also tracks tricky financial transactions like stock splits and corporate takeovers. You can download up to five years of stock quotes for trend analysis and record keeping. Quicken can also help you calculate your capital gains taxes (not an easy task with today's tax laws).

Quicken 2001 Deluxe has a feature called Online Investment Tracking. This feature connects individuals to financial institutions for online banking, online bill paying, and online investment tracking through the Open Financial

Exchange Server. As before, you can download broker statements, download stock and mutual fund prices, get investment research and news, and track your overall portfolio value. Recent enhancements allow you to optimize your RRSP, optimize your asset allocation, and customize investment alerts. Investments can also be tracked in multiple currencies.

Intuit's online Investment Tracking (www.intuit.com/ofs/invest_tracking. html) allows participating brokerages to download current account statements directly to individuals, which allows investors to stay up to date by seeing recent transactions, holdings, and balances. (Intuit recently bought Quicken.) In other words, investors don't have to wait until the end of the month to see exactly what they own. The Quicken 2001 Deluxe program costs $60 U.S. (or $80 Canadian).

Here's how to automatically update securities:

1. **Choose Features→Investment→Portfolio View.**

2. **Pull down the Update Prices menu and select Get Online Quotes and News.**

   This page provides the required Internet information (if this is the first time you are using the program). The program assumes that you want to update all the quotes of your securities. If you want to update only a few quotes, click those quotes to check them and make certain that the securities you don't want to update are not checked (check marks would appear next to the security name).

3. **Click Get News For The Last, and enter the number of days you want to know about to download any headlines, if you want the latest news on your investment.**

4. **Click Update Now.**

Portfolio management programs

Several hundred portfolio management programs are available for your investment tracking. The programs vary in price from free to around $500. Many of the freeware and shareware portfolio management programs include an amazing number of features but are somewhat cumbersome to work with. Some brokers give free portfolio management programs to customers who open an account. Financial data providers frequently give free portfolio management programs with a subscription to their services. Other portfolio management programs are components of larger investment analysis applications. To discover what works for you, try some of the free demonstrations or trials that vendors offer. They require no obligation, and after sampling several programs you can get a good idea of which features you need. Following, we list a few examples of PC-based portfolio management programs:

BB Stock Tool (www.falkor.com) tracks, charts, and analyzes stocks. The program includes charting, technical analysis, portfolio management, market timing, buy/sell signals, profit testing, customized high/low alerts, automatic stock split detection and management, most active volume, and price movement summaries. You can access daily quotes with your modem and Internet access to automatically update your portfolio. Software developer Falkor Technologies Inc. provides an owner's manual and sample data. The BB Stock Tool uses Windows 95 or Windows NT 4.0. You can get a 30-day free trial, and the program costs $89 U.S. if you decide to keep it.

Fund Manager for Windows (downloadable at rocketdownload.com or www.zdnet.co.uk/software) is a top-rated portfolio management program for stocks and mutual funds for the average individual investor. It takes a short time to get the hang of it, but samples help shorten the learning curve. Fund Manager provides many easy-to-read graphs, charts, and reports that are printable. You can update prices by clicking Internet. Fund Manager imports from Prodigy, MSN, Quicken, and other sources. Retrieve the latest quotes from AOL Canada or many international Internet sites. Fund Manager tracks your investment performance quickly and easily. The program uses Windows 95. It's free to try, $34 U.S. to own, and $5 U.S. to upgrade.

WinStock Pro (download.cnet.com or www.zdnet.com/downloads) is a stock market tracking and portfolio management program using your Internet connection. You can set up several portfolios that use the Internet to update prices. The program converts foreign currencies and features a ticker toolbar and printed reports. You can import or export to Quicken. The program includes e-mail, automatic dial-up, paging, audible alarms, and flexible reporting. WinStock Pro runs on Windows 95 up to the most recent Windows version, and is free to try. It's $30 U.S. if you decide to keep it.

Using Online Brokerage-based Portfolio Tracking

Usually, you must update Web-based portfolio management programs when you buy or sell securities, pay a commission, or receive a dividend or stock split. This is time-consuming and it's possible you could make an error. Such inconveniences can be especially troublesome for active traders. The portfolio management function of your online brokerage eliminates this problem. Following are several electronic brokerages that provide portfolio management programs:

Charles Schwab Canada (`www.schwabcanada.com`) provides customers with a portfolio management feature. The portfolio shows the ticker symbol of the security, the quantity of shares owned, the name of the security, and the current market value. For company news or charts of the security's performance, just click the appropriate links. Charles Schwab Canada also provides an asset allocation toolkit that shows the current allocation of assets for your trading account. The asset allocation model, which shows conservative, moderately conservative, moderate, moderately aggressive, and aggressive asset allocations, is used for comparative purposes.

E-Bond (`www.ebond.ca`) lets you track the value of your bond holdings, but only if you hold them in an E-Bond account. This independent Canadian bond brokerage firm allows you to access your account 24 hours a day.

TD Waterhouse (`www.tdwaterhouse.ca`), shown in Figure 16-6, has a Portfolio Tracker that can be used to monitor a portfolio (containing up to 10 stocks from any major North American exchange) to analyze returns and percentage gains and losses. You can also track up to five portfolios in real time. Each portfolio can contain a combination of up to 10 stocks, options, mutual funds, and/or indexes. Their stock quote service is top-notch.

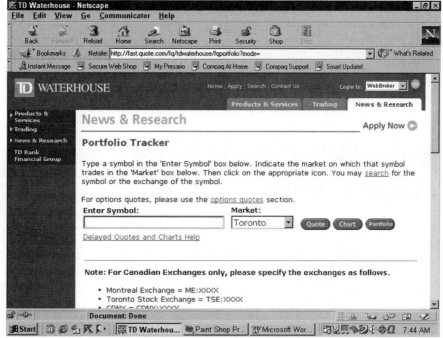

Figure 16-6:
TD Waterhouse clients can track their actual investment portfolios in real time.

E*Trade Canada (www.etrade.ca**)** provides a portfolio management tool with your free registration. To create your portfolio, simply enter the name and a description (for example, Registered Retirement Savings Plan). Enter the ticker symbol, type of security, quantity, cost, and the date the security was acquired. The portfolio management program displays your portfolio performance. You can manually edit, add, or split investments into multiple portfolios (the college account, the retirement account, and so on).

Royal Bank Action Direct (www.actiondirect.com**)** gives you the ability to create custom portfolio reports and produce graphs to monitor information such as capital gains, profits, losses, and rate of return. You can perform more detailed analyses by exporting data to other software programs. It also includes a diary function that allows you to set up price alerts and reminds you of maturing investments.

Keeping the Winners and Selling the Losers: Measuring Performance

Measuring portfolio performance is often difficult. For example, suppose that you invest $2,000 in a mutual fund that returns 15 percent in the first quarter of the year. In each of the next three quarters you invest $2,000, but the fund doesn't provide any returns during those months. Your return on the first $2,000 is 15 percent. Your return on $6,000 for nine months is zero. The fund reports an annual gain of 15 percent, not counting dividends and gains distributions. However, these percentages don't mean that you should measure performance on a short-term basis. Market prices vary and returns fluctuate for many reasons. What really counts is the true rate of return, which can't be measured from quarter to quarter.

Another problem in measuring portfolio performance is risk. Risk is defined as the variability of returns. In other words, the more the returns vary, the greater the risk. One of the disadvantages of using standard deviation (a measurement of the variability of historical returns around the average return) is that it doesn't take into consideration *good variability*. Good variability means that returns are exceeding expectations. This event increases the stock's volatility and standard deviation. The stock is now considered more risky because returns are higher than expected. What this shows is that standard deviation isn't always a good way to judge risk. In other words, standard deviation is just a measurement of volatility. Risk enters the picture only if volatility is *below* the investor's return target.

You can use many ways to measure the performance of your portfolio. One way to measure performance is to use benchmarks — that is, comparisons of the performance of your investments to top performances and indexes. For example:

✔ Divide your stocks into capitalization groups (small-cap, mid-cap, and large-cap) and rank each group by P/E ratio. Compare your investments to top-performing stocks in each capitalization group daily and weekly.

✔ Divide your fixed income (bonds and treasury securities) investments by quality rating and then rank each group by yield. Compare your investments to the top-performing bonds in each asset allocation class.

Doing this type of work by hand is time-consuming. Figure 16-7, on the following page, shows the download registration screen at Total Sum (www.totalsum.com). Total Sum develops financial analysis software programs that help investors account for risk factors when analyzing a company. One such product is called RiskView — a comprehensive program that provides risk analysis for individual investors and even institutional traders. RiskView lets you do the following:

✔ **Track historical equity performance:** Stock analysis to determine price-to-return ratio, risk/return over a period of time with risk/return graphs

✔ **Conduct risk/return analyses:** Risk/return analysis, historical risk, risk/return table, and return versus risk comparisons

✔ **Forecast volatilities:** Volatilities and correlation, introduction to correlation, limits of correlation, and sensitivity graphs

✔ **Perform personal portfolio performance analyses:** Portfolio returns analysis, portfolio/benchmark analysis and graphs, daily portfolio returns, and the distribution of daily returns

✔ **Conduct customized risk-management analyses:** Portfolio risk analysis, introduction to volatility, forecast of risk estimates, daily risk estimates, and risk-adjusted returns

Developed by Infinity Financial Technologies, RiskView is a free, single-source tool you can use to monitor total returns on individual equities or indexes and perform *what-if* risk scenarios using more than five years of daily historical data. The site provides daily updates to stocks and indexes and Value-at-Risk (VaR) analyses based on Infinity's EquityMetrics, a full set of return volatility and correlation estimates. VaR information can be obtained at Gloria Mundi (www.gloriamundi.org/var/software.html). This site is a repository of reviews of software packages that calculate value at risk, and includes a review of RiskView.

RiskView's database includes the Dow Jones Global Indexes (DJGI) and its underlying stocks (which represent more than 80 percent of the total stock-market value in 29 countries), and provides over 3,000 indexes for tracking stocks in 29 countries, 9 geographic regions, 9 economic sectors, and 121 industry groups.

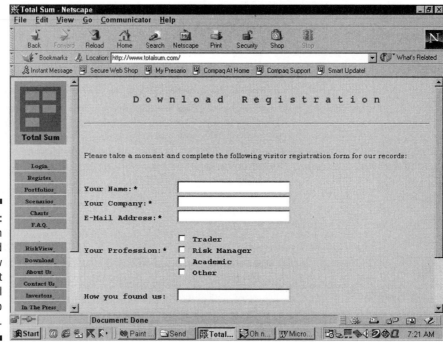

Figure 16-7:
You can download RiskView software at the Total Sum Web site.

Chapter 17

Avoiding Online Fraud

∙ ∙

In This Chapter

▶ Recognizing potential online investment scams

▶ Identifying pyramid schemes

▶ Requiring real financial disclosures

▶ Unmasking dishonest brokers by asking the right questions

▶ Knowing where to complain online if you receive an unscrupulous investment offer

▶ Evaluating the security of Internet transactions

∙ ∙

*D*on't become a victim on the Information Superhighway. Investment watchdogs estimate that a combined $12 billion a year is lost in investment fraud in Canada and the United States. That's about $1.25 million every hour.

In the past, swindlers used Canada Post mail and telemarketing boiler rooms to exploit unsuspecting investors. Fraud artists have now invaded cyberspace in a big way. Research from some organizations shows that in each of the past few years, individuals in Canada and the U.S. reported losses due to online investment scams ranging from $3,000 to as much as $700,000. Their research indicates that the average loss per investment victim is $20,000.

Investigating potential or real investment fraud is difficult. In Canada, the situation is much worse than in the U.S. since many of the Canadian watchdogs have no teeth. That's because they don't have either the right number of staff, or the right type of staff. Investigating fraud is also made difficult by the fact that the terms of an investment transaction may be hard to understand, and investment literature and salespeople may omit key facts. You can spot warning signs of potential scams, schemes, and deceptions, however. Doing so involves a little effort, homework, and investigating, but isn't that what investing is all about?

In this chapter, we introduce you to some Canadian securities watchdogs. We warn you about online investment information and offers that may be too good to be true. We provide guidelines for checking out brokers and investments, and tips for identifying a pyramid scheme. We show you how to read financial disclosures to get the facts, and we explain how to complain online. We also offer a few thoughts about the online security of your personal and financial information.

Canadian Watchdogs

To be frank, Canadian securities regulators have not done a good job of monitoring domestic corporate governance. Bre-X and YBM are just two of many examples that come to mind. Even certain Canadian banks have governance problems over how their staff execute stock trades. Foreign investors know this, and they discount the price of stocks traded on Canadian exchanges such as the TSE or the CDNX. If you have two identical companies — one in Canada and the other in the U.S. — the U.S. company's share price is almost certainly going to be higher. That market is indeed efficient in its due diligence!

Nevertheless, watchdogs do exist in Canada. In much the same way you'd still reach for a nearly broken umbrella when it's raining hard, don't hesitate to call a watchdog when in doubt of an investment. Regulation of Canadian financial intermediaries is split between federal and provincial governments. In general, banking is regulated federally, and securities-related matters are governed provincially. However, there are some twists:

- **Chartered banks** often own stakes in securities dealers. The federal government oversees these large enterprises.

- **Large brokerage firms** operate around the world, so the scope of their business is beyond provincial or federal jurisdiction.

- **Insurance companies** are regulated by both federal and provincial governments. The federal government oversees matters related to corporate solvency. The provincial government oversees consumer and contractual issues.

- **Credit unions** can look much like banks but they are under provincial jurisdiction.

- **Stock exchanges and other self-regulating organizations (SROs)** have rule-making powers of their own. The Investment Dealers Association of Canada is another SRO with powers to audit brokerages and enforce rules.

It's easy to see now why the first question a complainant may have is — who can help me? Because of all the changes in the Canadian financial-services landscape, the answer to that question can be quite blurry.

Complaints, Complaints

The Internet provides many ways to complain about online investor fraud. The Office of the Superintendent of Financial Institutions (www.osfi-bsif.gc.ca) is a federal regulator of banks, trust companies, federally registered pension plans, and certain lenders.

Each province has a securities commission, but the scope of their powers varies widely. The Ontario Securities Commission (www.osc.gov.on.ca) is the largest body, and it even provides services to smaller commissions in other provinces. The British Columbia Securities Commission (www.bcsc.bc.ca) is also fairly large. Provincial securities commissions govern their respective SROs and act as appeal bodies if an SRO's decision is contested. Stock exchanges are mainly responsible for regulating trading activity.

The Canadian Investor Protection Fund (www.cipf.ca) acts as an insurance fund to cover certain investor losses, subject to limits. Their services, and complaint processes, are described on their Web site.

The Investment Dealers Association of Canada audits brokerages and conducts inquiries if a broker has violated any regulations.

Here are other watchdogs of interest to investors in U.S. stocks:

- ✔ **Better Business Bureau** (www.bbb.org) has an online complaint process, and promises to follow up within two weeks of your complaint.

- ✔ **Securities and Exchange Commission** (www.sec.gov) has an excellent online complaint process.

- ✔ **National Fraud Information Center** (www.fraud.org) forwards your complaint to the appropriate organizations and includes it in their Internet fraud statistics (which may not help you get your money back but may be helpful to other online investors).

Don't Believe Everything You Read

Every investor dreams of being an early shareholder in a Microsoft or an Intel Corp. Dishonest brokers and stock promoters prey upon this greed and offer unsuspecting investors low-priced stocks in companies with new products or technologies. Often these companies are like a milk shake: frothy at first from all the hype, but when the froth settles, it just doesn't look as good as it first did.

A government watchdog has posted more than ten *teaser* Web sites on the Internet. These sites are registered with Internet search engines. Some of these teaser sites have even been singled out as *new* or *cool* sites of the week. Teaser sites purport to achieve fabulous success through some sort of business opportunity, multi-level marketing, or franchise. Users click through to the final page and discover a sober warning: "If you responded to an ad like this, you could get scammed." The warning pages provide advice on how to avoid fraudulent business opportunities and tell consumers where they can find out more about investing in franchises or business opportunities.

The Internet allows swindlers to reach millions of potential victims cheaply. To put things into perspective, more than 12 million Canadians and 100 million Americans have ready Internet access. In contrast, the popular *Canadian Living* magazine has fewer than 1 million paid subscribers. The Internet's reach is vast, and easy to extend.

Online fraud can be compared to phone or mail fraud. Many Internet bulletin boards and newsletters provide general stock-picking advice or mention other investment possibilities. However, some online resources tout specific stocks, moneymaking ventures, and service providers. Some investment chat rooms even have sales pitches that offer further details by private e-mail and toll-free telephone numbers.

Investment swindlers can work anywhere, from dingy telemarketing offices to expensive hotel suites to cyberspace. They may be friends of friends, and they may wear natty suits or hard hats. They may be so-called recognized experts or they may have no connection to the investment community. They all have one goal, however — to get your money into their pockets.

If an Offer Seems Too Good to Be True, It Usually Is

As the popularity of the Internet grows, millions of people are flocking to this new global village. Inevitably, criminals follow the crowd. They seek to deceive the innocent, the hopeful, the naïve, the poor, and the greedy.

Online investor fraud often starts when you receive an e-mail message with an appealing offer. Offers that seem too good to be true usually are. Here are a few of the warning signs to help you identify potential scams:

✔ **Exceptional profits:** Usually the profits are large enough to get your interest but not large enough to make you suspicious.

✔ **Low risk, high return:** All investments involve some risk. If a fraud artist advertises "no-risk," this should be an immediate red flag that something is wrong. Don't invest if you don't know exactly what the risks are. (Remember, fraud artists don't honour money-back guarantees.)

✔ **Urgency:** Fraud artists usually offer a reason why you must invest as quickly as possible. They may tell you that delays can mean the loss of big profits or that they're limiting the offer to just a few individuals. Fraud artists often play on new technological advances that create a brief market that tempts you to get into it right away. If you feel that the posting is valid, however, wait before you respond. Others won't be shy about posting their opinions.

✔ **High-pressure tactics:** Fraud artists often act like they're doing you a favour by letting you get in on the investment opportunity. Don't be afraid to ask questions publicly. Post a follow-up message. If the original post is valid, the person who sent it will be happy to post a public response.

Although you can find plenty of helpful investment-related postings online (after all, that's what this book is all about), the Internet, like other places, has its share of fraud artists. The British Columbia Securities Commission Web page, at www.bcsc.bc.ca, has lots of fraud-related articles. Some of these articles can help you stay alert to various schemes and scams. To access a list of fraud-related articles, you can use this Web site's search tool. Just enter the word *fraud* or a similar keyword to access these articles.

Check It Out Before You Put Your Money Down

The explosion of the Internet has created new opportunities and new dangers for investors. If you're an online investment victim, the chances of getting your money back are slim. Even in cases where Canadian government agencies recover money, the consumer usually gets back less than 10 cents on the dollar. The best defence is to thoroughly investigate an online investment *before* you put your money down.

Here are some suggestions about how to investigate that "once in a lifetime" offer:

✔ Check with your city or provincial consumer protection agency; it may have information about the firm you're considering investing in. As well, a consumer protection agency can direct you to other organizations that may have information about the investment.

✔ Contact regulators. Organizations that you can contact include the Canadian Investor Protection Fund, Office of the Superintendent of Financial Institutions, or a provincial securities commission.

✔ For the name, address, telephone number, and other contact information of your securities regulator, go to your provincial government home page. Provincial government home pages can be found at "www.gov." followed by Alberta **ab.ca** (i.e., www.gov.ab.ca); British Columbia **bc.ca;** Manitoba **mb.ca;** New Brunswick **nb.ca;** Newfoundland **nf.ca;** Nova Scotia **ns.ca;** Ontario **on.ca;** Prince Edward Island **pe.ca;** Saskatchewan **sk.ca;** and Quebec **www.gouv.qc.ca.**

✔ Write or telephone local or provincial police if you encounter an obvious scam. Fraud is illegal in every province in Canada. The Better Business Bureaus of Canada (see www.bbb.org/bureaus for a list of provincial bureaus) provide firm reliability reports that can be helpful to you. You need to read reliability reports before you purchase the firm's securities. Each report indicates how long the firm has been in business, how long the Better Business Bureau has known about the company, complaint patterns (if any), and whether any government agencies have taken enforcement actions in the past three years.

What Real Financial Disclosures Include

If you're considering investing in a new public company, you may want to download and print a copy of the investment offer. If the sales literature doesn't include a prospectus with audited financial statements, ask for one. If you're told that the company doesn't have a prospectus, request a written financial disclosure about the company. All in all, you should have the following information:

✔ **Offering circular:** Sales literature that presents the investment.

✔ **Prospectus:** A formal written statement that discloses the terms of a public offering of a security or a mutual fund. The prospectus is required to divulge both positive (opportunities) and negative information (risks) to investors about the proposed offering.

✔ **Annual report:** A written report that includes a statement by the chief executive officer and management's discussion and analysis of last year's performance and future prospects. Financial statements include a balance sheet, income statement, a statement of cash flows, and retained earnings.

✔ **Audited financial statements:** Financial statements audited by a public accounting firm.

Telltale Signs of Dishonest Brokers

Dishonest brokers often ask their victims a steady stream of questions designed to derail honest investors from asking the right questions. Dishonest brokers don't want curious customers. In contrast, honest brokers encourage you to ask questions, provide you with additional educational materials, and make certain that you understand the risks involved in your investment decision. And if you decide not to spend your money, they are untroubled by your investment decision.

The National Futures Association in the U.S. has collected a set of questions that are turn-offs for dishonest brokers (`www.pueblo.gsa.gov/cic_text/money/swindles/swindles.txt`). We've tailored those questions to meet the needs of online investors:

- **Where did you get my name?** The dishonest broker may say "a select list of investors," but your name was probably obtained from a Usenet newsgroup question you asked, a bulk e-mail response, or from a mailing subscription list. Individuals who have been duped in the past may be on the "select" list. They were conned before and probably can be conned again.

- **What risks are involved in the investment?** All investments except treasury securities have some default risk. (Treasury securities are considered to be *risk-free*. The Canadian government backs these securities just as it does the *legal tender* — the money — in your pocket. The Canadian government isn't likely to fail, so the securities — and your money — are risk-free.) Some investments have more risk than others. A salesperson who really has a sure thing won't be on the telephone talking with you.

- **Can you send me a written explanation of the investment, so I can consider it at my leisure?** This question provides two turn-offs to dishonest brokers. First, swindlers are reluctant to put in writing anything that may become evidence in a fraud trial. Second, swindlers are impatient; they want your money right now.

- **Would you explain your investment proposal to my lawyer, financial planner or investment adviser, or banker?** You know the investment is a scam if the salesperson says something like "Normally, I would be glad to, but . . ." or "Unfortunately, we don't have enough time," or "Can't you make your own decisions?"

- **Can you give me references and the names of your principal investors and officers?** Swindlers often change their names so you can't check their histories. Make certain that the reference list contains the names of well-known banks and reputable brokerage firms that you can easily contact. The Investor Protection Web site at `www.investorprotection.org` includes links to resources you can use to check out a broker or other financial professional.

✔ **Which exchanges are the securities traded on? Can I have copies of the prospectus, the risk-disclosure statement, or the audited financial statements?** For legitimate, registered investments, these documents are normal. A legitimate investment may or may not be traded on an exchange. However, fraudulent investments never are. Exchanges have extensive rules for competitive pricing and fair dealing. Those that don't follow the rules are subject to severe sanctions.

✔ **What regulatory agency is the investment subject to?** Tell the broker that you want to check the investment's good standing with its regulatory agency before going forward. The possibility of having to talk to a representative of a regulatory agency is a real turn-off to a swindler.

✔ **How long has your company been in business, and what is your track record? Can I meet another representative of your firm?** If the broker or the investment doesn't seem to have a past, the deal may be a scam. Many swindlers have been running scams for years and aren't anxious to talk about it.

✔ **When and where can I meet you to discuss this investment further?** Legitimate brokers can tell you how much of a return investors have enjoyed in the past. Even if you do get this information in writing, keep in mind that past performance doesn't indicate future performance. However, dishonest brokers often won't take the time to meet with you, and they don't want you in their place of business. Legitimate registered brokers are happy to sit down and discuss your financial goals.

✔ **Where will my money be? What type of accounting can I expect?** Often, funds for certain investments are required to stay in separate accounts, at all times. Find out which accounting firm does the firm's auditing and what type of external audits the firm is subject to. (Make certain that a well-known accounting firm is actually the auditor.)

✔ **How much of my money will go to management fees, commissions, and similar expenses?** Legitimate investments often have restrictions on the amount of management fees the firm can charge. Getting what the firm charges in writing is important. Compare the firm's fees to charges for similar investments.

✔ **How can I get my money if I want to liquidate my investment?** You may discover that your investment can't be sold or that selling your investment involves substantial costs. If you're unable to get a solid answer in writing, the investment may be a scam.

✔ **If a dispute arises, how will it be resolved?** No one wants to go to court and sue. The investment should be subject to a regulatory agency's guidelines so that disputes are resolved inexpensively through arbitration, mediation, or a reparation procedure.

Anatomy of a potential "pump and dump" scam

A few years ago, a newsgroup user called "dennismenis99" posted the same message to a dozen high-tech investment newsgroups touting AvTel Technologies (NASDAQ:AVCO), an unprofitable California network provider. The erroneous message stated that AvTel would launch high-speed Internet access to about 10,000 Santa Barbara customers using ADSL (asymmetric digital subscriber lines). The message stated that this new modem-based technology provided a dedicated Internet connection that was up to 50 times faster than conventional modems and worked over existing telephone lines. The result would be no more waiting or busy signals.

By noon, the Nasdaq-traded stock skyrocketed from $2 a share to $10 a share. By 3:30 the stock was selling at $31 a share. Around this time, short selling began. (Short sellers borrow shares of stock from a broker and sell it. When the stock price drops, they re-purchase the shares and return them to the broker. The difference in the original selling price and the new, low purchase price is the trader's profit less brokerage fees.)

At 5:40 p.m. Nasdaq halted trading. Over 3.6 million shares were traded in one day compared to an average of 3,300. AvTel's stock price increased in after-hours trading to $38 a share resulting in a 1,400-percent increase in one day. During this time, newsgroup messages were filled with misinformation about Nasdaq's actions, the company, and stock trading in general.

On November 13, 1998, AvTel admitted that, contrary to its earlier press release, it had no proprietary technology or products. AvTel also had no existing plans for national expansion. As a result of this information, when trading resumed on Monday, November 16, 1998, shares were trading at $3 per share. Over the next week, three law firms filed class action suits against the firm on behalf of the damaged November 12, 1998 AvTel share purchasers.

Your Bank Account Number, Security, and the Internet

Just as you protect your home and its contents, you must prevent online thieves from accessing your personal and financial assets via the Internet. Locked doors, alarm systems, and nosy neighbours can help safeguard your home. Precautions on the Internet are firewalls, passwords, and encryption of important information.

Dan Farmer, an individual investor and consultant, conducted an informal (and absolutely unscientific) survey of 2,200 Internet computing systems in December 1996. The survey results indicate that approximately 66 percent of Web sites have potential security vulnerabilities (see www.fish.com/survey/). For example, in December 1996 several catalogue companies installed an

Internet shopping program incorrectly. Consequently, hackers were able to get the credit card numbers of the catalogues' customers. Today, the use of effective Internet security software is more widespread, but security leaks still occur.

To illustrate further, many Canadian online banks use a distributed Internet security system. Security is on your computer during the transmission of information and also in the bank's own computer system. Online banks use several types of security systems simultaneously:

✔ **Encryption:** *Encryption* is a high-tech word for encoding and is used by people other than spies. It is used so that your banking information is gibberish to unauthorized individuals.

✔ **Passwords:** Personal passwords are necessary to access your account information.

✔ **Automatic sign-off protection:** Your session terminates when you sign off, so that no one can continue in your absence.

✔ **Browser security:** Your browser isn't allowed to save any of your bank information.

✔ **Monitoring:** The system constantly scans for unauthorized intrusions.

For Canadian banks, the Canada Deposit Insurance Corporation (CDIC) insures your money, but online securities firms don't have similar insurance for consumers. To date, electronic theft has been slight, but as more money flows over the Internet the need for insurance is certain to change.

Part V
The Part of Tens

The 5th Wave — By Rich Tennant

"No, that's not a pie chart. It's just a corn chip that got scanned into our portfolio summary."

In this part . . .

You get the scoop on some valuable online investing-related tips, conveniently organized in chapters made up of lists. Overcome common misconceptions about online investing. Know when to buy — and to sell — a stock. Check out some retirement-planning Web sites, and find out how the Internet can help you plan and prepare your taxes.

Chapter 18

Ten Common Misconceptions about Online Investing

To many Canadians, there is little that can be more intimidating than planning their investment strategy. But when they are asked to do this through the Internet, they are faced with an added layer of complexity. Complexity often breeds misunderstanding — and this often creates myths. In this chapter, we check out your possible fears and misconceptions, and try to dispel some of the common myths about the world of online investing.

An Army of Hackers Wants to Get into My Investment Account

It is amazing how willingly people give out their credit card numbers to total strangers. For example, if you use a credit card in a restaurant, do you really know how many people are handling it? Is the card being duplicated? What happens to the duplicate slips? Most Canadians don't even bat an eye at this issue. Yet, when your investment account information is encrypted and is transmitted online to or from the intended recipient, a state of worry sets in.

Since 1996, when online trading technology was introduced, there has been no rash of break-ins or illegal access activity resulting in lost investment funds. If there have been problems, they have not been publicized.

To dispel fears of illegal access, most banks and brokerage houses have gone all out to develop or purchase the very best in encryption and authorization software to prevent anyone other than you from accessing your account. They have gone all out because the foundation of their business is trust. They don't want that trust to be weakened. And it may take years for a hacker to break a code that encrypts your personal data!

To help prevent unauthorized access, make sure that your broker provides a password option. Use a password that is unique. That way, no one can access your portfolio without knowing your password. Also, seek out SSL encryption. This online protocol ensures portfolio and other sensitive personal data are never sent across the Internet unencrypted. Disconnect from the Internet when you are not online using it. If you use a cable-based service — where you cannot disconnect — get firewall software that will act as a smart gateway to your computer. In other words, anyone trying to get into your computer will have to get by a "virtual wall" of security precautions. You can install personal firewall software from eSafe (www.esafe.com) or McAfee (www.mcafee.com).

I Have No Privacy!

Even if you don't worry about the issue of illegal online access to your account, you may have fears about online privacy — the possibility that people may be able to obtain personal information about you. You can protect your online privacy in several ways. The most basic is to skimp on giving out personal information. Give out only information that is essential and reasonable. When you use investment Web sites, favour those that let you access information without asking you to sign your life away when you register. Try to make sure that the benefits you get from the Web site exceed the risk taken if you do give out personal information.

I Can't Trust Anything I Get on the Internet

No one has a monopoly on common sense. You need to use yours, especially when you visit an investment chat site. Chat sites can be full of hype that tries to herald in the next Qualcomm, Dell, or Microsoft. It can also contain messages of doom and gloom by "shorts" — traders who place an order to sell a stock they don't yet own, in the hope of covering that sale with a future purchase of actual stock at a lower price. Both types of hype are typically based on false or misleading information that has some potential to affect stock price.

Also be wary of the media and of brokerage houses. Business media occasionally "get it wrong," especially when they do not do enough due diligence on companies they report on. Media may also slant a story a certain way, without providing the total picture. They have only so much time to report on things, and often miss out on a chance to give a balanced picture. Brokerage houses sometimes underwrite new public offerings, and at the same time have their own analysts tout that stock as a strong buy. Be wary of this bias. Always ask yourself whether the brokerage house the analyst works for also underwrote the stock issue.

Can Online Broker Fees Really Be that Cheap?

Brokers fees appear to be a real bargain at first glance — and in many cases they really are — but be on the lookout for hidden charges. For example, many Web brokers offer a tiered fee structure where market orders may be $15, limit orders may be $20, and broker-aided trades cost $25. Also be on guard for hard-to-see mutual fund fees, account inactivity penalties, and real-time quotes charges. All of these prices should be fully disclosed on the online broker's Web site, but they are not always easy to find. They are the online equivalent to "fine print"! If you are not sure about the fees you may be asked to pay, call the brokerage's customer service representative.

On Busy Days, I Won't be Able to Access My Account

During the sudden October 1997 market correction, online investors jammed the telephone lines of brokerages and many could not log on or execute trades due to the volume. Since then, there have been more market corrections and heavy-volume days. Yet, fewer complaints have resulted. On the whole, online brokers responded to the challenge of high-volume trading days and system crashes by increasing the capacity and reliability of their hardware and software.

In late 1999 and early 2000, there was another big surge in trading volume. But rather than being based on fear, this recent surge was based on more people participating in online investing. Again, the brokerages responded — albeit not as fast as they could have — and hired and trained more staff. During these busy periods, some resourceful investors even opened multiple trading accounts with different brokers. That way, if one broker was too slow, an investor could try her luck with another broker! Today, with the recent Nasdaq bear market over, volumes have settled down, and the issue of system crashes is all but dead — for now.

Online brokers are constantly improving their computer systems with a view to eliminating future system backlogs and crashes. Many systems are now prepared to trade at four to five times the average daily volume.

Reaching a human customer service representative may still be a problem during heavier-volume days, however. Systems will still crash from time to time, creating access problems. Some online brokers do not offer 24-hour service, seven days a week. These issues will continue to exist. The key point to remember is that service is improving, not deteriorating. It's in the online broker's interest!

My Broker Gives Me Advice I Can't Get on the Internet

More and more online brokers are providing top-notch financial advice on a pay-as-you-go basis. They often provide portfolio management and stock-reporting services as well. TD Waterhouse (www.tdwaterhouse.ca) is an example of a value-added broker that provides research reports, and more, to its clients.

Timing the Market Maximizes Returns

Many investors successfully time the market — buying low and selling high. For investors, nothing beats the feeling of getting the investment decision right on both fronts!

But timing the market is hard for even a seasoned investor to do. The movement of a stock's price is based on so many interrelated economic, political, and other variables that even the most sophisticated computer in the world could not consistently predict market movements. There is much research that statistically concludes you cannot time the market effectively over the long term.

Does this mean that it does not matter what securities you pick and when you pick them? Even the most statistically inclined academics do not go that far. Active management still has its respected followers who argue that timing the market produces higher returns over the long term. At the start of the recent Nasdaq bear market, the prudent investor recognized the stock price bubble, and headed for the exits just as the hype about technology stocks was peaking. By the same token, the smart investor recognized some oversold technology stocks with great financial statements and prospects, and loaded up on them just as the headlines were screaming doom and gloom!

In the end, if you have a diversified portfolio, your decisions about when to buy and sell individual stocks, bonds, or mutual funds may not be as critical as you think.

The Internet Can Teach Me All I Need to Know about Online Investing

A basic understanding of investment fundamentals is critical if you wish to trade online effectively. Although the Internet can provide you with many useful investment primers, the information is often not well organized. That is why we discuss investment basics in Part I of this book. Even so, this information only skims the surface of the true body of investment knowledge.

The Internet is simply a tool to help you invest. Just because you own a tool like a chisel does not mean that you are ready to carve out a true work of art. You have to learn how to wield it properly first!

Online Investing Is Geared to Technology Stocks Only

Although it is true that many of the original online investors favoured "technology stock" trading — after all, they were the first to master the underlying technology — today's online investors trade stocks in every industry sector. As well, online investing is about more than just stocks; it's also about bonds, options, mutual funds, treasury bills, foreign securities, derivatives, and more.

I Need to Be a Techno Geek to Trade Online

Today's personal computers are of a "plug and play" variety. You can get your computer up and running in under an hour. The software needed to get you on the Internet is easy to install, and technical support is usually available through your Internet service provider if you need it. Finally, setting up an account with an online broker is easy, and most software is user-friendly.

Chapter 19

Ten Green Flags for Buying

In This Chapter

▶ Buying low so you can sell high

▶ Checking out earnings forecasts

▶ Watching for bargain stocks that are trading under book value

▶ Buying for value, not price

▶ Selecting a P/E ratio strategy that works for you

*R*ecent surveys show that over one-third of all Canadians have investments. Furthermore, if they have pensions, they're likely to have at least half their pension funds currently invested in the stock market. Despite all this popularity, equities (such as stocks) have a serious drawback: They don't offer the security of interest-bearing investments (money-market funds, Canada Savings Bonds, and guaranteed investment certificates).

Interest-bearing securities offer consistent returns. In contrast, stock price fluctuations just "happen." Every stock investor can count on market increases and decreases. We recently witnessed a slow but savage correction in the Nasdaq, which caused the value of some stocks to evaporate by as much as 98 percent! These fluctuations aren't always company-specific, but that doesn't offer much comfort. Over time, stock investments tend to reward patient investors with good, inflation-beating returns that are greater than those of any other type of investment. For many individuals, investing in equities is the only way that they can reach their financial goals.

Over the years, avid investors have developed many methods to help others decide which stocks to buy and when to purchase them. No hard-and-fast rules exist. The approach that's best is the one that works for you. The following sections offer a collection of investor wisdom that can assist you in maximizing your personal wealth.

Buy If the Stock Is at Its Lowest Price

This principle is more easily said than done. Excellent investment candidates are stocks that are selling at their lowest price in three to five years (assuming that the company's financial position hasn't deteriorated). Wait for the price to stop declining and the company to show some strength, however, before you put your money down.

You must condition yourself to work against the crowd. The time to sell your stock is whenever it's "hot," its prices are high, and everyone wants to own it. See Adviceforinvestors.com, at www.adviceforinvestors.com, or Zacks Investment Research, at www.zacks.com, for charts, quotes, and online company profiles. Of these two information sources, Adviceforinvestors.com has the more extensive coverage of Canadian companies.

Buy If a Stock Is Oversold

In 1998, a Nortel Networks executive made an inaccurate offhand comment to analysts attending a press conference held by the company. The next day, the seemingly negative comment was made public and the price of the company's stock plummeted. The miscommunication had little to do with the growth prospects of the company at that time.

Even today, despite rumours of its imminent death, Nortel's growth prospects remain strong because of its dominant market position and its efforts to contain costs.

Check Out the Earnings Forecast

People use *earnings forecasts* in fundamental analyses to determine the fair value of a stock. If this fair value is less than the stock's current price, the stock is overpriced. If the fair value is more than the current price, the stock may be underpriced and represent a bargain.

Financial software developers and most brokerages have analysts that develop earnings forecasts for companies. Prices for these reports vary from free to several hundred dollars. The Internet provides many sources for earnings forecast reports. The following are a few examples:

- ✔ **Canada Stockwatch** (www.canada-stockwatch.com) provides earnings forecasts for many Canadian companies for a fee.

- ✔ **Financial Web** (www.wallstreetguru.com) provides free earnings upgrade and downgrade information in addition to other related information. While this Web site focuses on U.S. equities, it does cover some of the larger Canadian companies.

Watch for Stocks that Are Trading Under Book Value

Book value per share is the company's net asset value — that is, assets minus liabilities divided by the number of outstanding shares. This amount appears in the company's annual report. See Yahoo! Finance at `finance.yahoo.com` (click Profile) and Zacks Company Reports (`www.zacks.com`). Companies that sell below their book value (if they don't have serious operating and other problems) can be good bargains.

Another indicator of a company's value is *book value less intangible assets*. However, intangible assets may not be assets at all, especially if their value evaporates. So this indicator paints a conservative picture of the value of a company. (An example of one such intangible asset is goodwill, which is the premium a company pays to acquire another company.)

Cash value is yet another indicator of a company's worth. Cash value simply indicates how much cash can be attributed to each share. The value of cash is fixed. That makes cash value per share the most straightforward and conservative measure of value.

Beware of Firms with High Long-Term Debt

Usually, the lower the debt-to-equity ratio, the safer the company. Beware of companies that borrow aggressively but never earn a high return on their new capital. They may not be able to pay off their debt! Compare the company you're researching to similar firms. Companies that have paid down their debt over the past two or three years, however, may be worth your serious consideration.

Get an industry report (go to the Industry Data section at the site) from Adviceforinvestors.com, at `www.adviceforinvestors.com`, and get an industry overview, the average debt ratio, and equity financing structure for the industry. Compare this average to the debt ratio of the firm you're researching. To discover which firms have low debt ratios, use the online stock screens described in Chapter 12.

Locate a rising company in a rising market. Small and mid-size companies are hungrier and more innovative than their older and bigger siblings. A company needs something new to create a startling increase in stock price, and these companies may have that something.

Successes in Canadian industry come from a major new product or service, new management, or an important change for the better in the conditions of a particular industry.

Select companies with entrepreneurial management — rather than caretakers who discourage innovation — that take risks and keep up with the times. Companies with managing executives who own a meaningful share of the outstanding stock are generally good investment candidates.

Bigger is not always better. If you're choosing between two stocks — one has 10 million shares outstanding and the other has 60 million — select the smaller company. All things being equal (that well-used economics expression), the smaller company is going to be a better performer.

To find out where the entrepreneurial companies are, see the *Globe and Mail* (www.globeandmail.com), the *National Post* (www.nationalpost.com), and the *Investor's Business Daily* (www.investors.com). All are free, but you only get selected offerings from the print versions. However, many of these offerings include helpful profiles of small-cap growth companies.

Invest in Industry Leaders

If you investigate a specific industry, determine which companies are growing the fastest in that industry and which are the industry leaders. By focusing on just these two elements, you're likely to reduce the number of investment candidates for your consideration in this industry by 80 percent. You also discover the following information:

- ✔ Many companies in the industry have no growth, or lacklustre growth.
- ✔ Older companies have slower growth rates than younger companies.

Remember that investment in industry laggards seldom pays, even if they're amazingly cheap. Look for the market leader and make certain that you have a good reason to invest in the industry in the first place. Be aware that all industries have their own cycles of growth; you want to invest in an industry that's in an upswing. For industry surveys and reports, see Industry Canada's Strategis (strategis.ic.gc.ca) and ValueLine Investment Surveys (www.valueline.com).

Buy Good Performers

Try to buy for value and not price. Select companies that regularly outperformed their competition in the past three to five years. Invest in companies that have consistent rather than flashy returns. Take into consideration the following guidelines:

- ✔ Check the company's stability and examine its five-year revenue and earnings record.
- ✔ Keep in mind that an annual percentage increase is desirable, but so is consistency over the past five years' earnings.

✔ Disregard a company's one-time extraordinary gains.

✔ Determine whether the company's annual growth rate is between 25 percent and 50 percent for the past four or five years. If so, it may be a winner.

Don't try to chase after last year's high performer — it could be this year's loser. For company reports, see Adviceforinvestors.com (www.adviceforinvestors.com) or Standard & Poor's Wealthbuilder (www.wealthbuilder.com).

Select Your P/E Ratio Strategy

Any analysis of investment candidates generally includes P/E (price-to-earnings) ratios. The importance of these ratios varies from analyst to analyst. The following subsections describe two worthwhile strategies. Select the one that works best for you. (See Chapter 12 for more information about P/E ratios.)

Low P/E and high dividend approach

Long-term investors often employ the "7 and 7" approach — they purchase stock in companies with a P/E ratio of 7 or less and a dividend yield greater than 7. Also, if the company's P/E ratio is lower than 10 and the earnings are rising, it could be a winner. But make certain that no major long-term problems can drive the P/E to 4 or lower.

High P/E ratios are worth the price

You often get what you pay for. From 1953 to 1985, the average P/E ratio for the best-performing emerging stocks was 20. At the same time, the Dow Jones Industrial's P/E averaged 15. If investors weren't willing to pay for the stocks that were trading over the average, they eliminated most of the best investments available.

For more information about how to use P/E ratios in your stock-buying analyses, visit the Investor Home Web site (www.investorhome.com).

Look for Strong Dividend Payout Records

If you're risk-averse, your timeline for investments is shorter than that of many investors. Or if you believe that the market is heading for a downturn, you seek companies with consistent records of paying generous dividends. These *income stocks* hold their value in volatile markets because investors are confident that they're going to continue to receive sizable dividends. The disadvantage of these companies is that, because they pay out such a large proportion of earnings, they may not retain enough capital to grow the company. This failure to invest in their own growth may cause their stock prices to drag. Income stocks are also more sensitive to changes in interest rates than are other stock types.

Chapter 20

Ten Signals to Sell

- -

In This Chapter

▶ Getting a grip on when to hold and when to fold

▶ Setting profit goals and maintaining them

▶ Facing your disappointments

▶ Moving out mediocre performers

▶ Watching what the insiders are doing

▶ Keeping an eye on the right economic indicators

- -

*I*nvestors often sell winners too early and ride losers too long. Knowing which stocks to sell and when to sell them is the hallmark of a savvy investor. From the moment you purchase a stock, you want to be considering the right time to sell and reap your rewards.

Know the Value

If you're pondering a sale, take the time to ask several questions and research the Internet for answers about the security's future.

When you purchase a security, you anticipate a certain rate of return. To examine your investment selection's performance, calculate what you have gained by holding the security.

> ✔ **For bonds,** measure the current yield by taking the annual interest payment and dividing it by the current price of the bond. (For details, see Chapter 13.)

> ✔ **For stocks and mutual funds,** calculate the investment's total return (ending value less beginning value plus income divided by beginning value).

To check the quality rating of bonds, read reports that may be available at bond-rating services like the Standard & Poor's Canada Bond Rating Service (www.cbrs.com) and other sources. For stocks and mutual funds, read the appropriate annual reports and fund statements. Remember that no scientific formulas exist to guide your selling decisions. Knowing some general rules and the kinds of questions to ask, however, can help you become a more successful investor.

The selling system that's best is the one that locks in gains and protects you if the value of your assets drops. Your personal selling system needs to work well with your investment time frame, investment style, and risk-tolerance level.

Know When to Fold

For beginning investors, the following selling rules are valuable. Veteran investors may have the same selling rules or quite different ones. Nevertheless, both new and experienced investors need to choose a personal system and stick to it.

A sure way to be out big dollars is to hang on to an investment that's losing money. Try not to become emotionally involved with your investment selections. In other words, never fall in love with a stock. A way to lower the likelihood of holding on to an investment for too long is to develop a few personal selling rules. Write your personal selling system in your investment plan and store the plan on your computer's hard disk. Your rules may state, for example, that you're to sell the stock if any of the following conditions occur:

- The stock drops below your predetermined trading range.
- Market experts call the company "steady," or dividend increases are behind the general market.
- You discover that the company's sales growth, profitability, or financial health is in trouble.
- You discover that the industry is in a serious decline.
- The company loses its competitive edge and market share is declining.
- The stock's trading volume increases but the stock price doesn't rise.

Set Profit-Taking Goals

Realizing your profit is what investing is all about. Profits may look good on paper, but money in the bank is what pays for your child's education or enables you to retire early. If your stock is selling for a high price and is now a large part of your portfolio, you may want to sell.

What's more, if you're contemplating selling the stock, you don't want to sell before the stock reaches its peak. In other words, you want to sell at the best price and before the stock starts to decline. What should you do? The following list gives you some ideas:

- Let's say that your stock is currently selling for 50 percent more than your purchase price. Take the money and run if the stock is not likely to go any higher.

- Set a target price that may not be your sell price but a benchmark. If your stock reaches the benchmark price, re-evaluate your investment plan. Make certain that you check similar companies to see whether they're selling at the same level or higher. If so, you may want to raise your target price.

- Consider selling if a stock shows up on brokerage buy lists, gets included in many mutual funds, or receives a lot of favourable press.

- If a winner now represents more than 10 percent of your portfolio, you may want to sell part of your holdings. That way, you lock in part of the profit and still benefit if the stock keeps rising.

- Don't try to sell at the stock's top price. You didn't buy at the bottom, so don't expect to sell at the very top. Even after all your analyses, you still need to rely on your gut feeling about the right time to sell.

Remember that you must pay taxes on your capital gains. Check out Chapter 22 for more on taxes and your investments.

You Can't Be Right All the Time

Selling a loser is often harder than selling a winner. If you purchase a stock with a certain expectation, but the company never lives up to your expectations, you should sell. The following list provides a few examples of such situations:

- Sell a stock if it declines 20 percent in a down market and 10 percent in an up market. If a stock drops 15 percent in a flat market, re-evaluate.

- The company's growth rate and earnings trends peak and then fall.

- The company cuts its dividend or stops dividend payments entirely.

If you sell a loser, note exactly why it didn't turn out as expected and include these notes in your investment plan. Such documentation helps you avoid making similar mistakes in the future.

Everyone expects strong performers to keep up the pace. Past performance, however, doesn't guarantee future performance. For more information, see comments about past winners at the Investor Home Web site (www.investor home.com/mutual.htm#do).

If the Stock Is Going Nowhere, Get Going

If the stock or fund in which you invested is a mediocre performer, you need to replace it. You may not want to rush to judgment, however. Give the company about a year to make any needed changes to bring its performance up to speed. Then sell it if you don't see any improvement.

You can tell whether you have a nowhere stock by comparing it to the appropriate stock market index. If the index is consistently matching your nowhere stock, you may want to consider selling. Doing so frees up funds for you to use in purchasing better performers. If you don't have any great investment candidates, think about spreading the proceeds among your portfolio's best existing ideas. Or, better yet, just hang in there — a good investment opportunity is likely to appear sooner or later.

Get some help to beat the crowd from The Online Investor at www.invest help.com.

Don't Be Fooled by P/E Spurts

Be suspicious of sudden jumps in the P/E (price-to-earnings) ratio. Such spurts may mean that a stock is headed for a fall. Soaring P/E ratios and depressed dividend yields can be signs that market prices are unstable. Consider selling if the P/E ratio rises more than 30 percent higher than its annual average for the past ten years. Say that the P/E ratio for the past 10 years is 20, for example, and then it suddenly climbs to 26. Consider selling the stock. (On the other hand, don't sell stocks that are in a temporary sinking spell.)

Watch Interest Rates

Bond investors must anticipate the turns and directions of interest rates. If interest rates increase, bonds and bond fund prices decrease because buyers are less willing to purchase investments with lower rates than those stated on new bond issues. Bonds with longer maturity terms lose more value if interest rates continue to climb. Bonds are subject to inflationary expectations, monetary demand, and changes in short-term interest rate expectations. Thirty-year bonds purchased in the '70s, for example, lost approximately 45 percent of their value after interest rates increased in the '80s (for details, see Chapter 9). Keep in mind the following principles for a personal selling system:

- ✔ Rising interest rates tend to divert money from the stock market and depress stock prices.
- ✔ Low interest rates usually indicate a good time to own stocks, because the economy grows or rebounds as a result, and stock prices are likely to increase.
- ✔ Declining interest rates indicate less fear of inflation.
- ✔ Income stocks are often more sensitive to changes in interest rates than other types of stocks.

Keep an Eye on Economic Indicators

Until recently, inflation averaged 3 percent a year since 1926. Financial instruments like guaranteed investment certificates, Canada treasury bills, federal agency bonds, and corporate bonds are fixed-income investments. Their yields don't vary, regardless of the inflation rate. Over the long term, therefore, low-yielding fixed-income securities can lose out to inflation.

Stock market declines often precede economic recessions. Indications of an economic slump may suggest to you that you should get out of the market. Stock prices often rebound at the end of a recession, however, and this argues against selling during a recession.

For more information about what to look for in economic data, see the Economy and Politics section of the CBS MarketWatch Web site (cbs.marketwatch.com).

Watch What the Insiders Are Doing

Do you want an inside tip? Watch what insiders do with the stocks for their own companies. The SEC and Canadian securities commissions require that officers, directors, and shareholders owning 10 percent or more of a company's stock report their trades. These reports are readily accessible on the Internet.

Insiders trade shares so that they can purchase shares by using the options that they receive as part of their employment contracts. Also, if a stock's value is significantly different from its selling price (either higher or lower), a lot of insider trading activity takes place. High sales activity by insiders may foreshadow a financial debacle. Consider selling your own shares if such trading occurs (especially if the sale price is decreasing).

For a report of Canadian public company insider trading activity, see Adviceforinvestors.com's (www.adviceforinvestors.com) Insider Trading Data feature. Free insider trading reports for many companies can also be accessed at Yahoo! Finance (finance.yahoo.com) by clicking Profile.

If the Company or Fund Changes

The company in which you own stock may have changed its core business since your purchase or the fund may have changed its objectives or increased fees. You need to think about the original reasons why you purchased a company's stock or a mutual fund. If the investments no longer meet these criteria, it's best to move on.

Similarly, if your own financial situation changes, you may want to sell some or all of your investments. A good reason to do so is if your risk-tolerance level changes; for example, you're getting close to retirement or your child is ready to start post-secondary education.

Have you witnessed a material change in the company? For the latest news, see CBS MarketWatch (cbs.marketwatch.com) or Yahoo! Finance (finance.yahoo.com).

Chapter 21

Ten Tips for Planning Your Retirement Online

In This Chapter

▶ Finding retirement planning tools online

▶ Using the Internet to establish and reach your financial goals

*E*very Canadian should have a formal investment plan. At the very least, you should do some basic financial planning (even if it's only noting the monthly bills that need to be paid on the back of your paycheque envelope). To be a successful online investor, however, you need to do a little more homework to get your financial ducks in a row — especially if you expect to spend your twilight years comfortably.

In this chapter, we show you how to use the Internet as a resource to find out more about retirement planning. We point out online tools to calculate your future income needs and much, much more. We give you some Internet tips to help you benefit from one of the last great tax breaks for Canadians — an RRSP. We direct you to Internet information resources to assist you with your financial planning. Saving for retirement and investing are inextricably linked: You need to save to invest, and you need to invest to build capital for retirement. One goes with the other. Let's see how the Internet can help you with your retirement savings goals.

The Internet's Role in Retirement Planning

The Internet makes planning for your day in the sun easier than ever before. The Web has hundreds of online worksheets, calculators, and other tools to put you on the right path. Keep in mind that the Internet's tools do not replace the development of a proper professional retirement plan, but they do simplify the process and make it more understandable. This chapter introduces you to some of these resources.

Calculate Your Current Assets and Net Worth

The first step in getting to where you want to go is to figure out where you are now. You need to know your financial starting point. What assets do you own? What debts do you owe? What's left over? With this information in hand, you can then craft a retirement plan. We know that calculating your net worth doesn't sound exciting, but the Internet can make this important process a bit less time-consuming with fast number-crunching tools. You may even find that you're having fun doing these calculations!

Many professional financial planners tell you that most people don't know their net worth and that their ballpark guesses aren't even close. The Internet's online calculators can help you draw up your exact net worth. They do much of the work for you. They prompt you to consider assets such as real estate, vehicles, jewellery, collectibles, and items you may have forgotten about. They also remind you of the debts you owe — things you'd rather forget! For example, Altamira Resource Center Net Worth Calculator (www.altamira.com/"icat/toolbox/netcalc.html) is designed to help you determine your current net worth and track it over time. This site suggests that as you go through life, one of your primary financial goals should be to increase your net worth.

Keep Track of Where Your Cash Is Going

Once you determine your current net worth, you must figure out how much money you need to retire. But first, you have to calculate what you spend today so you can determine what housing, family, living, and leisure expenses will continue or end after retirement. What you need to help you along is a budget, which identifies and spells out your expenses.

The Internet has budget calculators, and once again all you really have to do is plug in the numbers. The Internet does most of the number crunching for you. Online budget and other types of calculators can be found at CANOE Money (www.canoe.ca/money) (click the Money's Tools Index icon to get there) and at Quicken.ca (www.quicken.ca). They will help you identify where your money is coming from and — just as important — where it's going!

Set and Reach Your Goals

To put the final piece in the retirement savings puzzle, you have to determine how much income you need between now and the time you retire. This requires a clear understanding of your current financial status (which you've just calculated) and your expectations for retirement.

Two Web sites give you a retirement game plan — they provide useful and independent (they won't try to sell you anything) information. They help you set financial retirement goals, calculate what you'll need to retire, and access RRSP loans. They also give you a heads-up on your insurance needs and your ability to pay off bills.

- ✔ **Human Resources Development Canada** (www.hrdc-drhc.gc.ca) has most of the information you'll need if you want to learn about its Income Security Programs (Canada Pension Plan, Old Age Security, and so on).

- ✔ **RetireWeb** (www.retireweb.com) focuses on the number crunching and the qualitative side of retirement planning. This Canadian site demonstrates the concept that you have to not only plan for your retirement, but also manage retirement issues if you've retired already. The developer of this Web site is an actuary who suggests that you spend a few hours exploring its content and online calculators. It is geared to Canadians at all stages of adult life. Check the figures to make sure they are current — it does take a while before the site gets updates.

There are also some helpful Web sites that will try to sell you something. Nonetheless, these sites have online calculators that are powerful:

- ✔ **AGF** (www.agf.ca) has a retirement calculator that can help you calculate the income you'll need when you retire.

- ✔ **Altamira** (www.altamira.com) shows you the savings needed to retire with "X amount of dollars."

Research RRSPs Online

As you know, the Canadian government created an RRSP system to encourage Canadians to save for retirement. An RRSP provides a tax deduction in the amount invested. The income earned within the plan is tax-free until you withdraw the funds. The amount of tax you can save by contributing to an RRSP can be significant. You can open an RRSP account at most Canadian financial institutions. Most bank Web sites allow you to open an RRSP account online. A list of Canadian banks, credit unions, trust and insurance companies — and their savings rates — is available at CANNEX (www.cannex.com).

The Internet also explains self-directed RRSPs, spousal RRSPs, mortgage versus RRSP issues, and more. Check out the Learning feature in GLOBEfund (www.globefund.com). This site features useful online retirement calculators. Also check out RRSP.org (www.rrsp.org), which offers a large variety of articles, financial tips, and products related to RRSPs and RRIFs (Registered Retirement Income Funds). Scotiabank's (www.scotiabank.com) RRSP decision guide answers many questions RRSP buyers may have.

Make the Most of Your Tax Bracket!

Retirement planning and taxes go hand in hand. You have to think about the tax impact of holding certain types of investments, or of making RRSP contributions.

Ernst & Young (www.eycan.com) is an international accounting firm that offers tax services. At its Web site, you can access a free calculator that will show you the taxes you save by contributing given amounts to an RRSP. The money saved can be used to build wealth through investment. This site has other helpful calculators too. See Chapter 22 for more about tax-related Web resources.

Move Some of Your Savings into Investments

Once you have figured out what you must save, you may seek advice to build your investment portfolio. That's where an investment adviser or broker should enter the picture.

There are three types of brokers, each offering a different range of services: full, discount, and deep-discount. Internet deep-discount brokers are the least expensive, but they offer bare-bones services. You can't get personal advice — at least not yet.

Check out Charles Schwab Canada (www.schwabcanada.com), which has both full-service and discount brokerage operations. At its Web site, you can access a service price list and the locations of its convenient network of storefront offices.

TD Canada Trust (www.tdcanadatrust.com) provides tips and advice for successful investing, and a series of strategies to help you meet your retirement goals.

Find a Qualified Financial Adviser

Proper retirement planning requires an integrated and "big-picture" under-standing of many issues, including budgeting, investing, taxation, estate planning, and insurance. A decision in one of these areas inevitably affects another. Making sense of all this almost always requires professional help.

As a starting point, check out financial planning books that show what to look for in a financial adviser (such as credentials and experience). CANOE Money (www.canoe.ca/Money) has archived articles, which you can usually find with the site's own search tool, that give tips on how to find a good adviser. Portals such as Yahoo! Canada (www.yahoo.ca) and search tools such as Google (www.google.com) can help you find the names, locations, and contact addresses of actual advisers in your area. Royal & Sun Alliance (www.royalsunalliance.ca) offers an online library of downloadable Adobe Acrobat pdf documents that discuss estate and tax planning principles.

Check the News to Stay Current

Early in 2000, the federal government brought in a budget that changed tax rates and introduced new RRSP and other retirement-related rules. In fact, what really happened is that the government changed the underlying assumptions behind your retirement plan! Legislative changes like these mean you have to adjust your retirement plan — otherwise it's based on old information.

Stay up-to-date with these changes. From time to time, use the search features of Canada's daily newspapers to review tax news. Check out the Web sites of the *National Post* (www.nationalpost.com) and the *Globe and Mail* (www.globeandmail.com).

Know Your Government Entitlements

For decades, the Canadian government has provided retirees reaching certain ages a variety of pension and other entitlements. Being aware of these benefits can help you draw up an accurate retirement plan.

Human Resources Development Canada (www.hrdc-drhc.gc.ca/) has most of the information you need if you want to learn about its Income Security Programs (Canada Pension Plan, Old Age Security, and so on). Its site is current and informative and is linked to related Web sites.

Chapter 22

Ten Ways to Make Tax Time Easier

In This Chapter

▶ Using the Internet to plan for tax time

▶ Getting help from Canada Customs and Revenue Agency

▶ Seeking expert advice

▶ Preparing and filing your income tax return

*W*e hope you strike it rich through investing online, or at least make enough to build a new deck to sit on when you're reading today's *Globe and Mail* or *National Post* financial sections, searching for your next sure-fire investment move. But (we know you've heard this a million times) paying taxes is one of the great certainties of life and the more you make the more you pay, no getting around it. Or is there? Here are ten tips to ease your tax burdens, the actual dollars you'll have to hand over, and the stress it might cause you to pay up. And — surprise, surprise — they all involve your trusty computer.

Planning, Returns, and the Internet

The sting of taxes can be reduced. That's because Canada Customs and Revenue Agency (the CCRA) and an army of tax professionals have jumped aboard the Internet. Internet resources can help you with the three fundamental areas of taxation: tax administration, tax planning, and tax-return preparation. Following are some specific ways to take the tension out of tax season with the help of the Web.

Getting in Touch with the Home Office: The CCRA

The Agency Web pages (www.ccra-adrc.gc.ca) are filled with administrative information: guides, publications, technical papers, brochures, and forms related to just about every Canadian tax issue around. In addition to tax information and guidelines, you can access Web pages that deal with trusts and your general rights as a taxpayer. Also, if you're missing a certain tax form and don't want to hear the CCRA's busy signal or wait in line at one of their offices, then pay the site a visit. You can download tax forms online with relative ease. After the recent Nasdaq correction, many Canadians were busy downloading the CCRA's loss carryback form!

Despite the abundance of CCRA online resources, however, not all Canadians can choose to actually do their tax return on the Internet. That's because the CCRA wants to be absolutely sure that the Net is secure. A tax return contains the single biggest collection of sensitive personal information residing in one document. (The CCRA has an ongoing project where selected Canadians file their tax returns through the Internet. If the project is successful, then this online option may eventually be extended to all Canadians.)

Planning Ahead

Most accounting-firm Web sites, like PricewaterhouseCoopers (www.pwcglobal.com/ca), have online tax schedules to help you determine the taxes you would pay at various income levels. These tools are handy if you want to determine the tax and cash-flow impact of selling investments. Click the Tax Facts and Figures links to get there. PricewaterhouseCoopers also runs a Web site that publishes tax news at www.ca.taxnews.com.

Making the Most of Your RRSP

If you feel a need to top up that RRSP before retirement, visit Ernst & Young's Web site (at www.eycan.com). It will allow you to calculate online the taxes saved at various RRSP contribution levels. The Web site has a user-friendly menu of tax topics. Click on the RRSP link to find the advice you want.

Giving the Taxman the Business

If business income is part of your tax picture, be sure to take the time to work through the impact it has on your return. Allocation of your business income can reduce your taxes in several ways (deductions, carryforwards, deferrals, credits, and so on). At KPMG's Web site (www.kpmg.ca), you will find tips on identifying and claiming allowable business expenses to reduce the tax you pay.

At TaxWeb (www.tax.ca) you can find online calculators and a daily update of currency exchange rates as well. TaxWeb has links to other tax sites and a list of courses you can attend.

General Tax Planning Tips

Like all accounting-firm Web sites, Deloitte & Touche (www.deloitte.ca) has lots of archived articles on a variety of tax topics. All accounting-firm sites have a built-in search tool that lets you type in the tax issue that concerns you and returns a list of articles by in-house tax experts. These general tips cannot replace the value of getting personal tax advice. KPMG (www.kpmg.ca/english/services/tax) has a capital gains tax tool to help you calculate capital gains.

The Certified General Accountants Association of Ontario (www.cga-ontario.org) now publishes a handy online tax planning guide that you can access from its Web site.

The Canadian Tax Foundation

As we noted in Chapter 21, any time a federal budget is passed, your financial plan probably needs retooling. That's because the assumptions that form the foundation of your plan may have changed. The Canadian Tax Foundation (www.ctf.ca) has the most comprehensive collection of tax information in Canada. From its Web site, you can access a catalogue of tax publications, read expert analyses of recent budget changes, and find links to related Web sites.

Carswell

If you can't find what you need at the Canadian Tax Foundation Web site, check out the publications offered by Carswell (www.carswell.com), one of Canada's leading publishers of tax and legal books. From there, you can access online newsletters or order tax publications.

Prepare Thyself?

Now that you've obtained the tax forms, educated yourself about tax rules, and sought online or personal advice, you're ready to file your return. But do you file it yourself or hand this task over to your tax practitioner? This is a personal decision based mainly on the complexity of your financial situation and how proficient you are with tax rules.

If you go the do-it-yourself route, you have more choices to make. You can prepare the tax return manually, or you can use tax-preparation software. If you choose the latter route, the two best-known tax software products are QuickTax (www.intuit.com/canada/quicktax) and CanTax (www.cantax.com). Both offer online support, free revisions or corrections, and other information to help you along. Along with technical advice, their Web sites give useful tax tips.

Filing Your Tax Return Online

It should eventually be possible for most Canadians to file a tax return on the Internet. Check out the CCRA's Web site (www.ccra-adrc.gc.ca) to learn about how you may qualify to participate in a pilot project in which participants file their tax return on the Net.

Index